DISCHARGE

**A Veteran's Lessons on
Outrunning the Pentagon,
Moving Stolen Military Art, and
Guzzling Civilian Freedom**

by Ames Holbrook

ISBN 978-1517431983

Cover art conceived, designed, and executed by
Julius C. Willis III

The DISCHARGE Press letter formation and stamp logo are
property of DISCHARGE Press.

Manufactured in the United States of America

To my daughter. Obviously.

And all you warriors coming home.

SLATE OF HONOR

DISCHARGE, this shining literary grenade and emblem of U.S. freedom, would not have been possible were it not for the sacrifices of those who signed on the line to keep America standing. I thank you vets foremost, with plenty of love left over for the rest of the awesome folks I name here.

VETERANS
William "B.T." Thompson. "Sweet Dick" Lew Carter. Rusty Spray. Julius Willis III. Team 3. Josephine "Tres" Hinds III. Word Roberson. Tyrone Bowman. Pat Uskert. "Johnny Handsome" Dever. Stephen Lile. Phillip Thompson. Erik C. McGee. Rob Sweitzer. Craig Robinson. Richard "Chez" Moriyama. "Diamond" Dave Grenon. Phil Miller. Chason Castro. "Johnny Seahorse" Seright. Sal Gonzalez. Geoff Wellein Anand Samtani. "Jammer" Vincent. Dave Webb. Ross Lile. Ted Harrop. Heather Hanson. Jeff Wheeler. Russell "The Band-Aid Man" Brown. Raymond Victor Brown. Dad.

LITERATI
Kevin Bruhn. Steve McGinn. Eddy Wang. "Mardi-Gras" Dave Finn. Kai Mander. Mel Berger. Mollie Glick. Craig Nelson. Mark Hejnar. Pablo Campos. Bob Brown. Maisonneuve Magazine. Carmine Starnino.

BLOOD
Sisi. Soraya. Mom. Stephanie Bowers. Sumalaya. Kishore Manghnani. Arayan Lias.

Contents

Foreword: The Truck-Driving Menace and the White-Hot Discharge

I drew the zombie shift and I've got the brand new Cadillac at about 85 miles per hour, my speed governed by the WIDE LOAD truck in front of me. He's swerving. There is some bizarre construction in progress to our left and there is a high concrete wall fortifying the left-hand boundary of the speeding lane.

He hits the wall, the metal-on-concrete scrape leaving a comet trail of sparks reaching back to the Cadillac. It's 4:30 in the morning, the guy must have fallen asleep. I've bounced my car off guardrails in my life in a drowsy state, so I understand. In some cases I recommend a minor road scrape for a sleepy driver when the window down and the radio loud are no longer doing the trick. Nothing big, something like knocking off an outside rearview with a sign or nicking the first water barrel at a freeway off-ramp. It's an inoculation against The Big Wreck.

The truck gashes the wall a second time, another comet trail, and now I'm confused. The first one should've been enough. When I am awakened by the tearing of metal that is my car, or the shattering of my driver-side mirror, I am awake for good. When I hear one of my lock-down hubcaps get sheared at the nuts and I open my eyes to see it bouncing in the tunnel like dropped change, I am charged as if I've had a full night's sleep. Most of the time I don't need to make contact with anything. When I'm speeding down a deserted rural highway, I find that just stamping on the brake with both feet will wake me up. That lone

1

vulcanized scream on the high plains is enough to make my blood pump. Bumping into something once should be enough for any reasonable man.

Thus I conclude that the driver in front of me is not a reasonable man. He is a menace. I have been on his tail for a quarter of an hour, all the while my life expectancy dropping. This drug-crazed, jelly-spined bastard is going to wreck and die, and he's going to ride to purgatory with the next ten carloads of fools like me who thought passing this lunatic would be more dangerous than flying in his wake. When a twelve-ton monster carrying the top of a domed stadium loses control on the freeway and tumbles like a senior citizen down a staircase, other people get involved. National papers put the obituaries in special tiny print columns so they don't seem longer than the article itself.

And here he is careening and jerking the load, defying anybody to guess his next move. His load takes up two lanes and there are only two lanes. And the shoulder. To the right of the shoulder there's a ditch.

The right lane is his base of operation. I guess he cuts left about twice as often as he cuts right. He favors the wall. That's the side I decide to pass him on. This maniac has no pattern, so no logic applies.

I crack my window and the air rips out of my eardrums in a suction rush. The Cadillac's a jet with the exit door kicked out at top altitude. My crotch is freezing from the Super Slurpee. I pull the cup from between my legs and tear the lid off along with the spoonstraw. I shake the frozen cherry-cola mix into my mouth. I'm in the left lane, twenty feet behind the truck, and I flatten the accelerator. Here goes. I see the inside of the Slurpee cup, my left hand is tapping its bottom, and my right hand locates music while I keep a firm grip on the wheel with my knee.

I eject Public Enemy's fourth album and slam in 2 Live Crew's first one, a true American classic. The soothing 2 Live harmonies meet my ears just before the Slurpee freeze bites my skull from the inside. I'm not dead yet.

I put down the cup and there's only road ahead. I have to be going

100.   Check the rearview and the madman is behind me, still wildly sweeping all southbound lanes, but fading. Randomness wins. Continue mission.

Straight ahead the hood is blazing platinum. White-hot, just like this entire discharge. The Army can reach for me now, but I'm just a mirage. A guy who used to be part of their machine, a highly-trained warrior with a fat file, one side of which sings my virtues – the critical missions accomplished, my soldiers always the top-performing team – and the other side which decries my flaws – reckless judgment, an authority problem like Nat Turner. The Army still has that file, but they don't have me, because I'm out here putting space between. A day at a time I sweat and bleed the soldier out. And in the end, if this mission is successful, I will look in the mirror and find myself staring at a civilian.

It all could have been perfect, if not for that cursed dog painting. God, I wish I'd never heard of that painting. I shake my head to get the stolen art out, I want my brain to stop reminding me that life can run opposite from how we dreamed it.

I drop the pedal into midrange, just enough to keep the truck behind me. We're off. Soaking every drop of freedom we gave up while we kept our nation safe. Another powerslide into a new city – living like lowlifes, but spending like the spoonfed rich kids we always hated – night after eye-tearing night. I feel free and powerful and I'm tempted to wake up The Band-Aid Man. Band-Aid is riding shotgun and he's been asleep for quite some time. But since we're coming into his hometown now where no money, maybe no job, and probably some community service await him, I told him I'd drive the last leg.

We make a great team. Band-Aid Man is the crazy one.

Dear Sisi,

I need to make one thing clear up front: I don't hate the military. Yes, I ridiculed it. I stood up to it. I hazed everybody in my chain of command who put it on a pedestal. The infuriating Military Machine drove me to do all that, Sisi, but this is a book about love, not hate. I love freedom. I am married to the uniquely American brand of freedom, till death do us part. But I learned the hard way that the U.S. military can take that freedom away from the very people who have served in its ranks… if we don't buck the power.

I'm writing this to you because what happened makes me think of you most of all. As I put the words down, I know you're not ready for this, but you will be one day when enough time has passed. I want you to know the truth to offset all the other accounts you've heard. This one you can trust. I've given this book to you personally, and you're safe. Dive into it with no fear. Laugh at the wild parts. Roll with the frightening parts. No matter how crazy it comes off, know that these tales are true. This really happened to me, but I survived. I'm better for it.

And I think you'll be better for knowing what you're about to know.

Wow, I just now realized that this story opens exactly as it closes. A telephone rings at an ungodly hour. The caller is an agent of The Machine. And the one picking up the phone is just a regular person living a peaceful life, wholly unaware that answering that call will take everything away.

Horse-pelt and the Recall Shock

"It's wartime, soldier. You are recalled."

The major's announcement blasted me out of bed like reveille. *What?*

"Do you copy, Lieutenant Holbrook?"

A wave of nausea hit me when I heard myself addressed that way. The man who identified himself as *Major Horse-pelt* kept yelling into the phone: "…report to Fort Sill, Oklahoma. We are carrying you AWOL. People are dying…"

"But Major," I managed, "I got out of the Army eleven years ago. *In the 20th century.*"

"You're listed as a deserter, which is prosecutable, but we can off-switch that when you report." The major's voice had no life. Every line was like a snapping branch. "I'm going to FedEx your mobi-pack overnight. We're required to give a month notice, meaning you'll enter active duty in three-zero days. Lieutenant, do you have any questions of me?"

I had so many questions, including *What is a mobi-pack?* that I almost couldn't get out the most important one. "Major, I've been a civilian for over a decade." There was only expectant silence. "I mean… how can the Army use me? Is there an interview to determine—"

"No!" he dismissed. "The process is fully automated. You'll plug a hole in some National Guard unit that needs a lieutenant with your skills."

"My *skills*, Major? They're…rusty…" Still no reaction. "How do you know what my skills are? Do you have my last OER?" *OER* stood for Officer Evaluation Report. The military jargon's roll off my own tongue frightened me. For an instant I regarded myself as a sleeper agent who'd just received his trigger code.

"Negative. Fax me that, pronto." My handler fed me the number and skimmed ahead as if all were resolved, "Any other questions?" He didn't wait for a response, instead read back my name in the phonetic alphabet – "…confirm HOLBROOK: Hotel, Oscar, Lima…"

The Army was sucking me into its shrapnel seam and there was nothing to grab hold of. "Need to cut this short, soldier. You'll find all your answers in the mobi-pack." The phone went dead.

Whaaaaaaaaaaaaaaat!

In true sleeper agent possession, I found my body drifting to a cardboard box buried in my closet. My hands descended beneath the flaps and emerged clutching my last Officer Evaluation Report. My eyes fell to the document that covered my final assignment with the U.S. Army. The date from the other side of this millennium jarred me.

Continuing my robotic spell, I set the OER page apart to be transmitted from the next fax machine I could find. My mind stretched to divine whether anyone used fax machines anymore. Apparently the military still did, but they were liable to be the only ones. I considered that my only option might be to drive to the nearest military base or recruiting station and ask if I could use their fax.

What was I doing? The Army was calling me up after eleven years? Eleven years ago was another world. In the Army and in civilian life we'd used paper maps to navigate. Back then, hardly anyone had cell phones. And even stylish ladies had pheromone-trapping pubic hair – *bush* in male parlance. If those random samples had changed that radically over the intervening decade, how lost would I be with modern military tactics and equipment? Was this really happening? Oh, God, something was terribly wrong with this picture.

Sisi, at that moment I got the phone call from Horse-pelt, I felt as civilian as you do now. Wait, I felt even *more* civilian than a regular citizen like you who's never served, because I hadn't been merely born into civilian status. I'd struggled to get there. I'd transformed myself all the way out of the soldier frame in a grueling road odyssey of self-determination.

More about that epic road test soon enough, but for now I just ask that you understand one thing: this recall of mine was unlicensed and out of nowhere. The Pentagon might as well have taken to America's streets in black SUVs, pulled random civilians into uniforms, and handed them orders to parts unknown. Remember, I didn't choose the word *random* – Horse-pelt did. You heard the major. He said I'd be assigned to some *random* unit. That alone ruled out the single justifiable excuse for reactivating me: some version of the Hollywood plot where the government had to call up the only guys who knew how to fly the old spaceship. I could have at least gotten my head around my country's needing me for a mission like that, however preposterous. But that wasn't what happened to me, obviously. Psychopaths like Horse-pelt didn't call people for schemes that awesome. Extremely cool Colonels showed up at your door to deliver the news. And those Colonels never described your world-saving assignment as *random*.

I shouldn't even mention that this Horse-pelt bombshell dropped at the worst possible time it could have in my life. That the Army recall would derail my universe just then was a calamitous bulls-eye of the most tragic timing. It's heartrending, I promise, but we're better off if I save it for the epilogue. This is a high-speed ride, you'll land at the end soon enough. Besides, a lesson I learned early is that when you can stand on principle, you should never bring in other excuses. And when the Army recalled me, all excuses were beside the point. Only one thing should have mattered: I was not in the Army.

From the minute I got that call from Horse-pelt claiming I was a deserter, there were only two ways the story could go: either I'd escape the Army, or I'd wind up in its clutches again. It was my sincere belief at the time that I wasn't a deserter – I had been discharged. What convinced me was something I've mentioned already. I had become a civilian not by default, but by proactive baptism. That's the key to all of this. That transformation was my evidence. You'll know too, once you see what I went through. If I can bring you along on that metamorphosis, I'm convinced that any doubt you may harbor will vanish. Let yourself be taken away, just as I was. Try to see that collection of road days beginning the minute my airplane's tires skidded down from my final overseas flight, Ames-the-Soldier flung up the gate ramp and into the civilian world like an uncontrolled missile.

There I am in the concourse, moving fast. I've got printed orders to report immediately to Ft. Dix for final out-processing. Racing around the D.C. airport, I can sense my whole civilian life in front of me, but I can still feel the Army at my heels.

I snatch my bags right away, but now I've got to lug them around the airport. My friend Jammer is supposed to pick me up here, but he's nowhere to be found. The Band-Aid Man was going to pick me up, but since he was driving from San Antonio I told him I'd meet him at Jammer's place. Nothing's coming together.

I see the military transportation terminal where I'm supposed to get on an uncomfortable Army bus and ride to Ft. Dix. My name's probably on some list there waiting for a checkmark that will never appear. I'll get to Dix my own way.

I'm excited to see America, I haven't touched its soil in three years. But much more time stalled and the sleep deprivation is going to cripple me. Yesterday's Germany farewell ran overnight, then high anticipation kept me wide awake over the Atlantic. I call Jammer's number. Jammer just got married two weeks ago. His wife's French-accented voice is on the answering machine and it's telling me that Jammer got delayed in his New York business and he won't be able to pick me up until late. Forget that. Band-Aid Man is probably already in D.C. I call Band-Aid Man's work voicemail in San Antonio and leave my information. Maybe he'll collect his messages from the road. If Band-Aid is in town, then that means he's driven from San Antonio in thirty-six hours. The more I think about it, the more I think the link-up is hopeless. Too little time, too many variables, not enough planning. Best just to get a hotel.

I see a hotel telephone billboard down the concourse. I approach it and pick up a direct line.

"Thank you for calling Holiday Inn, this is Dwayne, how may I assist you?"

"I'm at the airport. Could you send me a van?" I hear a sound behind my head. It is a familiar sound and I would have identified it easily even if the spray hadn't wet my neck at the same time. It is the sound of the tab being lifted to open an aluminum can. I turn around and he speaks.

"Want a beer?"

"Cancel the shuttle," I say excitedly. I hang up the phone, I grab the beer, and I embrace the smiling giant before me. We release and take a few steps back. Memories rush me as I take in the legendary white suit, the pale blue eyes, the strong jaw, the slick and immaculate black hair, and the adhesive bandage on the earlobe.

Just as I remember, his handsome head is small for his frame, and his buttocks are enormous. Now in one of his favorite poses, he's standing up straight with his arms bent at the elbow and his hands in the vicinity of his Adam's apple. The picture brings to mind a Tyrannosaurus Rex whose head's been shrunk by a witch doctor. It's been a long time, nearly two years. But at last I am reunited with The Band-Aid Man.

The white Cadillac is rolling, The Band-Aid Man is driving, and we're talking. I am overwhelmed. My window's down, my hand in the wind. Before I can catch my breath we roll across the Potomac and I'm seeing buildings and monuments that I haven't seen since I was a child. I haven't seen any of America in three long years and now I'm in our nation's capital. I'm blown away.

"You look like shit," Band-Aid angles the wheels and hits the brakes and we screech into a curb. The roads are wet, I guess it just rained.

"You obviously got no beauty sleep the whole way over here. And lose the geek travel glasses. How am I supposed to get any bush?"

Bush. I haven't heard it used that way in a long time, but as soon as he said it a wave of memories hit me. The Band-Aid Man loves women. He loves everything about them and he loves sleeping with them. I've met some players, but Band-Aid is a different brand. He refers to women as bush, bitches, and even whores, and he genuinely respects them all. He's a reckless romantic. He wants to sleep with every female on the planet, but he'll never make a false promise to make that happen. When he wakes up next to a woman, he quietly slips out of bed and exits the room. He heads straight for the refrigerator and a half an hour later he's waking her up with a giant omelet and muffins and coffee. If her fridge is empty, he goes to the store. He'll take out the trash, everything, that's how he is. He just loves making women happy. And I've never seen Band-Aid lose the slightest interest in a woman after he's slept with her.

Anyway, that's a part of the man, a big part. "The relentless pursuit of bush" was his motto for a while. Then some smart guy saw him in action and changed it to the more apt: "the mindless pursuit of bush." It's laughable, but it's a healthy, old-fashioned laughable, and there's something so honest and innocent and childlike about Band-Aid's enthusiasm for women that a guy can't hang around him without getting swept up in it. I know, because he infected me when we ran together in Europe. Of those wonderful ladies who have been kind enough to seduce me in my lifetime, most did so during the nine months I spent with the Band-Aid Man.

"Come on, Ames. Are you dreaming about your days as a janitor again? Take those Army-issue glasses off and put in your lenses. That can be your Step One in becoming a civilian."

"You don't have to stop the car, Band-Aid. I'll do it."

He pulls a die out of his pocket. "I stopped so we can decide where we're going. Odds, Jammer's house here in D.C.; evens, we head straight for New York City."

"Jammer's expecting us," I counter. "How about one through four, Jammer's house; five, New York; and six, Topeka."

"Here goes." He accepts the Topeka option without blinking. He's shaking the die in his big hand over the dashboard and I can hear it clicking off his gold Aggie ring before the cube springs out across the great dash, and I realize I'm excited about what it will say, but no outcome would disappoint me. I could have an awesome time in Topeka with The Band-Aid Man.

"Single snake eye! Jammer's it is," he shoots back into traffic.

I put my glasses in the glove compartment, Step One toward civilian-hood down, and I grab my bag out of the back seat and snatch my lenses. I'm wetting the first one and I start hearing the horn. Cadillacs always have loud, powerful horns and this one is among the finest. I've been hearing those annoying cheap European horns for so long that this Cadillac horn is charming me. I think it's the most solid, wonderful sound I've heard in my life. To this soundtrack, I get both lenses in. I sink back into the blue leather interior and I flick a switch that reclines my seat.

"Lose the flight clothes too. I can tell you were in the back row, they smell like the goddamn lavatory. Have another beer."

I change into a fresh T-shirt and Levis outfit, my standard. I grab the bill of my black and gold New Orleans Saints cap and pull it down straight and low. This is how I've dressed for ten years. I'm not a pretty guy, so it's never made any sense for me to dress up – the fancy paint job on the beat-up car that just makes it more pathetic. I crack another Miller.

"Ames, can you do anything about your hair besides put a hat on it?"

"Like what?"

"I don't know, don't you have a toupee or something?"

I laugh. My hair's another thing. I was born half-bald and no more hair ever saw fit to show itself on my head since. The good thing about it is it's a condition that grows more acceptable as the years go by. These days I'm merely taken for a luckless slob with a prematurely receding hairline. But I caught hell in elementary school, boy. And I was getting good grades in those years, which didn't help. "Let's beat up the alien!" was a popular rallying cry among classmates.

He's still pouring on the horn. We're both smiling, grinning like lottery-winning idiots because not only are we reunited, but we're reunited in the Promised Land. I'm excited about the open road ahead, but nervous too, and full of questions for my mentor. "So, what's the plan?"

"Plan for what?"

I'm momentarily disheartened that I have to remind him of our purpose, "For making a civilian out of me. Do we have an itinerary?"

Band-Aid flicks his hand dismissively at the itinerary concept, "This is a fluid process. We can't limit ourselves with a script." He takes note of my expression and allows, "I can tell you what I have planned for the end."

I sit up straighter, "Tell me!"

"We're gonna turn in Reveille."

"What?"

"The historical Texas A&M painting. We're bringing it back to the A&M Corps of Cadets."

"Your dog painting?"

"Not just a dog, goddamn it. That's *Reveille I*, the original Corps mascot. There's a shitload of history in that painting. Back during World War II hardly anyone had money, but they took a collection all around campus and finally raised enough to commission Marie Haines to do the painting before Reveille died. It's a priceless historical painting by a famous artist."

I've known about the painting for almost as long as I've known Band-Aid, but only now get around to asking, "Why do you have it?"

"They were doing renovations at the Military Science Center and someone set it next to a dumpster. I thought they were throwing it away, so I took it. But now apparently they think it was stolen, so there's this big commotion."

"We're returning stolen priceless art as the closing ceremony to my discharge?" My mind jumps straight to my being jailed as an accessory.

"It's not considered stealing in the eyes of the law if you didn't know you were stealing."

"Yes, it is, in the eyes of the law, exactly."

"Well, eyes of *the Lord*, then, which is more important," Band-Aid counters. "14th Street, this is it." He U-turns and bounces the car up on the sidewalk on my side before killing it.

"What's this? You're allowed 18 inches."

"It's a high curb and we're heavy, I didn't want your door to catch. Bring your shit."

Jammer's home. He pops his head out the upstairs window and buzzes us in. I met Jammer early in my military career at artillery school in Oklahoma. The Army paid for this guy's college too, only he managed to perform so marginally in ROTC that he never had to serve a day in a regular unit. After that stint in Oklahoma, the rest of us scholarship boys got shipped all over the globe in battle dress while Jammer went and made some real money selling strange computers from some office that got raided every other week by federal marshals.

We all tackle each other and roll around on the ground. I haven't seen Jammer since he visited Europe over a year ago and he looks exactly the same. A big, wide-eyed, spaced-out, good-looking lout. His wife's shuffling around the room, moving furniture out of the way so we don't break it. She's shaking her head at the ridiculous male ritual of wrestling to show affection.

Band-Aid rushes downstairs. While I'm talking with Jammer and his wife, I hear the trunk slam outside. Band-Aid rumbles back in with a bottle of Jägermeister. The Band-Aid Man has a way of making an entrance. Everyone in the room, bar, holding tank, whatever, always knows he's arrived. Part of it, of course, is his size. At six feet, five inches, he towers over most crowds. But the real agent behind his attention-grabbing entrances is motion. He's almost never still and he displays keen showmanship in every action. He's a very inefficient machine – he'd drive a physicist to anger at the incredible wasted energy. His simplest gestures are exaggerated with his audience in mind. He ducks dramatically under doorways, walks with something like a tenth-speed gallop, bobs his head slowly and grandly, and flashes a perfect giant-toothed smile. He might carry that smile all night, but it always seems to have just appeared. His arms are constantly swinging, cracking, and popping, often with some object in his large hands feeling the brunt of the whip effect.

Right now that object is the green bottle of Jägermeister. He cracks the top with an outward hand twist that jingles his gold wristwatch. He rummages through the cupboards, forever at home at a friend's house, and he flips out four shotglasses. The bottle's on the counter now and he's juggling the glasses. He's worked as a bartender before and he can never resist dazzling the crowd with some trade tricks. Glasses are clinking, the bottle is somersaulting, suddenly there's a stack, then a pyramid, bottle in the middle, bottle on top, finally bottle tipping and glasses filling to the brim with brown liqueur.

We're all looking at the glasses, and I'm sure we're all putting together our own personal Jägermeister follies films. Band-Aid has to be thinking about the date he became The Band-Aid Man. That was a mad September dice-night, the kind that transforms a man and did.

Band-Aid raises the first glass. "And the first toast of the road trip is to our current mission in life. Here's to turning Ames into a goddamn civilian."

There is a slight pause before the glasses move, perhaps a shared reluctance to kick off anything by gulping down cough syrup, but we drink the Jägermeister just the same. It's freezing, and I start to feel warm.

"Feel the bottle," Band-Aid holds it out to me. It's so cold that it burns and it would probably be broken on the hardwood floor right now if my fingers weren't frozen around it.

"Oww! My hand is dead. Where'd this come from?"

"I had the bottle on Dry Ice."

"You savage, you could've killed us all. Like those guys who break into cabins in Alaska and drink the liquor at a hundred below and lock up their internal organs. Where is this Dry Ice?"

"In the cooler in our trunk."

Good Lord, what else is in that trunk?

Jammer kisses his wife good bye and we all three go barreling down the stairs. The air feels nice and even warm compared with Germany.

"Everything's closed," says Jammer. "I could show you some monuments."

"I'll drive," says Band-Aid. I whisk the beer out of his hand and down it.

"Pop the trunk, Band-Aid."

"Not yet, I'll open it tomorrow. I want you to see it in the light."

"Can we at least get a beer out?" Jammer asks.

"Get in." We do and Band-Aid is looking and speaking as if he's been insulted. "Get your beer, fuckers. I downloaded the small cooler." He jabs his thumb next to Jammer where the "small cooler" is taking up most of the back seat.

"Dude," says Jammer, "sorry we doubted you."

I'm shotgun, Jammer hands me a Genuine Draft and I don't pop the top. It is my turn to make an offering, so I hand Band-Aid a leather case. "Blow the dust off this," I tell him.

He slowly unzips the case and his eyes swell with the joy I was hoping I'd see, "You brought the classics."

Jammer cranes over the seat to get a view, "You guys still have cassettes? How did you even rent a car with a player?"

"Ames's and my love for the finest car made is shared by others like us who have our level of experience and wisdom," Band-Aid answers. "Old people. Cadillacs still have tape decks."

Jammer finishes scanning the titles, "From a fifteen-year period notorious for bad music, you two have managed to collect the very worst."

The Band-Aid Man turns to me, "What did he say?"

"He put in a request for Sir Mix-A-Lot."

"Hell yeah!" Band-Aid slides in the tape and Jammer frowns bitterly. The tires screech, my side of the car falls off the high curb with a roller-coaster-like dip that sends us all sagging into the leather upholstery before the shocks catch up and spring us back toward the ceiling, and then I open my beer. Band-Aid's been on his good behavior tonight and I'm suspecting that's about to change. The black asphalt tearing toward us, we jet into the night.

Jammer and the Plea to Hillary Clinton

Jammer knows his way around. He's spitting out directions and Band-Aid's reacting well. When you've got a smart backseat guide who's identifying sights and packing explanations between instructions to the driver, you need a good man behind the wheel. Band-Aid knows just when to risk that wide turn into the oncoming traffic lane and when it's better to bounce his knee into the shifter to knock it from overdrive to reverse. And he recognizes the occasional need to use the emergency brake when he wants to throw the back end around. These maneuvers he performs at no expense to the horn that is still bleating up and down the streets of our great capital. This keen driving sense combined with Jammer's D.C. expertise is making this one of the best high-speed tours I've attended.

We see the White House. Right in front, Band-Aid Man slams on the brakes and steps out of the idling car. Jammer and I join him on the sidewalk, Band-Aid holds his panoramic camera out with one long arm while looping our necks with the other. Click, a white flash fireball blows through our faces and past the black iron fence behind us, bowling up the Presidential lawn. Our first trip picture. Band-Aid about-faces to deliver an impromptu speech at the top of his lungs: "Hillary! First Lady, Goddess of Bush! You're the strongest and most involved first lady ever. It is in your power. Get us laid!"

We roll on. The great thing is at three-thirty on a Monday morning in northwest D.C. there's no one on the streets. Not this Monday morning, anyway. It's a ghost town. Wait a minute, flares in the road ahead.

"Do you want me to go there?"

"Of course. Let's investigate." Now I can see police cruisers, lots of them.

"It's a crime scene, let's turn around."

"No way, Jammer. You're relieved from tour guide status. Go, Band-Aid." I realize Jammer's extreme nervousness has snapped me into a confident mood. It's a supernatural shift-by-contrast that reminds me of when I've had a pretty good buzz in a club that's invaded by hell-raisers way drunker than I, and those clowns make me feel suddenly sober.

Pink flares are burning just ahead of us now. They're marking some kind of perimeter. There's a cop on foot standing between us and the flares. The white Cadillac advances and I'm guessing Band-Aid is about to stop and roll down his window to ask the officer what's up. But the car speeds up and we roll over the flares, right past the officer on foot.

"What are you doing?" Jammer asks. He keeps repeating his question with increasing emotion.

Now there's a row of metal barricades. They make a wall, but one has been pushed aside and Band-Aid threads through. Now our headlights shine on a cluster of blue uniforms. Band-Aid angles in a few feet from the cops and steps on the brake.

It's an abrupt, official-sounding stop, and before anyone can think, Band-Aid springs from the car to stand among the officers at the scene. I quickly leap out too, slamming my door.

"What's going on here?" Band-Aid demands.

Initially the cops straighten up. The Band-Aid Man has just acted the role of the internal affairs Captain with an obscure but important job at headquarters, come to check on the troops.

"Uh, still filming, sir," an officer answers slowly.

"A movie, eh? I want to be in it."

The officer's expression changes. Maybe he sees the Texas license plate – Texas has front and back – or maybe it occurs to him that Band-Aid is half his age. He asks, "Who are you?"

"I'm The Band-Aid Man."

The eyes of several cops shift to me and I give the thumbs-up sign.

"Get back in your car and get out of here," the first officer says.

We comply. We swiftly cruise in reverse, through the barricades, over the flares, and past the cop on perimeter watch. Our horn is honking wildly, as if we've all been just married in a three-man wedding. It is only then that I remember the stolen dog painting. I'm all at once shaken by the idea that Band-Aid so cavalierly breaches police lines despite the fact that we're art thieves. If this dog painting is in the news even half as much as Band-Aid claims, then all it takes is just one sharp-eyed cop and this whole trip blows up on night one. But then the idea that Jammer would be arrested with us – as an accessory after the fact, minimum – makes me crack up to myself. My vision of Jammer's being muscled into handcuffs alongside me and Band-Aid over stolen art Jammer had no clue about makes me so delirious that I forget how nervous I was about my own fate a minute ago.

"Never do that again," Jammer says tearfully, still unaware of the true stakes.

Two blocks later we pass a cop cruiser on the right, and I feel my heart pound in an anxious way that I now understand it will pound every time we see any police vehicle on this discharge – until we've turned in that stolen painting. The cruiser peels off and at the next light we find ourselves next to a car with the stereo cranking. Chevy Cavalier, rental car white, two females. The passenger rolls down her window, Band-Aid's has been down. Their driver speaks: "That was pretty smooth of your friend to raise his beer right in front of a cop."

"Told you," Jammer scolds.

"Do you men want to party?"

"I drove 1600 miles to party, darlin." Nice, Band-Aid Man. Playing up the Texas angle.

"Follow us." They take us to a gas station where they get out to fill up, and I'm not sure what to make of this. I mean I know American women are more spontaneous than their European cousins, whether they're spontaneously seducing you or, more typically in my case, spontaneously asking me never to talk to them again, but this is too quick. Suddenly I'm struck with a wild possibility. Has Band-Aid Man's plea to Hillary somehow magically paid off?

The driver leans in my window, "Give us ten dollars for rubbers."

Band-Aid opens up the armrest storage bin that I notice is full of condoms. He holds up a handful.

"This look like ten dollars' worth?"

The driver gets back in her car. The other girl hasn't said a word. They lead us back onto the road.

I take another look in the armrest. "I'm glad you came prepared, Band-Aid."

"I knew you'd be proud." That was an issue in Europe. He wasn't always careful.

We drive for a while.

"They're taking us to the Super 8 motel," Jammer says. There's no motel in sight.

"The driver's just all right."

"Her friend is awesome. She looks like that model Paulina."

Five minutes later we pull up to the Super 8. Band-Aid and I both look over our shoulders at Jammer.

"Get a room," says she, the one who talks. She flashes a breast for some reason.

I'm wondering why we can't just party in the parking lot. Even Band-Aid doesn't seem too psyched.

"Let's get a room!" Jammer demands.

We do, it's cheap, and we follow the girls upstairs.

Band-Aid pulls me aside, "I guess Jammer figures he's only got two weeks invested in his marriage." Our door opens and I head straight for the bathroom. When I walk back out I hear Band-Aid say, "Get the fuck out of here."

"What's going on?"

He turns to me with an annoyed expression. "These girls are whores," he explains. "They want 300 dollars."

"What?"

"How about one-fifty?" the driver compromises. "That's only fifty apiece."

"Get the fuck out of here!" Band-Aid Man suggests.

Jammer's still got this shrug on his face. I can see he's thinking fifty apiece seems pretty reasonable. I feel like a fool for not having known all along that these women were prostitutes.

The girls storm out of the hotel. "Have fun putting it in each other's butts!" the driver taunts. We never did hear a word from Paulina. I hit the bed face down.

Jammer's waking me up. I look at my watch, it's 5:30. I've been asleep for ninety minutes. The length of a good kung-fu flick.

I finally get to drive. This Cadillac is beautiful, magic. The emergency brake pops automatically when you put it in gear, the stereo is powerful and clear, and the computer figures out everything. The car jumps off the line and it completely ignores speed bumps. The fact that it corners like a waterbed just adds to its character. I feel safe, comfortable, and invincible. And there's that horn. Once you squeeze it, once you hear that deep, resounding blare, you can't stop. They have horns like this on steamships, and I know now what Band-Aid Man was feeling. He knew he could crush anything in his path.

They open my door from outside to pull me into Jammer's house. I'm not just sober now, I'm amped. That Cadillac charged me. Everyone else falls asleep, but I can't. I do a hundred pushups on the hardwood floor. I've been doing a hundred straight pushups for years, every weekday morning as soon as I get up. I figure even if I don't get any more exercise during the day, at least I did that. I slip into the bathroom and take an unsatisfactory shower. A terrible no-pressure/cold-water combination. The Band-Aid Man is laid out on a mattress in the living room. I tap him on the shoulder, "Band-Aid.

When do you want me to wake you up?"

"Who the fuck cares? Just get up when we get up. We've got a long drive, perdente."

Aah, "perdente," I hadn't heard that in a while either. It's Italian for loser. Italy's where Band-Aid and I were stationed together until he was thrown out of the Army by a whacked-out, God-playing commander named Tony Whorlander. I was used to it. Band-Aid was my third lieutenant buddy to be served an early discharge, and it would have come for him sooner or later. He's too wild for the Army. But thanks to a computer glitch, he showed up to his unit in Italy days before his background check came through. When it did, you could hear the whistles coming from headquarters. His record showed, among other highlights: disturbing the peace, DUI, two convictions for reckless driving, damaging public property, a motorcycle theft arrest, and roughly a lieutenant's annual salary in revolving credit card debt.

His commander nearly passed out. All he could do was keep Band-Aid Man busy at work, he had to let him go home every night. Rome may not have been built in a day, but legends rise overnight in Italian towns. Band-Aid took little time to develop an after-hours reputation as a party animal and wildman. The commander was so scared that Band-Aid was going to do something crazy, maybe even seduce his fiancée, that he wouldn't let the poor guy rent an apartment, retrieve his shipped boxes from storage, or even get a driver's license.

When I met the character we now know as The Band-Aid Man, he was flanked by two beautiful Italian women. He introduced himself and said that he'd been warned to stay away from me and that he'd like to go out with me that night. He already had our dates, "Two different girls, not these," he said in rapid English. I told him I had overnight duty, so tonight was out. He was disappointed and he went on to explain how he was being mistreated at the unit, trapped in a hotel, not being allowed to drive and all. I liked the guy right off, the way he spoke with an easy Texas drawl. And how he was standing there in a light-blue suit, giant necktie, nodding pointlessly and grinning like a wild horse. I gave him the spare key to my downtown penthouse apartment. I'm usually on target in my initial assessments of people, and this time I knew I was. This guy was reckless, charming, and out of control – absolutely dangerous. He had no business in the United States Army, and the criminal tendencies his background check revealed were probably just the tip of the iceberg. He appeared sober, so I also lent him my car.

America had seemed so far away back then, but here I am. I feel the civilian in me thawing like a caveman picked out of the permafrost.

Jammer finally leaves for work, we all three walk downstairs together and our host departs. Band-Aid Man and I go to Walgreen's for some snacks and he buys a fancy blue-flame lighter. Outside I notice that the rear of the car is sunk. There's not much space between the back tires and the wheel wells, whereas in the front there's plenty. This gives the Cadillac a sort of taking-off look. Band-Aid Man says, "Oh yeah, you wanted me to open this." He pops the trunk. For a full minute I stare dumbly.

The whole picture is given a supernatural quality by the curling smoke of the evaporating Dry Ice. I've never seen an assortment of alcohol like this one. The cooler is giant, I think you could fit four spare tires in it. It's easily as big as an average car's trunk and it's full of ice, beer, wine, cans and bottles. But as big as that cooler is, it takes up less than half of the Cadillac's cavernous trunk. And the trunk is full. My eyes reel around the scene and Band-Aid Man recites inventory. Two bottles of Crown Royal in their purple sacks; a fifth of Bacardi; a jug of Mezcal; two suitcases of Miller Genuine Draft and another of Lite; a twelve-pack of Schlitz; two six-packs, bottles, of something I've never seen before called Zima; and the most breath-taking sight of all, running and splashing through the entire stock like a glittering river, several dozen loose sixteen-ounce cans of malt liquor, all different brands. I haven't seen some of these malt liquor brands in years. In fact, I spot one can of Power Master – a malt liquor I'm pretty sure was pulled off the market in the very early 1990's after a public boycott.

"See anything you like?"

I say nothing, only reach cautiously for a St. Ides.

"We'll get back to this later. I know how you feel about drinking and driving, so we'll stick to the small cooler for now," he grabs one of the bottles of Crown and slams the trunk. "Besides, I've got something else up front, something you'll like."

I take the passenger seat, wondering if I dreamed the contents of that trunk. There is a black and silver can in my hand, though, and the malt liquor I taste is genuine.

"Here you go, bro," Band-Aid lifts the lid on a wooden box. "Fifty Cuban cigars, take one."

I bite off one end of my Montecristo and he lights the other with his new blue-flame lighter. Awesome.

He gives me a one-armed hug. "Can you believe you're Army royalty and yet you're leaving it all behind?"

Army royalty. I shudder a little. "With your help, Band-Aid, I will leave it all behind."

"We need to eat," he decides.

"I'm all right."

"We're gonna need more nourishment than just cigars and alcohol, Ames. We've got a long drive ahead of us."

"So you keep telling me. Where are we going, anyway?"

He looks at me seriously, takes a long drag on his Montecristo, and says, "I don't know."

Major Bivens and the War Gone Sideways

That's how it started, Sisi. Not even 24 hours on the ground, and the azimuth had already been set. I wasn't a civilian yet, but I was off the Army's leash. You know Band-Aid spoke the truth, Sisi, we do descend from military royalty. Holbrook. Graham. Herr. Patton. Stanley. Hoyle. De Russy. People who Google those surnames find rock-star Army legends all. These military heroes are the names at our family reunions. West Pointers, battlefield commanders, infantry, artillery, armor, paratroopers – six generations of warrior blood in two Army lines circulate in my veins, recycled iron in the forge. But, I'm unlike my ancestors in a couple of ways. Number one, although I served in the combat arms of the U.S. Army during wartime, I saw no action whatsoever. I achieved absolutely no distinction in uniform, unless you count exhaustive training for spectacular combat missions that never came to be.

The other significant difference between my ancestors and me is that I cut my military career short. For them, the only ways out were retirement or death. I chose a different path. Twenty-five years old, I set out to make my own tracks in the civilian world.

I will always have some of the Army in me. I'll always be proud to have been part of it. But I made the decision to leave the Army and it was my mission to live up to that decision. I was going to put some distance between the Army and me on that first discharge day. Some more distance the next day. Under Band-Aid Man's guidance, I was going to use every mile of that discharge road trip to outrun my Army life. The transition wouldn't be sudden. It would be a gradual chipping away of the mindset and the burden. And then, some special time down the road, I would realize I was a soldier no more.

Eleven years later, I needed the Army to realize it too.

Following the shocking phone call from Horse-pelt, several days went by with no contact. I obsessively checked the mailbox for the promised *mobi-pack*, and found nothing. Had that phone transmission really happened? I began hoping the call-up had been a practical joke. I even felt out some mischievous friends. None of them confessed, but I was actually starting to relax.

And then all comfort went out the window when the Army called again.

"Lieutenant Holbrook, this is Major John Bivens from Deserter Tracking Command, St. Louis. I got your OER, I'm trying to figure out what you want me to do with it."

"That was for Major Horse-pelt."

"He's out now. I'm grabbing the slack."

"Sir, he told me I've been recalled. That's my last Army evaluation to help you place me."

"Jesus!" Bivens exclaimed. "I knew this war had gone sideways, but I had no idea we were calling up guys like you."

"I know," I concurred. "Eleven years."

"What about eleven years?"

"That's how long ago I got out, sir. Isn't that why you said 'Jesus?'"

Bivens said, "No. I was looking at your raters' comments: *'Inability to adjust to military life.'*"

"But—"

"'Disregard for authority?'"

"All right, sir." I licked my lips while Bivens got further off track.

"Oh, I like *'Talents will be best served outside the military.'* That's especially helpful in war—"

"Major Bivens," I cut in. I resented his misplaced emphasis on my record. "I think the point is that I shouldn't have been recalled in the first place."

"I'll say."

I swallowed. "Because I've been out for so long. Do you mind if I ask, sir, if eleven years is in the ballpark of normal recalls?"

"I don't know what normal is. The process is automated." *Nuts*, even Major Bivens said 'automated.' And he was angling to a hang-up, which was the last thing I wanted. He already liked me less than Horse-pelt did, but Bivens sounded like a human being. Given the cold Army monolith I faced, I found it reassuring that Bivens had emotion enough to despise me.

"Major Bivens, if I have a duty, I'll honor it, but I was commissioned *fifteen* years ago."

"Where?"

"Where what, sir?"

"Where did you get your *Army* training? Your *college?*"

"University of Hawaii."

"God. That doesn't count for either."

"Sir, I just want to know if this is a computer error."

He crinkled my evaluation report. "You served during some hot times – Gulf War, Somalia, Bosnia."

"Hot combat zones on three continents *way back then*," I emphasized for dinosaur effect. "But I didn't set foot in any of them."

"No? What were you doing during the Gulf War?"

"I'm not at liberty to discuss that, sir."

"You've got to be kidding!"

"I'm sorry, sir." I felt his frustration, but I spoke the truth: "In the debrief they ordered me never to discuss it. It was a Top Secret unit, there's not even a record anymore."

"Next time, make something up," Bivens stated irritably.

"Yes, sir."

"If the Army called you, then you're going to have to show up. There's a reason."

"I have trouble accepting that, sir. I want to know what the reason is."

"That's too bad. I've got to go. I'll forward this OER to your rec—"

"Sir, who else can I talk to? Your boss?"

"Colonel Rosato? Why not? I'll enjoy this."

I heard nothing for a long minute. I considered that Bivens, in a final insult, might have hung up on me.

Then a fresh voice greeted my ears, "This is Frank Rosato."

"Ames Holbrook, sir. I'm a former lieutenant who's been recalled and I'd really like to talk to you."

"Okay, Lieutenant, what do you have?"

Rosato's tone was warm and open. He was one of those teddy-bear colonels. This time I explained my situation over the phone with a measure of real of optimism. Rosato asked, "Was Major Bivens able to help you at all?"

"I don't think he was trying to help me, sir."

"Ahem. Well, Major Bivens is in my office now, so we'll keep this on speaker so we can all learn."

I liked the *Ahem*. I took it as a grunt of obvious disapproval for Bivens. I said, "Colonel, I really appreciate your giving me your time here."

"You're welcome. I've always got time for a young lieutenant."

"I'm not a young lieutenant, sir. That's the thing. I'm a thirty-six-year-old man who's been out of the Army for eleven years and I'm trying to figure out why I've been recalled."

"Wow. What's your civilian job? Is it something the Army has a particular need for?"

"I'm unemployed, sir. I'm writing a book."

"Then this is a blessing!" Rosato declared. "Here you are out of a job, down on your luck, and along comes the Army in the nick of time."

"Sir, I *quit* my job. I desire this free time."

"I can see it now," Rosato said excitedly. "Hero lieutenant writes the Great American Novel about the war."

"I don't want to write about war, sir. Even if I go."

"What! Why not?"

"Everyone else writes about war. I like the less traditional conflicts."

"What kind of soldier are you?"

"Sir, this will help you answer that," Bivens stated acidly. I could hear the paper shift hands.

"Let's see, forward observer assigned to the 3rd Infantry… he's *talented and aggressive in the field.*' That's just what we need over there. And you're questioning why the Army mobilized him?"

Bivens snorted, "Sir, why don't you start on the first side? *'Questionable judgment in dealing with higher ranking officers.*'" Bivens was out of control. I no longer wanted him around. "Keep reading, sir," he urged. "It gets better."

Rosato let out a low whistle.

I jumped in. "Please, Colonel, my fitness for duty is not in question. What we need to focus on is that I've been out of the Army for *over a decade.*"

There was a frustrated exhalation and I heard my report being slapped down. Rosato asked, "Aside from this tour of infamy, what else did you do in the Army, Holbrook?"

"I was in the 10th Apple Division, Belgium. I took my orders directly from General Red Buckles."

A dramatic silence ensued, finally broken by the Colonel.

"Tenth *Apple*… What the…?" Rosato demanded, "Is there such a thing?"

"No, sir. Major Bivens told me to make something up."

"Unacceptable, John!" Rosato upbraided Bivens. "At West Point didn't you have something called the Honor Code?"

"Yes, si—"

"Get out of my office!" Rosato screamed. The teddy bear had some wrath in him. I heard rapid steps and the hinging door. I could feel the colonel stare at the telephone, wanting to be *completely* alone.

"Lieutenant Holbrook," he said, "this might not be what you want to hear, but you'd better just go downrange and fulfill your obligation."

"What obligation, sir? I've never heard of any soldier having a fifteen-year obligation. If someone can cite for me the obligation I have, I will fulfill it."

"Can you prove you *don't* have an obligation?" Rosato posed.

"I wouldn't even know how, sir. But all the facts…"

"You served your full term of active duty?"

"To the day, yes, sir. I honored my time requirement and resigned unconditionally."

"Maybe you were never truly discharged," Colonel Rosato declared, clapping his hands sharply at the finality of his solution.

Whoa. My career may not have been flawless, but I took special pride in my inspiring liberation. Was he out of his mind? How could teddy bear Colonel Frank Rosato even suggest such a thing? I had recorded much of the discharge road trip, and that wasn't all. I'd saved the receipts for the Cadillac, high-octane gasoline, lodging, and bar tabs, and when the event concluded, in one of my all-time great civilian coups, I'd gotten the Army to reimburse me for it.

"I've got paperwork to prove it, sir. My discharge happened."

"Sounds like you *think* it happened, LT. But maybe it didn't."

FIDO and the Burger King Directions

I click Band-Aid's lighter a few times, admiring the blowtorch hiss of the blue flame. "So, this is going to help make a civilian out of me?"

"Don't rush it," he emphasizes. "That's central to this whole fucking thing."

I have to trust him, because he has done this before. He's been a civilian for nearly two years. Just the same, if I were a more financially conscious individual, I would question some of his budget allocations. The blue-flame lighter is on the list, but there have been several extravagant outlays since he picked me up. At our last freeway stop, we topped off the Cadillac with high-octane gasoline. I have never put premium gasoline in a vehicle I owned, much less a rental car, but Band-Aid insists the new Cadillac will need the high-octane fuel "for performance" when we start really putting her through the paces. I quickly realize that my second thoughts about the expensive fuel are irrelevant in the face of the major financial crime, which was the renting of the Cadillac, and I decide to enjoy life and avoid dwelling on any of Band-Aid's expenditures. I ask, "Where'd you get all that malt liquor?"

"Most everything back there I got from guys at work." The Band-Aid Man works for Miller Beer, delivering kegs for special events and hanging neon signs.

"But half that stuff isn't made by Miller. You've got fifteen kinds of malt liquor."

"Guys I work with. I didn't get everything from the company. I called in some favors."

"I guess so."

"Some Mexicans gave us the malt liquor." The Band-Aid Man is half

Mexican himself, his father is Mexican.

Balancing my cigar on the edge of the ashtray, I adjust my sun visor so my mirror reflects through the back window and I've got my own rearview. I call out some late directions and Band-Aid Man swerves right as directed, cutting hard across four lanes to make our turnoff.

"Sorry, man."

"No problem, Ames, we made it."

I look at my mirror again and I see a Ford Crown Victoria, its roof flashing red and blue.

We pull over and the New Jersey Highway Patrol car is right behind us. The idea that Band-Aid Man and I are art thieves crossing state lines is the only message my brain is broadcasting right now. My heart's beating through my clothes, something no cop would miss. The patrolman is making his way to our car, and I'm afraid I'm just going to blurt out "Stolen Painting!" as soon as he's in earshot. Considering this discharge began well under a day ago, I feel we've had way too much police contact already. The officer walks up to my window. He crouches and speaks across to The Band-Aid Man, "You just made a perfect letter Z on the interstate and you didn't touch your brakes once."

"Yes sir, I downshifted, sir."

"Oh, you did?" he nods. "Do you have your license and registration?"

I see myself in the patrolman's sunglasses and I'm surprised to see I look pretty cool. The positive energy in my reflection makes me think this will go well. If I can just fill my mouth with other words, maybe I won't blurt anything about the dog painting. While the cop scans the documents, I do some explaining, "It was actually my fault, officer. I'm the navigator and I told him to turn way too late."

"You're telling me. I've never seen something like that done intentionally, driving perpendicular across the lanes. I thought for sure you'd had a blowout, the way you swung around so suddenly, until I saw you swing back and keep driving as if nothing had happened." He scans the paperwork some more, "Car is registered as rented to a Bob Brown, this says he's the only one who can legally drive it…"

"Bob's my brother, sir," Band-Aid Man answers quickly. "It's my buddy's first morning back in the states, sir. He just got out of the Army. Now we're on a trip to turn him into a civilian."

"Oh yeah?" he seems interested. "Do you have your military IDs?" We hand them over and he studies them, Band-Aid Man's card identifying him as a reservist and my regular army version with "Indef." in the expiration date spot.

"First day back? Where were you stationed?"

"Italy then Germany."

"We were artillery officers in Italy together, sir. Then I came back and Ames went to Germany."

The patrolman looks at me, "Have you been shot at?"

I shake my head, "Nowhere near."

"Artillery and you never got sent? How'd you pull that off?"

I smile, "There's an old Thai saying I learned from my girlfriend's brother: *You can beat anything, except destiny.*"

The patrolman smiles back, "My brother was stationed at Ramstein with the Air Force, he loved it. He says Germany was nothing but crazy fun, sexy girls, and great beer. Sound pretty familiar?"

I nod, "Except for the fun and girls part."

"The sexy girls are the Italian babes," Band-Aid Man announces. "I got Ames more Italian bush than I got myself."

"I guess Ames liked that," the patrolman laughs. Circle of smiles, stories from everybody, first names tossed around with warm respect – this whole scene has taken on a close, brotherly air. We each contribute bits to one story that makes us all laugh together and I look at the patrolman. I think we both remember at the same time why we're here together on the side of the freeway in the first place.

He leans in to The Band-Aid Man, "In your estimation, were you in control of this vehicle the whole time?"

"Yes, sir, I was."

The lawman hands everything inside. "Be careful." And to me, "Welcome back to America."

We're in traffic, roaring down the freeway, and I see the New Jersey Highway Patrol officer turn around. The fraternity of protectors, two Army and one peace officer, got us off the hook. For as long as a veteran lives, he or she will carry the mantle of having served. It will open doors sometimes in the civilian world, and, even more often, it will reinforce the veteran's self-image. Large swaths of civilians may not fully grasp what it means, but veterans can always take pride and comfort in that service, no matter what life throws at them down the line.

At the moment we're on our way to Ft. Dix so I can out-process from the Army. All discharged Army personnel have to exit officially through a designated out-processing station. This is federal law, something that was not considered when we made our decision. We're going because we think we can get some money at Dix, in the form of a travel advance. My official home of record is San Francisco, three-thousand miles away, and the Army is supposed to pay to get me there.

"Hey, Ames, didn't you say you wanted a Roy Rogers?"

"Yeah, man."

"There's one coming up, with a gas station too."

They don't let you pump your own gas in New Jersey, but fortunately they let you eat your own roast beef sandwiches. I haven't eaten Roy Rogers in three years, it's strictly a northeastern U.S. joint, but it's as delicious as I remember.

He puts us back on the New Jersey Turnpike, me with extra sandwiches for the road, and in no time we're looking at signs for the Ft. Dix exit.

"I hope these guys have better gate personnel than they did at Quantico. When I was coming to pick you up, I had to stop at Quantico Marine Base to write a check and this perdente gate guard stopped me and waved me through. I told him, 'I've got a friend who was a Marine and he's always telling me how squared away the United States Marines are. I can't wait to get back to San Antonio and tell him that I ran into a Marine gate guard who didn't even know how to pay proper respect to an officer.' Then he said, 'Sorry, sir,' and he gave me a swift salute."

"That's a terrible story," I say. Officers straightening out enlisted men on matters of military courtesy always embarrass me a little bit. The salute for officers, in particular, strikes me as pointless. There are no salutes on a battlefield, so why practice them?

But that's just my opinion, and I respect The Band-Aid Man's too. After all, he started out in the Army as an infantry grunt, and then he went and got his officer commission through Texas A&M's Corps of Cadets, where they made him pay hell to get that bar. He had to know the rules, had to respect the courtesies, and he was drilled and drilled more than I'll ever understand. When he got his gold lieutenant bar, he knew exactly what it meant to him and he expected everyone else to know too. I, on the other hand, got my commission from the University of Hawaii with a hui of laid-back local boys. The most stressed thing there was physical fitness and the hardest drill we ever went through was the swim test without board. So I won't curse The Band-Aid Man's game, even if I don't play it.

We see the gate for Dix on our right and Band-Aid Man turns late again, this time not my fault. With much squealing and rumbling, he cranks right and the left front hubcap chips the curb on the far side of the waving guard. She's waving with both her arms. Ricocheting back toward her, he slams on the brakes and we screech to a halt right next to the guard shack. We are still and, aside from the unmuffled rumbling of our 200 horsepower V8 engine, we are silent as well. The muffler initially worked fine, until Band-Aid ran over something on the freeway that tore it open on our first night out. Since our muffler's collision with the freeway scrap metal (that I saw with my own eyes) happened soon after the bitter surprise Band-Aid suffered from that pair of seductresses who brought us to the Super 8 motel before revealing themselves as prostitutes, Band-Aid remains convinced that the whores detached our muffler in a willful act of sabotage. It's unfathomable to me that money-driven hookers took the time to drop under our Cadillac in their skirts and pumps to unbolt our muffler, but The Band-Aid Man is always mistrustful of women who won't sleep with him for free – or at least pay him the respect of announcing their prostitute status from the beginning.

Though the muffler has been broken for hundreds of miles already, the Cadillac has never seemed as loud to me as it does right now. The military policewoman runs around to our side of the shack, "You're in the exit lane."

"We're officers!" Band-Aid Man shouts, stretching across to hold his ID card next to mine. "Conducting officer business."

"This is an outside investigation," I say, brandishing a Roy Rogers roast beef sandwich still wrapped in foil.

"Not a word of our visit to anyone."

"Yes sir," she says, delivering a shaky salute.

The Cadillac jumps forward ten feet, Band-Aid Man leaning on the horn to chase back cars that are approaching us head-on and, clear of the guard shack, we dart into the right lane.

He made a good call, identifying us as officers. There is a certain mystique surrounding the officer corps, owing mostly to the fact that they are a highly confused group of individuals when it comes to their jobs. Ask any officer to define his job and he'll give you a very abstract answer with all kinds of offshoots and he'll wrap it up with a line about national security. I was in the Army for years and I never figured out just what I was supposed to do. I defined my own job as: to train my men to stay alive and clean house in battle; and I handled everything else as it came up. So as uncertain as officers are about the function of the officer corps, the enlisted soldiers have no idea and really don't want one.

I'm not too worried about military police right now, anyway. Even as much as mustachioed MPs on power trips are something to consider at the outset of any on-post drive, the kind of irregular motoring our

Cadillac is liable to be doing here is outside the MP scope. The MPs are looking for 30 mph in a 25 and guys weaving away from the club at night – not Band-Aid Man's style. What I'm more concerned about is gung-ho Cro-Magnons wearing field-grade officer rank. Every post has a handful of colonels and majors who view themselves as enforcers and love to flag you down and straighten you out. Nothing infuriates these guys like creative driving. They can accept a little speeding and half of them are drunk when they pull you over, but show some ingenuity behind the wheel and that's your hide.

I take a delicious bite of a barbecue-sauce-soaked sandwich. "Where's the out-processing building?"

"You asking me?"

"You've done this already."

"I came in a bus like I was supposed to."

"Let's ask this guy." There's a young, lean, straw-haired man in sweats on the sidewalk, looks like one of those marathon-running captains. *What in the world?* His sweats are among the strangest I've ever witnessed. Crazy stitching, I'm guessing a Korean custom job from an assignment in Taegu. "King Kong" is written boldly on the back, with a harmless cartoon monkey face stitched in the middle. Worst of all, "King Kong" is also written vertically up and down both pantlegs. (In the 21st century arena of Juicy Couture and Victoria's Secret Pink, the King Kong sweats might strike some as fashionable, but I promise this outfit was an eyesore. Like Band-Aid Man's long-arm camera-snap selfies, the King Kong sweats were a decade ahead of their time.) I call out to him, "Hey, bud. Can you tell us where the out-processing station is?"

He turns and shouts over our idling engine: "All right, if you're facing the back of Burger King, you take a right on that intermediate road..."

Oh no. The Burger King thing, how could it have slipped my mind? Burger King has a contract with the government and they've got an outlet on just about every U.S. Army post in the world. Somehow, as a result of this, no one can give directions on an Army base without using Burger King as a reference point. I don't understand this either, but it's verifiable fact. The Army spends millions every year training soldiers to navigate in the field and our troops are great at it. An average American trooper can drag himself over miles of desert with only a compass and stars to guide him to arrive at a precise link-up point on the side of a mountain. Put him in garrison, though, and he needs Burger King. That's his North Star, and he'd be helplessly lost without it, starving and whimpering like a dog pushed out of a pick-up on a lonely rural road.

The man in sweats wraps up his directions and I say, "We just got here, we don't know where Burger King is."

He stares unseeingly and his face loses all expression.

I turn to Band-Aid, "Am I mumbling?"

"No more than usual."

"Are you all right?" I start to open my door and he snaps to. He looks as if he just woke up, he doesn't know what he's doing here. I remind him, "Those were great directions, but do you think you could tell us how to get to the out-processing station again, this time taking into consideration that we don't know where Burger King is?"

He's standing right outside our car in his King Kong sweats. His eyes are starting to lose focus again. "Hey, man, can we give you a ride to the emergency room or something?"

"Here, have a beer," says The Band-Aid Man, whipping a bottle of Miller High Life through my open window in a tight underhand spiral. I guess the man, from his angle, doesn't see the bottle until it's about to slam into his groin. He releases a high shriek that starts before the bottle hits him and dissolves into a low wail as he doubles over from the pain. The bottle shatters on the curb.

Our tires squeal and we break traction and The Band-Aid Man curses, "Fucking perdente. Goddamn beer-waster!"

"Stop!" I exclaim and he steps on the brakes, the bewildered man in sweatsuit a full block behind us. "Let me ask this guy." The Band-Aid

Man throws the gear-shifter into park with a huge upward swipe of the arm. He's scowling unbelievably.

This guy's in his class A uniform, gold major rank shining on his shoulders. "Excuse me, Major, where's the out-processing building?"

"Well, when you drive past Burger King..."

"Hold it, Major, we don't know where Burger King is."

"Oh, so you need directions to Burger King *and* the out-processing facility."

"No, actually, we don't have any reason to go to Burger..." I start to explain, but the Cadillac tires are squealing and my head's pulled back into the headrest.

"What a bunch of loser motherfuckers!" Band-Aid screams, setting the cruise control at 45 and taking a hard left onto an empty straightaway. "We'll find this place ourselves before those fuckers figure out what planet they're on!"

Sure enough, he gets us there. We roll up front and go inside together. It's after six, so everybody's gone home except for a sergeant and a specialist who got staff duty tonight. I approach the female sergeant at the counter.

She takes my paperwork. "Germany, sir? You didn't come on the bus from the airport?"

"He came in a Cadillac," says The Band-Aid Man, smiling before taking a swig of his beer.

"Hey, you didn't get me one?"

He grins again and draws a Genuine Draft from inside his coat, tearing the top off and flinging it across the room. It lands in a garbage can. "Prior planning prevents piss-poor performance!" he announces as he hands me the bottle. "That's my favorite Army expression."

"Mine's *FIDO*."

"*Fuck It, Drive On!*" Band-Aid unzips the acronym. "How's that your favorite when you don't even curse?"

"It's a motto to live by. And it's not cursing if you just say *FIDO*." I take a gulp and my eyes come back to the counter personnel. The specialist appears to be suppressing a smile. Many of the smartest people in the Army work up to specialist rank before getting out. The sergeant gives me some papers and tells me where to report at six-thirty tomorrow morning. She also tells me how to get to where we'll be staying tonight.

"Thank you very much," says The Band-Aid Man. "Y'all have an Airborne day."

We walk toward the door and the sergeant calls out, "Sir, you're supposed to be in uniform when you out-process tomorrow. And definitely clean-shaven."

Night is falling. We get in the car and roll to the Doughboy Inn, the post's motel for officers just passing through. The Band-Aid Man flirts with the woman at the counter and she upgrades us to a nice suite with two beds. In our room, he calls out the game plan: "We need rest for tonight. We'll get a wakeup call for nine and we'll be in Philly by ten."

I lie on my bed for half an hour. "Band-Aid," I finally say, "I can't sleep."

"Me neither, let's go."

We take showers and pull the Cadillac in front of the lobby. We leave our doors open, AMG's "Bitch Betta Have My Money" cranking on the stereo very loudly. I walk into the small lobby while he dives in the back seat.

There are four or five young male officers around the counter talking with the receptionist. Fortunately I've missed the "I could tell you, but I'd have to kill you" line that was undoubtedly spoken shortly after introductions. I catch only the tail end of that part of their rap where they boast about their Army positions and experiences. I hear one guy ask, "What's fun to do on post?" And another adds, "What do *you* do around here for fun?" So they've moved on to the social angle, letting their one-woman audience know that not only are they Army officer studs, but they're party animals as well. I start to worry that the conversation is contaminating me, that somehow just hearing it is making me more military when I'm supposed to be pulling the other way.

The Band-Aid Man hauls the backseat cooler through the automatic doors and drops it heavily on the lobby floor. Conversations cease and eyes turn to us.

"Going on a picnic?" an officer with glasses asks, trying to be witty for the good-looking receptionist.

"Philly," states The Band-Aid Man.

"That's a lot of ice chest," someone remarks.

"This is the small one."

There are no more comments from the other officers.

"Darlin', you got an ice machine?"

The receptionist smiles, "Right through those doors."

He lifts the cooler and stomps through the doors. He's looking at the machine, which dispenses ice through a little shutter one scoopful at a time. He's making measurements of the machine with his arms. I think he's trying to see how he can fill the cooler directly.

I join him and I look back through the glass doors. The officers at the counter are trying to make a comeback, but the lovely receptionist is looking right at us. "Band-Aid, go ask her about Philadelphia. I'll handle the ice."

He carries the cooler back through the doors and drops it on the lobby floor for the second time. While he's talking with her, I grab an ice bucket out of the maid closet. My uninspired plan is to put ice in the cooler one bucket at a time. I've got energy to waste right now. I bring the first bucket in and dump it in the bottom of the cooler, which he has already lined with full bottles. Each time I return to the ice machine, he returns to the car. I come back with ice and he comes back with alcohol. "Layering is the most important principle for packing a cooler," The Band-Aid Man explains to the roomful of pupils. "You can't just fill the cooler with ice and stick the beer in. The transfer of heat is all wrong then, your temperatures vary from beer to beer, and they're not as cold on the average."

We both make several trips back and forth and finally I glaze the top with our last bucketful of ice. My partner performs some fine-tuning, switching a few cubes around like a pool shark setting the rack.

"We're ready," he announces, grandly winking at the receptionist. "You want a beer?"

"I'm sorry, I can't."

"Another time, darlin'. Thanks for the information. We'll be sure to give you a rundown on South Street when we get back." As we push past the boys at the counter, he adds, "Here's a strawberry wine cooler for you guys to share," extending a bottle to the apparent ringleader. Band-Aid sets the strawberry bottle on the counter when the guy won't take it.

I see those other officers as we're rolling away and I almost feel sorry for them. Their rap was blown so completely. All they wanted was to make a good impression and that's nothing but a shattered dream now. You can't make any kind of impression at all when an immaculate four-thousand pound Cadillac appears from nowhere, and four-hundred pounds of fat-free men start shuttling ice and alcohol through the room, and a Greek god starts asking your lady about the big city when you were just asking what to do on post, and the soundtrack to the whole scene is "Bitch Betta Have My Money" in stereo surround. And then there was that wine cooler bit, standard Band-Aid Man overkill. But there will be other nights for those boys.

"Ames, you feeling sleepy?"

"Not yet."

"It's an illusion, you're running on empty. You'll need some E."

"What's that, man?"

"Hold out your hand." A couple of white pills fall into my palm from a white plastic bottle and he pours two into his own hand. He throws those into his mouth and says, "Ephedrine hydrochloride. It's a bronchial dilator and they keep you from getting sleepy."

"Band-Aid, I thought you didn't do drugs."

"I don't do illegal drugs. You can get these at 7-Eleven. They make your hair tingle when you take a piss."

I stare at the pills in hesitation. (The FDA would go on to ban this brand along with the rest of the "Stay Alert" ephedrine pills in 2004, following the deaths of 30 military personnel and a Major League Baseball pitcher, so don't look for them in 7-Eleven now.)

"Goddamn it, Ames, you're panicking over pills models pop to lose weight."

"Oh boy." I gulp mine down with Miller High Life. I'm not sleepy, but I am curious about the hair tingling part.

"Pour me a shot of Crown."

I pour us both one. This is a short drive and a couple of drinks on the way won't be a problem, but I'm going to have to watch him on this trip. He has trouble giving up the keys sometimes. The Crown goes down nice and smooth. We cross the Delaware River and hang some turns till we're in a parking lot at the foot of South Street. A bunch of meters, but it's after ticketing hours. We crack a couple beers in the lot.

"Welcome home, bro. Welcome to America."

"Thanks for welcoming me."

"Tonight's practice point: Talking to civilians as a fellow civilian. Your identity is no longer military. Bush will no longer be impressed or disgusted by your career as a trained killer. You will have to provide a new image of yourself."

Fair enough. There's very little I'll ever be able to say about the work I did in the Army anyway, aside from what was unclassified from the start, the parts that anyone could read about my team and me on our formal orders. I was the leader of thirteen other young men on a special weapons team based in Italy. We were a Trojan horse inside a much larger Italian combat unit. I don't know who hatched the plan, but whoever did was a genius. The irresistible premise was that no enemy fighting force in the world could suspect anything devastating might spring from the Italian army. A full Italian artillery division could set up camp on Saddam's back lawn, and he'd keep partying, content that no harm could come of it, thanks to the resounding lack of military threat that the Italians posed. And yet, buried in that Italian unit, my men and I were geared for harm of the highest order. Devastating casualties for the enemy was our program, and anticipated devastation for us too, because we were barely this side of a suicide run.

Before I even reported to my Top Secret unit in Italy, I spent more than a year training for it. After that, we were on our own. When we did get evaluated, as all military units must, it was by strange ghost ops guys – the type that emerged solo off the tailgate of a C-130 at an alpine air base before the plane ripped right back into the sky. The ramp would lower, and the first thing you'd see was the lenses of their reflective sunglasses in the dark cavern of the plane. I don't know where the military got them, these wordless cyborgs who would eye our patrols and, we rumored, take mental notes for reports they would deliver in some secure far-off facility to some general who was itching to use us for something.

Our missions carried names like "Minus Zero" and "Neverwas," the Army laughably overt in its covertness, and in fact (this I can say because it's a matter of public record) I was once awarded an Army Commendation Medal for a real-world op titled "Silent Echo."

And then it was all over. No parade. No change of command. No ceremony. No record of our unit's existence, because, in compliance with our final order, my men and I literally burned the last trace of it to ash.

I know my military experience was different from the next guy's. And every veteran's experience is different from every other's, from the stateside records clerk at air-conditioned HQ to the explosive ordnance disposal troop unhooking roadside bombs amid flying bullets in an overseas combat hell. Let me be the first to say that my tour was on the less hellish side of that range. But I know all of us share the feeling of *having served*. And, once we're out and it's time to go home, we all share the question of: What's next? Right now, at this second, it feels too soon for me to try to answer that. The question intimidates me. I can still feel the Army breathing down my neck. I just want to go.

We're parked right outside TGI Friday's, so we head in there first. The Band-Aid Man points out two unaccompanied females eating dinner and I snag a waitress.

"Hi. Do you think you can bring two extra bottles of ketchup to their table?"

The waitress smiles and goes. When she drops off the two bottles, the girls wrinkle their brows and look up at us suspiciously. I raise my own Heinz bottle suavely in their direction before they jump back into their meal. Our waitress comes back to me and says, "They aren't very fun."

She won't take my tip for the task. "I liked that. I'm Dominique."

I tell her who I am. The Band-Aid Man is talking to the female bartender on the other side of the counter. She's making him some kind of map on a dinner napkin and he keeps insisting, "More detail, more detail," in an obsessed way.

Dominique is straight beautiful. Brown skin, brown eyes, lots of twisting black hair, and a soft fluent voice that's hypnotizing me. She's at Drexel University for engineering, and she's working for credits this year instead of taking classes, which is how Drexel does it. She's telling me about how she's developing something to improve fluoride. She's not talking down to me. I want her to keep talking even though I don't know what she's talking about. I don't know anything about science, not like The Band-Aid Man. He would understand. But he's too involved in his map. "Draw it right," I hear him say, "There won't be any second chances."

Dominique turns the conversation to my civilian-conversion-by-road-trip, it excites her. She asks if we'll be here tomorrow night and I tell her no. She asks where we're going and I tell her I don't know. She smiles and I notice I'm smiling too.

Randomness had been an invigorating jolt to my system back then in the previous millennium, in TGI Friday's with Dominique. But in the modern day, in my own darkening universe, I was absolutely hating it. *"Automated."* Major Horse-pelt had voiced that toxic term first and Major Bivens had repeated it.

Sisi, in the wrong situation, that word promises nothing but ruin. I couldn't get it out of my head. According to the wisdom of Horse-pelt and Bivens, since I was classified as a deserter and therefore didn't belong to any particular unit, the U.S. Army was going to select my assignment through its own automated process. No aspect of my recall nightmare disturbed me more than that proactive disconnection from human reason. To Major Horse-pelt, the word "automated" conveyed an impressive scientific character that any good soldier would buy into: *Who could question the U.S. Army's supercomputer – envy of the world's armies' supercomputers – in its power to plug a soldier into the spot where he'll do the most good?* Personally, I had the same faith in a computer's picking an appropriate military assignment for me as I had in a computer's ability to choose my friends. It was computers' notorious *inability* to assess human beings that helped internet dating services generate endless stories of hilarity and horror. Sure, Army computers could measure materiel with admirable precision, but as soon as humans were thrown in the mix, then automated became another word for random. And randomness, which had been life-affirming during my road odyssey to civilian-hood, was the opposite now. *Adventitious* was just right for Army-spirit exorcism – morphing a soldier into a civilian – but it was the worst possible strategy for going the other way. And why in the devil *was* I going the other way, anyhow?

Sisi, my girl, they say you can't fight city hall. It's probably true, but I would advise that if you're given the choice of fighting city hall or fighting the Pentagon, you should go ahead and fight city hall. You're better off just flying in the face of idiom. City hall can hear you at least. Something will register. With the Pentagon, the military's mighty gears just grind you down and they never once feel you at all.

It didn't matter whether I talked to a psychopath like Major Horse-pelt or a teddy bear like Colonel Rosato, they simply couldn't feel me. I couldn't get through. I'd just told Rosato I was a civilian, and he'd replied that maybe I wasn't.

I squeezed the phone in ferocious protest of Colonel Rosato's suggestion till my forearm muscles pinged with snapping tension. *"My discharge happened!"* I repeated. Oh, God, I knew that as surely as I knew any beautiful thing in this world.

Rosato drummed his desk. "Son, why don't you report to Fort Sill as ordered and bring up your questions there? Maybe they'll give you some light duty and you won't even have to go to the war."

"Sir, you describe my greatest fear. If I have to derail my life and put on a uniform, then I want to be on the front lines, contributing. My nightmare is: I show up in Oklahoma and the Army sees how old I am and how long I've been out, and I get assigned to guard some tennis court on Fort Sill for the duration of the war."

"You're a pessimist, LT. Next time call me with something happy. 'Cause I gotta tell you: all you're bringing me so far is grief and bananas, and it looks like you forgot the bananas."

The colonel laughed and I laughed along. That grief-and-bananas quip hadn't been in circulation during my stint in the Army, although I knew it was now. Career military officers never cracked jokes that hadn't already enjoyed wide approval among the senior cadre.

Just the same, I tried injecting a little humor of my own in hopes of winning Rosato over. "I have to say, Colonel, this recall after eleven years is too bizarre. I think I may be part of some terrorist sleeper cell."

Rosato shouted, "Holy schmaltz!" His tone suggested eyes frantically seeking cameras and fingers pulling the telephone apart for bugs. "Are you shitting me? We don't shit about things like that in the Army! What the hell is wrong with you, son?"

"I'm sorry, sir, I jus—"

"Good bye, Lieutenant. Hope you find your answers."

"Thank you, Colonel. God is great!"

He hung up abruptly, leaving me in a spiral.

I wandered my home stunned as the certainty of my future sank in. I imagined putting on the uniform again. I remembered the shadowed yellow-ceramic corridors of Fort Sill's Army buildings, the vague disinfectant air. I pictured myself stepping on the swarmed walkways outside, jerking my eyes in all directions as I tensely sorted whom in this disturbed hive I had to salute and whose salutes I had to return. I saw the bleached grays and tans of the hard Oklahoma landscape. I imagined the tennis courts and my endlessly marching around them in a trance. Oh, Lord, help me right this ship.

Sisi, again I ask you to put yourself in my shoes. There was no draft, but the military machine still drafted you into service. You kept trying to call their attention to the mistake, to the injustice, but the reactions you got ranged from cold indifference to shrugging suggestions that you go along with the crazy plan and just see what happens. Wouldn't you have been just as astonished as I was?

Well, wait, don't answer yet. You've only just started to experience what I went through on my road to become a civilian. You still have much more to see.

Sugar and the North Philly Ride

In TGI Friday's, Dominique crouches down to my level and leans in, her fragrant black hair spilling around me. "If you don't have to go anywhere, why don't you stay here another night?"

"We can't. It's the road."

She smiles, white teeth and a wet tongue. "I admire you guys."

"I admire you, Fluoride Improver. Can you come out with us tonight?"

"I won't. I'd be an anchor."

I look over my shoulder as I leave, dreaming she'll change her mind. Even out on the sidewalk, I feel her pull, an elastic tension that eventually snaps in a final whiplash of disappointment as my partner and I charge on without her into the open night.

The Band-Aid Man and I rush the Philly clubs. We spin in and out, hearing tales, telling some, collecting phone numbers by accident. We stop at the Irish Pub to drink some Guinness motor oil and he pulls out his map.

"This is it," he says, eyes glowing.

"What?"

"The bartender chick gave us this map to Philly's biggest sports bar. She says it's huge."

It's an easy map to follow and we roll up front in no time. Inside we are greeted by two completely hot waitresses and no one else. We walk downstairs and it's the same story. We're the only customers in the whole thing. Surprisingly, The Band-Aid Man doesn't try to start anything with either of the waitresses. He leaves with me.

"Great scoop from your bartender, Band-Aid. Did you tell her we

49

don't like people?"

"It's a good map, dude, a detailed map. Use it to get us back to South Street."

"Man, I remember how to get back. I don't need –"

"Use the map to be sure, Ames."

Dominique told us to get cheesesteak sandwiches, so we stop and eat some great ones. The Band-Aid Man clicks his lighter in the air, and a girl walks up to it, her blue eyes seemingly drawn to the matching blue flame. Her girlfriend approaches next and asks us if we want to go someplace else.

We hop off our stools, find the Caddy, and the girls are pulling beers out of our backseat cooler. We loop the block in search of a hopping joint.

"It's winding down," says one girl. "Everything's closed."

The other girl says, "Except the Black Banana." So they lead us to it.

He and I are getting swept with metal detectors and the girls are going through some ID hassle. *Oh, our dates are underage.* We give them a ride. Double-parked next to their old Plymouth, we say good-bye. They tell us they'll be in New York tomorrow and to look them up. The Band-Aid Man yells out, "Next!" and hits the accelerator around the corner.

I study my friend. I'm high just because my civilian transformation is underway, but my partner is a little more complex. I feel for him, the man could have gone home with any of a half-dozen women tonight, but he just kept riding the swell. Now it's deep in the morning and he's here with no women and no prospects in sight. There's always a remedy, though. We've moved only one block. Spotting a man on the street, I tell Band-Aid to slow down.

"Hey, sir! Where are the ladies?"

It's up north, way off Band-Aid's favorite map, but the man gives us excellent directions. It's getting cool now and I like my window down, so we've got the Cadillac climate control set for 75 degrees to balance things out. He's still driving and I'm navigating.

"I could go for a good Juanvig right now," Band-Aid announces. Juanvig was a girl I knew way back in the eighth grade and then ran into later. She was a cool girl and a smart girl, and she also had a remarkable talent for oral sex. Well, that was a long time ago, but when I ran with The Band-Aid Man in Italy, I was treated to an endless barrage of his sex stories. Pressured to give him something in return, I once recounted the first time Juanvig tore into me. By the time I'd finished my report, Band-Aid was in a high state of excitement. In fact, he made me U-turn and take him back to the same girl's house I'd just picked him up from. And from then on, he'd called that sexual act a Juanvig.

"Right here," I point down a one-way. The rush of women toward our car instantly demonstrates that our man on the street had a particular brand of ladies in mind when I put the question to him. Well, who are we to challenge his notion? Band-Aid puts his foot on the brake, I dive over the seat, and two women reach for the door handles outside the white Cadillac.

"What do you boys want?"

"Uh… my friend," I stammer from the back.

"How much for a Juanvig?" Band-Aid asks.

"You want me to blow you?"

"A Juanvig, yes ma'am. How much?"

"Twenty-five, baby."

"Hop in."

She does and the other woman gets in back with me. The cooler's in between us. "You sure you don't want nothin, baby? My shit is sweet."

"I just had an operation," I explain. "Go ahead and have a beer."

She grabs a Lite out of the cooler and we hit our beers together. She asks me what I'm up to and we move on to her business, which she says has been good lately. She tells me her name is Monique and I instantly know that I will mix her name up with Dominique and I will never remember which was which. That frustrates me for an instant, but I don't think about it for long because there's too much going on. There's this pretty woman with a ring in her nose talking with me over a beer in the backseat. Forward and left of me, The Band-Aid Man's neck is stretching back over the headrest. And every two seconds, a giant bundle of hair flies into view, snapping and floating at the high point, before it drops out of sight again. I also remember we're parked right in the middle of a one-way street. It's one lane, we're completely blocking it.

Monique starts to ask me something, but The Band-Aid Man interrupts: "The E, Ames. It's fucking me up."

The woman up front breaks her routine long enough to say, "You got to try, baby."

"I'm on E!"

Monique says, "Sugar, is he as big down there as the rest of him is?"

The woman snaps her head up and glares over the seatback. "I don't know, but right now he about a two! I know it ain't my fault."

"It's the E, I tell you!"

"Everybody knows Sugar does that good," Monique vouches for her friend.

"Ames, I took four of 'em and my dick's a limp noodle!"

"Let me take you to a room, baby. I'll make you right," Sugar insists.

"How much is a room?"

"Eleven, baby. It's worth it."

"It sure is worth it," Monique seconds.

I slip my partner a hundred, all I've got is hundreds. "Bring me receipts for everything," I order. We pull around a couple blocks and here's the Apollo hotel. It's a doorway with a sign that you can't see until you're right up to it. The Band-Aid Man and Sugar are out the Cadillac doors. I step out to take comfortable control of the wheel and Monique doesn't budge. Four new women suddenly pop out of nowhere and jump in with us. There are two up with me now and three in the back.

"Oh yeah, it's nice and warm in here."

"Go ahead, baby," Monique tells me from her original seat. "We can take a ride."

I throw it in gear. We're moving.

"I'm glad they did get a room," Monique says. "I sure was tired of him ranting and raving about some E this and E that just 'cause his shit don't work."

"Oh that's all the time," someone pipes in.

From up front comes: "I know that's right. Seem like everybody got they own fancy way a sayin they impoten."

"Thank you."

"Hold it now, love. We don't need an accident around here."

A few seconds go by and I realize that last line was addressed to me. "Don't worry about that," I say, hooking a swift right down a narrow alley. "I've never had an accident." My left-side mirror is coming close to the brick wall until I swing another right, my wide chrome bumper missing a parked Cutlass Supreme by an inch or two.

"You still need to slow down."

They need to stop worrying. We're barely going 30. I think that gutted muffler is tricking them. Every time I accelerate out of a turn, the thing buzzes like a chainsaw, plus these brick buildings so close to us on both sides are bouncing the sound right back at us. I drop it down to about twelve miles an hour. They want to cruise, we're cruising.

"Thank you."

"Help yourselves to the beer. We've got Bacardi on the floor back there too." I hear some can tops popping and I hear the safety ring on the Bacardi crack. The woman next to me tunes the radio in to a song she identifies by group name, the Isley Brothers, and a bunch of the ladies harmonize with it. It's a slow, soulful jam, the kind I've never really gotten into, but right now with a beer in my hand and the prostitutes talking and laughing in the Cadillac rolling through the streets of North Philly, it sounds just right. Everything's just right.

We circle completely and we're back in front of the Apollo hotel. That sign cracks me up, totally temporary. It looks as if the hotel changes names every week. Some woman comes jumping down the steps and some of these ladies in the Cadillac call out to her. The woman outside reports: "There's some tall white boy in there tweakin, keeps talkin about some E."

"Oh! I know we heard enough about him! You keep moving, love."

So I hit the gas and I'm about to take a new route through the neighborhood and a white lady clips up to the back window in her high heels. She's looking rough and panicked. "Those guys went and got Honey too," she cries. "She in the hospital."

I stop. There's a collective gasp in the Cadillac and now all kinds of crosstalk.

"Oooh, you know they had banked Honey and fucked her in the ass," a girl bemoans.

"Yeah. She in the hospital right now," the white girl repeats before I drive on.

Amid the uproar, Monique starts explaining to me: "Some men been posing as vice cops and pulling our girls in, but they really just beat 'em and take the money."

"Man, that's rough. Have they messed with you?"

"Nuh uh, they won't mess with us. So far they only doing the white girls."

Well, the furor over Honey has the ladies talking shop now. What's nice is Monique's leaning forward and explaining things to me while the conversation is flying. The lady riding shotgun talks about a white girl who steals all the time. Monique taps me on the shoulder says, "Well, the white girls are supposed to make more than the black girls, but I make more than they do 'cause my shit is sweet."

"Who holdin the Bacardi?" someone asks.

"I got it. I just need two shots to the brain."

"That's what you gonna get if your folks see you drunk and dumb-actin."

"You better keep that bottle movin, girl." The bottle is making rounds. The lady right next to me isn't drinking any and neither am I. I've still got my Miller. Easier to keep an even buzz on this stuff.

"I just need two shots to the brain," the girl behind me says again. She continues to repeat this between multiple two-shot sets.

I have no idea where we are now. The girl next to me turns up the radio really loud. We're not talking much anymore, but the mood's good. The lady next to me guides me back. I guess I wasn't paying attention, I took us far from the Apollo. We're coming in, though. I'm rolling right by the front door and a girl says, "Oh no, that's our folks right there. Stop."

In my headlights is a hefty man in a long gray coat. "Folks is pimp," Monique explains to me as three Cadillac doors open. "Ask for me if you ever come by here again. Monique. Thank you baby, bye bye."

Car doors slam and ladies rush out into the cold to greet the man in the gray coat. This guy is staring into the windshield, walking toward me, his face crunched up. He's trying to figure out who I am, what I'm doing here, and why four of his girls just hopped out of my Cadillac.

"Drive away, love. You don't need to talk to him right now," says the woman next to me. She's the only one left.

FIDO.

I'm kind of relieved when I see the man's face as I roll by him. It doesn't look angry the way I thought it would. It looks confused. I zoom off. "Where do you want to go?"

"Just around. My folks isn't here. He's out of town."

We make another slow loop, radio playing, car crawling, the girl hasn't drunk a drop. When we come back around to the Apollo, she says thanks and steps out. No Band-Aid Man in sight. I get out of the Cadillac and stretch. The pimp is twenty feet away from me on the sidewalk, but in my mind I didn't do anything wrong. I skip up the stairs to the hotel door.

The man inside the door is seven feet tall. Serious-looking. I ask him, "Have you seen another tall guy? Came in here with Sugar?"

The giant lets out a slow chuckle. "He's right in there," he says in a voice deeper than mine. "He's on girl number five right now."

I bang on the room door. "Band-Aid, time's up."

"It's the E!" he protests.

"I know," I say sympathetically, "but we've still got to go."

"Lemme put my pants on, dude."

The door swings open and a girl is standing in front of me, shaking her head. "Big, beautiful man like that, uh uh uh."

The Band-Aid Man is suited up and we're stepping down to the car. "Gimme the keys," he insists.

"I got it, man."

"Yeah, right," he laughs. "I've been hearing you gunning and peeling out for the past hour. At first I thought someone stole our Cadillac. I couldn't concentrate hearing you drive around like a maniac."

I throw him the keys. "Are you trying to blame me?"

"Yeah." We're rolling out of North Philly with Schoolly D in the tape deck, special passenger request. "You should be inside with me next time. Fuck your never-pay-for-sex shit – we can't make a civilian out of you if you're gonna be that uptight."

"I'm not uptight, I just haven't found the *right* hooker yet. She's out there somewhere," I muse dreamily.

Band-Aid shakes his head. "Man, that E fucked me up. You'll see, Ames, it makes your dick limp."

"You can come back some other time. The hotel manager invited you to."

"I'll be back, all right, but god damn."

"Well, tell me what happened."

He launches into his tale, and at it's exactly as I'd pictured. A procession of girls tried to bring him to orgasm, each in her own way, and thanks to the ephedrine hydrochloride, they all failed. But the story takes a rough turn. It starts to get worse than I'd pictured.

"When this blonde white bitch with huge tits started going at it, I thought I was finally gonna come. But then right in the middle of it, she gets up and pisses in a trashcan. Super high pressure pissing, like a seltzer bottle."

"Oh no! That is terrible."

"Then she comes back for me like I'm still gonna be interested after I saw that."

"What about Sugar?"

"That was even worse. She got me kind of hard with the Juanvig, so I asked her if I could doggy-style her. So I stood behind her and she bent over the bed, and suddenly this reeking diarrhea smell from Sugar's unwashed asshole rose up into my nose and mouth and made me puke."

"Stop! Oh my God, Band-Aid Man, just don't say any more." There were four or five words in his description that almost made me gag by themselves. This is not a good sign for our journey. It's not easy to overcome something like Sugar's anus, and I'm hoping we still have a chance. That's the type of experience that can lock us on a path to damnation.

We're winding back toward Ft. Dix on this disturbed autumn night and I'm reminiscing about how innocently our visit to Philadelphia started out. Those two bottles of ketchup sent to the ladies' table, think of how differently the night would have gone if it had continued in that spirit. Why hadn't they called us to sit down with them? Or Dominique, beautiful Dominique. She would have been an anchor, all right – just the anchor we needed.

Misgivings about my mentor start to swarm me like a fever. In whose hands have I put my civilian destiny? I managed to pull my entire Army career with no hooker encounters, and now it's been two in two nights. What kind of a civilian is Band-Aid turning me into? Glimpses of my future as a whoremonger flash through my head – me falling in love with one prostitute after another, them draining my bank accounts until I'm flat on my back broke with no prospects in sight. This can't be the way to become a civilian.

Mind frazzled, can't think, if only I could get a night's sleep. But there will be no night's sleep for me, because we're rolling onto Dix now and it's twenty after six.

"Did you see that guard's fucked-up salute?" he asks me.

I didn't. I'm dizzy. I have ten minutes until I'm supposed to report for my official separation from the military.

Joe Shit the Ragman and the Battery of Clichés

You see what I went through, Sisi?   I'm not asking you to be convinced already that I was a civilian at that point, for even I would not make that claim. But at least you can see *the process was underway.* I was on the road to civilian status, that much is plain. If only the Army had taken the time to review these facts before they'd tried to recall me, it could have prevented so much pain on both sides. But that's not the Army's style, is it? Why would it review the circumstances, when the Army is always right?

By the way, Sisi, although I'm convinced that by the time this is over you'll see the evidence is ironclad and that I indeed became a civilian, I know there is always the fear of a technicality, some kind of scenario where I demonstrate beyond a doubt that I was a civilian, but I also neglected to sign some critical document that would've made it official. Society has conditioned our minds to assume the looming presence of at least one smart-bomb technicality that wipes out every other established truth, like the thief who was caught red-handed with the stolen goods, but was not properly read his rights by the arresting officers and therefore was not convicted and, as far as his record was concerned, was never technically a thief at all. But, I can assure you, that doesn't apply to me and my identity as a civilian. That technicality is one of the first things I eliminated, that very day at Dix.

Direct from the Sugar fiasco, I walk into the Ft. Dix out-processing center on schedule and I try to figure out what office I'm supposed to be in. I feel borderline sober with a gathering confidence that things will go better from here. A bald lieutenant colonel sees me in the hallway and says, "You look like you zigged when you should have zagged."

"Excuse me, sir?"

"You're all ate up. You are a no-go at this station."

"Sir?"

He bears down on me, fluorescent light reflection gleaming off his shiny head. "Let's you and I get on the same sheet of music, soldier. State your business."

"I'm here to out-process, sir... to separate from the Army."

"Not like that you're not. You still belong to Uncle Sam until I sign your paperwork. And I don't sign your paperwork until I see a United States Army soldier come through here, and by that I mean meeting Army regulation grooming standards, i.e. no facial hair except for a small, trim mustache not extending beyond the corners of your mouth; and you will report in the proper uniform, that is Class A's or Battle Dress Uniform, pressed and starched. All brass will glitter and shoes and boots will be polished to a high shine. Do you understand me, *Joe Shit the Ragman?*"

Wow. I had heard of the infamous Joe Shit the Ragman many times in my career, but this was the first time I had personally been *called* Joe Shit the Ragman. I did not know much about Joe, at least beyond what I'd gathered from context: that Joe's grooming and dress habits fell short of the military standard. I was pretty sure that if Joe Shit the Ragman was my starting point with this bald lieutenant colonel, I was not going to be able to get by my new adversary using any conventional means. I'd have to think of something dramatic.

"Yes, sir. Actually, sir, I was robbed at gunpoint at the Burger King on post earlier this morning. My assailant stole my uniforms and razor and my King Kong warmup suit. I wasn't planning on filing any charges, but now I see I have no choice but to sue to have Burger King removed from this post altogether. It's nothing more than a magnet for thieves, junkies, and overall bad apples."

"Not so fast, soldier," he says quickly. I can tell by his expression that he's troubled. The last thing he wants is to lose his Burger King. That's been his post fast-food outlet for the past fifteen years and he's hooked on Whoppers until he dies. Not to mention he's got to find his way to work in the morning. He realizes the best thing to do is to shuttle this hot potato out of here as quickly as possible before I make any noise. "Of course your ass is covered this time. You have my permission to out-process as you are. I'll look into the Burger King incident personally, so consider the matter out of your hands. A King Kong warmup suit, you say? I'll get to the bottom of this, I'll allocate the necessary resources. Mine is bigger than yours," he adds finally with a wry smile, tapping the silver oak leaf on his shoulderboard.

"Thank you, sir," I snap to attention.

"Your paperwork has to be squared away," he says importantly, recapturing his original vigor, making sure I know he's the boss despite his compromise.

Much has been made of the military's use of acronyms. There hasn't been a military comedy yet that didn't have some lines about acronym dependence in the script. Even dramatic war movies are packed with acronyms and some people would have you believe that the military couldn't communicate without them. Those who have served know better. Acronyms exist, but they're not the foundation of military communication. The real language of the military is the cliché.

In the Army, a field grade officer can spot a hotshot young lieutenant bucking for captain in a minute just by hearing his skillful turning of recognized expressions. By the time a man makes lieutenant colonel, he's gotten his clichés down and speaks in little else. I'm certain there are rooms in the Pentagon where generals make dire decisions on our national security using only a handful of the most hackneyed phrases to do so.

The bald lieutenant colonel starts to make his way down the hall, but he stops and turns for a final pronouncement. "Get your ducks in a row!" he shouts.

"Yes, sir!" I shout even louder, snapping to attention. I hold that tense posture and stare right through him until he finally turns away.

Out-processing goes smoothly until I get to the travel portion and the lady asks me for my vehicle registration. I say I don't have it. She says she can't pay me unless I do, so I show her the Cadillac registration. She says the Army won't pay for rental cars, only private cars that were shipped. Man, and that travel advance is why I'm here. Oh well, I'll file a claim later and I will get paid.

Now's the time for that approving signature on my packet. Bald LTC is out somewhere, but a female substitute is on hand to sign me out. She explains a condition of my release from the Regular Army. Although I'm signing all the paperwork now, my discharge will take official effect at the end of this month. This is a circumstance of my own careful design. The active duty term I owe the Army will not run out for another 30 days, so I have arranged to take what the Army calls *terminal leave* from now until then, burning my accrued vacation at my career's end in order to slip out of uniform early while still satisfying my commitment. For the rest of this month, the Army still owns my life, but I will be mobile, in the Cadillac, and they will never find me.

I excitedly listen to the woman as she explains that my release from the Regular Army will become official at the end of the month. It is all set in irreversible motion, she assures me – once I sign the paperwork here with her, no further action on my part is required. As I lower my pen to the paper, I am overcome with both relief and exhilaration that I will never wear the uniform again. I sign. She signs. Thank you, ma'am. I'm free.

That was where the official part happened, Sisi. You see, the technicality was taken care of – the technicality only works in my favor. The paperwork established that I was a civilian, no comebacks on that count, so the single glaring piece that remains to be sold is that I was not merely a civilian on paper, but that I also became a full-on civilian in real essence.

I hope and pray that what you read from here forward will convince you I did.

The Manhattan Art Professor and the Nude Model Short Circuit

We pop out of the elevator on the top floor of the Empire State Building, walk through the glass doors, and my eyes sting from the wind and the view.

"Hey Ames, because of the altitude, kisses up here can be shocking," Band-Aid reads from the brochure.

There's a cute redhead in front of me whom I wouldn't mind kissing. She smiles at me. While we're smiling at each other, The Band-Aid Man leans over and kisses me on the cheek. I jump and the redhead laughs and turns away.

"Did you feel a shock, dude?"

I rub my cheek with my shoulder, "I felt a chill."

"Ames, by the way, I called up my boss this morning and I convinced him to give me another week off."

"Yeah!"

"I had to after last night. We can do a lot more in two weeks."

"Three weeks would be perfect."

"Shut up, fucker, I'm losing enough income as it is. Not to mention I'm already on shaky ground at work. They'd probably fire me if Rodeo wasn't around the corner." He lifts a silver flask out of an inside pocket and we both take a sip of Crown Royal. He holds the camera out with one long arm and pulls me in with the other. The dense city landscape and the harbor are behind us. Click, our highest trip picture.

It's nice up here, but the city below us is inviting. We come out at ground level and start our march. Every block seems to hold dozens of happy, gorgeous women. Some of them are smiling obviously at The Band-Aid Man and looking over their shoulders at him when they walk past. He's loving it. One brunette in dark glasses breaks away from her girlfriend to ask him if he's from Texas. Their sidewalk conversation ends and he's acting as if that was a supernatural act, some girl popping up and guessing where he was from.

"God damn, dude, my bag's not that big, I've got no map, no camera, no cowboy hat, no belt with my name on it, and I'm wearing a tie. Why couldn't I be from here?"

I look at him against the backdrop of this crowd and I have to laugh. He sticks out like the state of Texas on a map.

"Dude, I should grow a beard more often. These girls are definitely noticing it."

"They're liking you despite that wimpy four-day scrub. I gotta be honest with you, it's not a winner."

"How's my hair?"

I look and smile, "Perfect."

We roam Manhattan for a while, through a string of bars and toasts with new friends, and at some point we find ourselves in a Mustang that's being hurled down the road by a girl named Lindy. Females who drive aggressively have a special place in my heart. All I know about Lindy is that her hands are all over The Band-Aid Man and she peels out at every light, so she's probably a cool chick. She races into a parking lot and drops into second gear so the tachometer jumps. We go to a club in the lobby of a Marriott, and my clothes don't make the dress code. Lindy argues with the doorman, says we're guests at the hotel. She shows her key envelope and I realize that she really has gotten us a room.

"You don't have to be the psychotic bouncer. You can be flexible on the dress code," Lindy tells him.

"Within reason, yes," the psychotic bouncer allows his eyes to skim over my outfit another time. "But in his case…"

I solve everything by volunteering to go up and sleep, something I've done for only ninety minutes in the past ninety hours. I pull one of the white plastic cardkeys out of the check-in envelope in Lindy's hand and

I'm about to tell them to have fun, but Lindy and Band-Aid Man are already kissing.

I have no idea how long I've been dozing when I hear The Band-Aid Man exclaim, "What an asshole!" The psychotic bouncer immediately comes to my mind, my last waking memory. I part my eyelids slightly to discover Band-Aid Man on the adjacent bed, Lindy on all fours in front of him. So, my friend is not cursing the doorman who kept me out of the club – he's simply praising Lindy's anus. *Am I dreaming?* I roll over to face away from them and quickly escape into sleep once more.

The next time I awaken, daylight's streaming in the window and The Band-Aid Man is snoring away. No sign of Lindy. Check my watch, I've slept eight hours and I feel awesome. I drop down on the floor and do ninety-five perfect pushups. Didn't make a hundred, started hurting around eighty, I guess I'm stiff after that sleep or something.

When I get out of the shower, Band-Aid's primed for another day in New York. My partner worked hard to sell his boss on another week off, which pays the immediate dividend of allowing us a second day in this thrilling monster of a city. Unfortunately, we're also at the brink of a serious cash problem. My bank card has failed at seven straight ATMs. Band-Aid, on the other hand, has no bank card in the first place, his financial institution having stopped mailing him replacement cards years ago, for the good of both parties. As we get out on the Manhattan sidewalk, I count the bills I have left in my wallet. It's enough to get us through the day, maybe, but the reckoning is coming soon. Our Cadillac is housed in an off-grid Indian garage, where the attendant made it a point to tell me repeatedly that ours was a cash-only deal. Band-Aid and I visited the garage a couple of times yesterday to replenish drinks from our cooler or grab new clothes, and both times the same Indian reminded me, "Just cash-money when you get the keys." I'm brooding about this impending confrontation when we run into the Academy of Art, and all of a sudden The Band-Aid Man is seized by the idea of doing nude model work to make us some quick dollars.

He pulls us inside the lobby where we're immediately halted at a staffed security checkpoint. "I'm here to hire myself out as a nude model," my partner announces in introduction. The female security guard listens to Band-Aid's explanation, ignoring the open beer can in his hand, and then radios to somebody that, "Two nude model applicants are coming in." I don't know how I became a nude model applicant too. I'm frightened. There are students crowding around listening, The Band-Aid Man has created a stir. This is a classroom building, so it's swarming with students. New York City art students, the brightest and the weirdest. Who knows what degrading ceremonies they subject their nude models to?

We sign in and the security guard escorts us to the elevator, that's as far as she goes. Evidently, public declaration that you'd like to take your clothes off for money is all it takes to be let loose in the building. We're in the car heading up with about seven art students and The Band-Aid Man is drumming up support for his cause: "Do y'all think I'd make a good nude model?" Impressed by the crowd's positive feedback, he commandeers a spiral notebook and starts a petition. "Band-Aid Man for Nude Model," proclaims the banner across the top of the page. Below it reads in smaller print: "Signature" then "phone # (girls)." Those are his written quotation marks.

The first teacher we find is in some workshop with rows of gray metal shelves. Students are scurrying between them.

"Hello, Professor."

Bearded, leering man with rolling head says, "Hello."

"I was told you might be able to use my services as a nude model."

The teacher's eyes lock on the beer in Band-Aid's hand. "I suppose you missed the sign on the door that says, 'No Food or Drink.'"

"I saw it, sir. I thought that meant 'None Provided'."

Head rolling, "No, we have important art here and we like to keep stain sources far away."

There is no change in the way Band-Aid Man holds the beer, "What about the nude modeling?"

"I can always use models."

"It has to be for today."

Eyebrows shooting up, "Today? I have nothing today."

Band-Aid shows the petition, "I can get more signatures, I just got these coming up here."

Eyebrows still up, "That's impressive, but I don't have anything for today. If you leave me your number, I'll call you when something comes up. Does your friend want to model too?"

I flinch wildly. Band-Aid says, "No, I don... Hell, that's a pretty good idea. He's got a great body, maybe we could do a job together." The teacher looks at me and I shake my head forcefully. I'm fit, but my frame is hardly art-worthy. No buttocks, gorilla-like hairy body – even the abstract artists would demand tuition refunds.

Band-Aid writes his number down for the teacher who I assume is now mistaking San Antonio's 210 area code for 201 New Jersey.

"Well, thank you. I'll give you a call."

"Do you want me to show you the goods? I can show you the goods," The Band-Aid Man is reaching for his belt, he's unbuckling it. Students have stopped scurrying for the time being. They're watching. The teacher's eyebrows are at an all-time high. I see the belt fly free in slow motion... now the button gets pushed through the slit in the trousers... the zipper is coming down…

"Stop!" I cry. I rush forward and grab The Band-Aid Man by the neck. He tries to whip me with the belt. The lashes are ineffective because I'm behind him, pushing him through the doors in the direction of the elevator. His belt swings grow slower and weaker. His fatigued arm drops and I release him.

"Band-Aid, what got into you? You can't just disrobe in the workshop for no reason."

"It wasn't for no reason, dude. I was showing him the goods. There are always last-minute cancellations."

"No, man, you had a short circuit. We'd better go." I drop the wide-lined spiral on the elevator floor as we descend and I assure my friend that the teacher will probably leave a message on his voicemail very soon. We get out on L. I continue to lecture him when we walk outside, "Man, you're supposed to be my mentor, but you're off the rails."

"Shut up, Ames, and start thinking about our mission here."

"I am! And I just discovered I'm trying to become a civilian under the mentorship of a pervert who's going to get us arrested."

"Bullshit. Open your eyes and recognize a goddamn milestone when you see one."

"Milestone?"

"Employment, dumbfuck. You don't have a job, and I just showed you how to get one."

I stop chastising and start listening.

"Yeah," Band-Aid rolls on, "Like just about every other discharged vet, your résumé tells employers you know how to kill people. That doesn't open any goddamn doors, trust me. So you need to try to find job angles wherever you can. If you even think there may be a job somewhere, try to sniff it out. You ain't in no position to be choosy."

The Band-Aid Man was on it, Sisi. I felt every word of his presentation sinking in, and I found myself just naturally tuning in more sharply from then on. It was the gift of experience-wrung wisdom that my brother passed on to me, as I snatched out of the air for free the lessons he'd scavenged through hard knocks. That whole fiasco in New York's Academy of Art meant something, and the same for so many other situations this journey would send my way. The civilian world was coming into focus, and I kept it tight as we continued to trip through Manhattan.

Laura Coffeecake and the Trade for the Cadillac's Freedom

When you look back across a lifetime, the nights run together like a pack of wild dogs. When you outlast a night, though, and honor dawn by greeting it, the dawn repays you by being memorable. Dawns never lose their identities.

Deep in the New York dawn, I try one last ATM right outside the garage. Band-Aid blows on his hands either for warmth or for luck, "Better hope this works, or the Indian's gonna repo our Caddy the way Laura Coffeecake repo'd my clothes."

Laura Coffeecake was Band-Aid's last girlfriend at Texas A&M. I've heard tons of stories about this chick for years running, but somehow unheard material continues to come out. "How'd she repo your clothes?"

"Fuck, I got my orders and the Army was sending me overseas. I'd been with Laura Coffeecake for two months, and I told her I couldn't take her with me. I wasn't mean or nothing, but she took it bad and she went out drinking at the Dixie Chicken, got fucked up, and then drove to my house when I wasn't there, broke in through my window, and took all the clothes she'd given me as presents during our relationship."

"Man, did you file charges or anything?"

"No, of course not. But all my friends were giving me shit for getting my clothes repo'd. And then a week later Laura gets fucked up again and calls me. I tell her, 'Think about it, baby, I never took back any of the gifts I gave you,' which was true – and then she brings all the clothes back to my place, bangs the shit out of me, and takes off in the morning."

"Wow," I punch my PIN into the machine and then hit the Fast Cash

70

button. "All's well that ends well."

"That wasn't the end, dude. Not a week later, I guess she talked to her mom, then she came back to my place and broke in and repo'd my clothes all over again."

"Talked to her mom? What does Laura Coffeecake's mom have to do with anything?"

"Oh fuck, everything. Mrs. Coffeecake was a piece of work. She called me up and promised to sue me for defamation of character."

"What? She wanted to sue *you* when her daughter repo'd your clothes?"

"No, not then. Like a year later over some different shit…"

This is the kind of endless labyrinth you get pulled into when Band-Aid Man starts talking about Laura Coffeecake. I'm not ready for it right now, since I'm consumed with frustration by what I see on the ATM screen. Same results as the rest of the machines: Unable to Complete this Transaction. My bank card is useless. We're out of options if we want to leave town tonight. Sometimes your destiny's slated and there's no avoiding it. We've been running long enough. It's time to face the Indian.

We descend the ramp into his den of vehicles. "Gentlemen?" He stands up. He's got a little stove going and he's flipping some kind of tortilla on it.

"Hello, sir. Aaahh, we need our Cadillac and I'm out of cash right now, but I've got a credit card."

"We cannot accept credit cards. We had a deal."

"Hold it," says The Band-Aid Man. "I've got some money in the car. Can you give me the keys?"

"The Cadillac is unlocked."

My partner pulls the door open and the Indian and I look at each other and nod awkwardly. We both glance over at the Cadillac and he probably experiences the same disappointment I do when we see The Band-Aid Man on his knees, scraping change out of armrests. I involuntarily turn away, my eyes running the escape path up the ramp and through the exit hole, into the twilight.

Band-Aid comes back with his hands full, but we're still way short. "How about a check?"

Shaking head, "I am sorry, that is not acceptable."

"Do you drink?"

"No."

The Band-Aid Man is pacing the floor, he's trying to think. He stops and turns. "Can I interest you in a Cuban cigar?"

The absence of an immediate rejection by the Indian compels me to turn back his way. His eyes are gleaming.

Band-Aid brokers a trade involving his last emergency dollar, all the change scraped out of the armrests, and two uncut Montecristos. The Indian holds out the keys, "Good morning, gentleman." There are handshakes all around. I pull down my shoulder harness and The Band-Aid Man slides behind the wheel and rushes the ramp. The garage's exterior mirror shows the coast is clear and I see our white reflection streak across it as we fly by. Our front wheels come down in the right-hand lane of Lexington Avenue and he stays on the gas to pull us right, into the brightening dawn. "Get us out of here," he commands, so I point him west.

I navigate us for a little while. I can't tell whether it's because we're way past regular waking hours, or it's his brain's full engagement in the struggle to solve our financial straits, but The Band-Aid Man is starting to lose his driving skills. He misses my twice-repeated directions, and now he's cruising nine miles an hour in a factory area. Red lights are blinking ahead and a train screams across our path like a rocket. "Wake up, Band-Aid! Where do you want to go?"

His eyes open and seem to register the speeding train on some level. "Well... we don't have a dime to our names and neither one of us has a bank card that's worth a fuck, and we don't have enough credit between us to take this trip on plastic alone, right?"

"Right. And can you back away from this train and take a right?"

He follows my directions absently, his mind focused on more pressing matters than the boxcars tearing across our fore. "And we've still got our military ID cards."

"What are you saying?"

"The only way we can keep this trip alive is to stop at military bases and write checks at the PX for the hundred-fifty maximum."

"Sweet Jesus! I thought I'd never have to see another post. I'm supposed to be getting *away* from the Army." I'm trying to come up with another way to get money, but I can't. I'm afraid he's right, we're going to have to go on post. *FIDO.* I squint into the rising sun and ask him, "Do you know a base around here?"

"Yeah, shouldn't be too far. There was this school that rejected me, West Point."

Zero Week and the West Point Military Relapse

Sisi, there's a line in the classic war movie Apocalypse Now where Captain Willard sifts through Colonel Kurtz's dossier and remarks in awe, *"The next youngest guy in his class was half his age. They must have thought he was some far-out old man humping it over that course. I did it when I was 19 and it damn near wasted me. A tough motherfucker. He finished."*

I've always suspected that Hollywood story was based on my grandfather, Ephraim "Eph" Foster Graham, Jr., who – in real life, not movies – completed airborne school at over twice the age of his next-youngest classmate. Grandpa Graham was real-life tough. In World War II, he commanded the 644th Tank Destroyer Battalion through five campaigns in the European Theater. 300 days in bloody combat, including the Battle of the Bulge. His unit was awarded the Presidential Unit Citation and the Belgian Fourragere. For his personal valor, Eph got two silver stars and two bronze. He was also seriously injured twice, but those war wounds never made it to his official record, because he didn't want the Army to hear about them and take him off the battlefield. Self-extract the bullets and get back in the fight. *FIDO.* And while he was the old man for airborne school, he became one of the youngest in the Army to be promoted to brigadier general.

I went to airborne school at the uninspiring age of 20. I remember riding into Ft. Benning, Georgia, on an empty shuttle, wondering where my classmates were. I reported to Delta Company and the crease-faced first sergeant tore my orders out of my hand. Gifted with a theatrical talent shared by many crusty first sergeants, he also managed to paw his hat off his head at the same time to accentuate the earthshaking nature of whatever situation he was about to reveal.

"You're here a week early!" he blasted. "Nice job, dumbass!" From the print in my orders, his eyes lifted to challenge mine. His grimacing skull telegraphed equal parts disdain and relish. "Whoever gave you these orders fucked you good. But I'm gonna fuck you better: Welcome to *Zero Week*! This is where you spend seven straight days and nights doing the most revolting details I can think of – and I am a sick-in-the-head motherfucker…"

He turned out to be that, and Zero Week retains its power as a chilling catchphrase to disturb me for all eternity. And just when the first sergeant left my life and the actual airborne course rolled around, I managed to catch the attention of my Black Hat instructor, a violently hard case in the first place, Sergeant Airborne himself, who, during an early bout of physical training, mistook my natural expression for a "smirk," and proceeded to make it his public mission to wipe it off my face. Since, as I mentioned, what Sergeant Airborne called a "smirk" is what I call sunup to sundown, seven days a week, just the way my face is arranged, Sergeant Airborne did not accomplish his goal, but he did see to it that by the time I stood up on that graduation rockpile, as a third-generation paratrooper, my dad pushing those jump wings into my blouse, that I had executed four times as many pushups, twice as many running miles, and seemingly half again as many frame-jerking hurtles out of the jump towers as any other soul in my class. Sergeant Airborne made such a spectacle out of me for three weeks that guys in other squads with entirely different instructors knew who I was. Going on five years later, soldiers I'd never known were still running up to me in the streets of Army towns and yelling out my helmet number.

That kind of thing – Sergeant Airborne's wrath, the Zero Week nightmare – never would have happened to Eph Graham, that I can promise you. Not to my father, either. Nor to any of the rest of the warrior heroes my family lines manufactured. I, on the other hand, have stories of that caliber for every leg and detour of my Army career. I am not Eph Graham, I'm not any of them. I am made of different stuff.

And, while it took me years in uniform to figure that out, I'm pretty sure the Army realized it from day one.

We're fast approaching West Point, where Eph Graham was commissioned over fifty years ago. He was a fourth-generation graduate of the U.S. Military Academy. I would have been a sixth, had I not opted for that other esteemed military institution, the University of Hawaii.

We're on 9W and Band-Aid comes honking into post at about sixty, which is all right because West Point is an open post and there's no guard at the gate. And he knows these roads. He's a graduate of West Point Prep School, normally a first step toward a degree from the United States Military Academy at West Point. For The Band-Aid Man, however, it was his final step, since the big school chose not to enroll him.

And sliding into these leafy S-curves now, Band-Aid's distaste is showing. He doesn't like this post and I'm glad because that means we won't waste any time here. We'll take care of business and get out. We come over a hill and down into the Post Exchange parking lot. There's a bank machine here, so I decide to give my card one last try. No dice, so I call my bank. A young-sounding lady is giving me the run-around. Band-Aid hears me struggling, so he takes the phone out of my hand and says he'll handle it. I take a walk and I come back to hear him describing himself to her. When he hangs up I ask him if my card's straight.

"No, but we've got another place to stay if we ever go back to D.C."

"Great. Let's get this over with."

"Yeah, time for me to write a hot check."

"Hot? You don't have any money in your account?"

"I've got a loan coming through pretty soon, but not in time to cover this."

"Don't write a check, then, Band-Aid. They'll void your ID."

"Fuck 'em. That's what they get for rejecting me."

We head inside and each write a check for $150. There's enough lag, where bad checks are concerned, that we can walk out of the PX and strap ourselves into the Cadillac as cool as watermelons. My partner's checks will blow up some time, but not now.

Band-Aid Man drives. I think we're headed off post, away from ground zero, but before I know it we're in the officers' club parking lot and our car is stopped.

"You're hungry, right?"

"Yeah, but not for this scene."

"Well, cash is scarce, dude, and I got my dad's officers' club card," he holds it up for me to see. Band-Aid is an Army brat too. Where my father was a paratrooper, Band-Aid's was a combat helicopter pilot who rose to be the first Hispanic helicopter squadron commander in U.S. Army history.

I glance through the windshield at the "Parking Reserved for General Officers" sign in front of us.

"For officers in general," Band-Aid Man explains, slamming his door.

We go through the cafeteria line and charge our food to his father's card. It's lunch time, so when we take our seats at our table, we're surrounded by officers in uniform. The food's good, but the atmosphere comes close to ruining it. I cut a piece of meatloaf and drag it through the mashed potatoes and gravy, and I begin to pick up the conversations from adjacent tables. It is military speak, politics at its worst, tattling and rubbing up to the brass. There are snide comments that so-and-so is "ate up" and someone else is definitely not "squared away." Recitations of Far Side cartoons and Seinfeld plots pass for humor, and all guffaws are in the appropriate military range. That laughter increases in exact parallel to the rank of the joke teller.

The Band-Aid Man starts coughing on his clam chowder. I leap up urgently and perform the Heimlich, and soon my partner is again able to speak.

"Get the fuck off me," he says gratefully. When conversations at adjacent tables resume, he adds, "Sure wish I could have passed the standard to be in these people's Army."

I can feel how hard it is for Band-Aid. This is ground zero for the school that wouldn't let him attend and we're dining in a stronghold of the Army officer corps that kicked him out.

The Army officer dialogues are cresting the levees again, inane conversations barrage us on three sides. I try to shake it all off, willfully stop listening. It's not hard, my head's in a different place. "I don't know what I'm going to do now, Band-Aid. With my life."

Band-Aid can take no more and he bolts from the table straight for the door. And I'm right there, neck-and-neck the whole way, right into the Cadillac, watching the ignition key turn.

"Rearward march!" screams The Band-Aid Man, clicking the shifter only one notch and accelerating us backwards out of the lot. "About face!" he shouts out his window as he executes a J-turn 180 by yanking the wheel hard left, letting off the gas, and knocking the shifter down to L1 all at the same time. We're spun around and he lets go of the wheel and stomps on the accelerator, letting the Cadillac straighten itself out. He overdrives it through the Colonels' residential area with the horn blaring a four-long-blasts pattern to indicate an air attack.

I glance at my friend. His eyes are unblinking and his face is unusually pale. I've been there, a lot of us have. It's thrashing, unsettling emotion, it's about carelessly slipping into a seam of the military and suddenly viewing it from up close, it's that smothering pressure, that dryness in the throat, that realization that you have been swallowed whole and you may never make it out.

"I gotta get away from this," he whispers nervously to himself. He takes a wide left, sending a pair of plastic garbage cans tumbling onto a Colonel's lawn. I would say something comforting, I'd tell him it's not real, but I don't want to startle him. He doesn't know I'm here.

My mentor in becoming a civilian is having a military relapse. If it can happen to him, I know it can happen to me. It can happen to all veterans, regardless of the particular character of their service. You can let go of the military, you can push it away with all the strength in your being, but the military will never entirely let go of you. It's something we vets learn to live with, even while we power through life as pure civilians of the highest order.

We're in Newburgh when Band-Aid finally comes to. There's a clearing off to the right and he drifts into it, stopping with our nose hanging over a ravine. We hop out and sit on the trunk, backs on the rear window, two Montecristos glowing, the valley spread out beneath us. He starts laughing, and his laughter rolls down the autumn-leafy ravine and into the Hudson River. That Army smother we just ran from doesn't touch me. Band-Aid Man broke us both out, because right now I'm feeling as free as I've ever been.

Everything's so beautiful that we can't resist breaking off on a random highway to trace the Connecticut coast. We stop for gas and the highest octane they have is 89. Band-Aid Man is not letting up on the necessity of premium gasoline for our Cadillac, and I've long stopped resisting. Now that I've gotten reacquainted with his driving behavior, I'm actually grateful for any edge the extra octane might provide. Band-Aid also sees a car wash, so we stop and roll it through.

We're glistening now, as white as a star, and there are people out, and he's honking and waving, and people aren't waving back, but they're not cursing us either. We find a dirt road that leads us to an old wooden pier. The pier's creaking underneath the tires and we're way out over the Long Island Sound. The sun's coming down behind us, not over the water. We get out and he takes a picture using The Band-Aid Man technique, camera extended at the end of one long arm, pulling me in with the other. Now I get behind the wheel and pull us away.

Cutting onto I-95, I ask him, "How's Boston sound? I have a friend there…" but he's fast asleep. It's all dark now, not many cars on the road. I find Paris' "The Devil Made Me Do It" tape and I let that spin, this rapper went to high school with me. I open the armrest, dig through the condoms and pull out the plastic bottle. Wow, I never noticed the label, glowing in late-eighties green and pink. I pop the cap. E, huh? I don't really need any. But I might. These are supposed to last for six hours. I tip a couple into my hand, put the cap back on the bottle, and close the armrest. I throw the pills into my mouth and wash them down with a handful of ice water from the cooler.

There's a truck ahead. This is a hilly freeway and I think these trucks are struggling a little. I start to pass him, still riding the cruise control. Whoa, there's a Corvette on my tail, where did he come from? All right, buddy, just let me get around this Freightliner. There's another truck ahead of this one, but I decide to pull between them to let this impatient Corvette shoot by. I've got the room, so I drift right, easing between the two trucks. Suddenly The Band-Aid Man gasps and throws his hands out at the dashboard. He slides and slaps his hands violently on the plastic in a deranged frenzy and in the next second he lunges at the steering wheel. He jerks madly at the wheel and I shout at him as I smack his arms away.

"We're gonna die!" he cries, assuming the fetal position and moaning like a shot wolverine.

The Corvette zooms past and The Band-Aid Man slowly lifts his head. He peers at me and allows his body to unfold from the giant cannonball contortion. "I'm sorry," he says.

I pull around the lead truck and advance into the clear. "You're sorry? What was that?"

"Feel my heart," he grabs my hand and presses it to his wildly pounding chest.

"You had a heart attack?"

"I thought I was still driving. I thought I fell asleep at the wheel and we were about to crash."

"Well, you almost made that part come true."

"I've driven so much that I can't think of myself as a passenger. I've driven 2,500 miles in this car. I like driving."

"I know you do."

"You know that feeling you get when you wake up in some girl's room and you have no idea where you are?"

"Not really."

"Did I ever tell you about the time I woke up and all I saw was white?"

"No."

"Yeah, it was all white, I couldn't see nothing else. And then I looked to my left and there was this girl there and she was sleeping, she was surrounded by white also. And I kind of recognized her from the night before, mugging at a bar and some shit like that. And all of a sudden there's a knock to my right and I look and it's a cop knocking on my window. I'm in a fucking car. I get out, I'm fine and the girl's fine too, but her car's got a tree where the radiator was. Evidently she was taking me to her place and she fell asleep and hit a tree. The white was our airbags."

"Band-Aid Man, please save all stories like that one until after this trip is over. If we start sharing car wreck stories, our subconsciouses are going to start devising a very creative way to total this Caddy."

"I told you about the time I drove off the bridge…"

"Band-Aid, go to sleep."

"Don't give me any orders," he mumbles dreamily. "You've got a long way to go before you're qualified to turn in Reveille…"

Geez, he won't let go of that dog painting. For his own reasons, he imagines the return of that piece of stolen art to its rightful military home as the capstone of my civilian conversion, a rite of passage to be earned, somehow, by whatever I manage to accomplish on this discharge. In the eyes of The Band-Aid Man, getting that framed dog back to the A&M Corps of Cadets will be a life achievement for which history will remember and honor us.

All I can see is trouble. Everything I know from my 25 years on this earth tells me that possession of stolen property comes with penalties. I can't recall an instance, ever, where thieves were given a heroes' welcome for returning something they'd stolen in the first place. At best, I can foresee a reduction in our sentence, something like what a bank robber gets when he turns himself in. I picture our court-appointed lawyer persuading the jury: "It may be true that my clients are not angels. Yes, they are the reason this painting was missing for many years, and they only returned it because they thought they would be celebrated like gods, but they *did return it!* And *that*, ladies and gentlemen, has gotta be worth something, am I right?"

Sisi, the dog painting hung like a guillotine blade over my neck throughout the discharge, but I think you get that already, so I'll leave it alone for a while and let it blindside you around the bend, same way it happened to me and Band-Aid, too late to do anything about it. You'll learn soon enough how the best intentions blew up, and how Band-Aid got us caught in a cat-and-mouse scramble with law enforcement, and how everything boiled over in a white-knuckle run to get the priceless art back to its rightful home before the cops picked us off. Looking back, it seems crazy that a painting we had in our possession generated hundreds of news stories – from early reports of its unsolved disappearance to the increasingly fevered cries for its return. Theories emerged, people and institutions were accused and slandered, and even a political administration got tarred by the Reveille fiasco before it was all over.

Forget about them. All the conspiracies were wrong. No one ever got the full, true story.

Not until now.

Mit and the Boston Pizza Negotiation

Looking out the windshield, all I see is blank horizon. There is nothing out there waiting for me, or even aware of me. I have no job, no home, nothing out there to help me. In this sense, I'm just like every other discharged veteran. There is no overstating the life change of a person separating from the service. In one instant, everything you knew is gone. There's no more security of a home base. Your friends, your rank, the bed where you laid your head for the past however-many years it's been, even your identity – you've lost it all. Identity might be the toughest. The military gives everybody two identities. The first one is your job. You are a cannon cocker (or the *best damn* cannon cocker), or a rescue swimmer, a paratrooper, a naval gunner, a flight mechanic, a surfman, a scout... and your unit counts on you to perform that role. Your second identity is your own personal spin on what you do. Are you the rebel who does everything your own way? Are you the joker? The perfectionist? Or are you the quiet one who nobody could get a fix on until the day everything went to hell and you were the one who didn't crack while you saved everyone else's skin?

Whichever it was, nobody knows anymore. Your hard-earned reputation means nothing today. The people you lived and worked alongside so closely that they effectively became your family? All lost. You had two identities, and suddenly you have none. I won't lie: it's not easy.

Inside this car, though, I'm all right. The Band-Aid Man came for me and that means a lot. I draw reassurance even from his sleeping form. When we roll into Boston, my partner is ready as soon as he opens his eyes, "Hey, that's downtown right there. Let me ask him where we should go." I slow down next to the guy on the sidewalk and Band-Aid asks, "Hey, buddy, we just got here, where's the action?"

"What kind of action?"

"Girls. We want to get laid." Band-Aid's mission statement discourages me as I unsuccessfully try to connect getting laid to making me a civilian, but I shake it off and resolve to stay positive with the understanding that The Band-Aid Man works in mysterious ways.

"Fair enough, there's plenty of 'em here. Start at Copley Square..." the sidewalk guy gives us directions. We thank him and take off.

"He sounded just like Ted Kennedy," Band-Aid marvels.

"They probably all do around here." I pass the intersection of Tremont and Tremont. The streets here are ridiculous. But I guess two streets with the same name is nothing unusual in a town where I'm seeing odd and even addresses on the same side of the street. I can deal with the other drivers, though. They're predictably aggressive. I rush the oncoming lane for a second to zip around a limousine.

"God damn, Ames, you can't drive. Pull over and give her to me."

"What do you mean? I'm a great driver, I've never been in an accident."

"All right, Ames, you never wreck, but you treat your passengers like shit. It's either gas or brakes with you. You know, there are times when a driver doesn't need to press either pedal down all the way, and occasionally he doesn't need to push them at all."

"So what are you saying?"

"Pull over, you're making me sick."

I park in a lot at Newbury and Dartmouth. There's TGI Friday's, and we know how well evenings end when we start out there. We make a beeline for it. They've got the heat cranked up in here, so I shed my jacket and sweatshirt.

"Ames with his personal climate control!" Band-Aid announces to the bar. "He's always got to strip down to his Saints cap and T-shirt." Some girls on our right laugh and Band-Aid introduces us. The streets outside are full of women, and there are plenty in here too. We get some beers, I ask the bartender for some change to make a phone call and he gives me a bunch of dimes. I call up my buddy, McGinn, and I tell him I'm right here in his town. He sounds excited and he says he'll meet us here. It's great to hear him. He was always a fun guy, high-energy and dramatic like The Band-Aid Man, but without the social graces. While Band-Aid Man is preoccupied with his image and always making a good impression, McGinn has no concept of image and regularly makes a bad impression on purpose. It's going to be fun to see the two together.

"Get over here, Ames. This girl says you have pretty eyes," Band-Aid Man is at the bar and he's got way too many shots lined up, even if the girls are doing them with us. I join him and the girls, but I tilt my head down so the bill of my cap cuts my line of sight off at their noses. They're from Michigan. I can't see their eyes and they can't see mine, this is fun. I'm going to do this for the rest of the night.

A hostess calls the Michiganders to a table, but the one I haven't even talked to doubles back, hands me her number, and mouths, "Soon." I put her number in my back pocket and I feel all the other napkins, matchbook covers, and slips of stationery from east coast cities in there. It occurs to me that I've worn this same pair of Levis every day since I landed.

New girls break into laughter at the end of the bar, so I ask our bartender to deliver a large tumbler of lukewarm tap water to each of them. The girls brighten in enchanted surprise when the glasses hit the bar in their midst. They thank us before they have their first sips, and then the tap-water taste seems to suck the laughing spirit right out of them. Our bartender shrugs and the girls take wing from their perches at the bar. Two young professionals still in their downtown attire introduce themselves to us. John's a handsome guy in suspenders. Chris wears glasses, seems a little more serious.

"Hey, let us welcome you guys to our city with some shots." The tequila glasses come out and John says, "Here's to being on the road."

That's a great toast and it occurs to me I've already heard it a few times on this trip, from new friends wishing us well.

The shots keep coming. Chris elbows John and reminds him they've got to go to work tomorrow, but John doesn't care. Some new pretty girls merge in with our group and Chris isn't so concerned about tomorrow's workload anymore.

They tell us we're in Boston on a good night and they tell us some places to check out. They're excited about our mission to turn me into a civilian and they're asking all kinds of questions while they order rounds of shots.

"Have you gotten any speeding tickets yet?"

"No. I got pulled over once, but the cop was cool and he let us go when I told him we were veterans."

"That's great. You guys are jugheads?"

Jughead from Archie comics? Or jarheads? Serious military geeks will correct civilians on the jargon, but I never have, and especially won't now, given my pressing agenda to become a civilian. For an instant, I even want to use the improper jughead term in solidarity – these civilians are *my people* now – but there's a momentum to this night that won't let me think it through. "Marines? No, Army."

"When we were stationed together, I got Ames more bush than I got myself," Band-Aid getting straight to what he considers the important part. "He was in a complete drought before I showed up."

"Well, not *complete*…" I start to defend.

Band-Aid cuts me off, "Oh yeah, there was this one chick – Ames finger-banged her tits or something."

"Jesus!" Chris exclaims. Chris and John stare wide-eyed, and it takes me several seconds before I form a picture of what Band-Aid has created, his vague idea of what an amateur like me might attempt with a woman.

"Poor bastard," John throws a pitying glance my way.

"I never did that," I protest, but I can tell that too many seconds have gone by and the concept has already been absorbed and associated with me permanently. For a moment, I can't figure out why I'm stinging, oddly worried about being judged by these people I just met. Then I realize it's because this is the first trace of my post-Army identity. *Ames the inept lover who uses foolish techniques to pleasure women.* This is part of the civilian Ames that's being forged.

I see Chris is now looking across the bar at a busty girl while sliding two fingers up and down in the air. I can't tell if he's messing with me or just trying to figure out how I performed the feat that Band-Aid described. "That was the old me," I struggle to set the record straight. "Now that I'm a civilian, I don—"

Suddenly I'm grabbed around my neck and pulled off my stool from behind.

"I tol you abou steal vegetable juice from my shop!" screams the San Francisco-Chinese voice of my attacker. "Where my V8 juice? Where my V8? If I don get my V8, my brotha will jack you shit to the sky! To the sky!"

I fall completely on my back and only now do I see my attacker. It's McGinn, my buddy from high school, and he's wearing a ridiculous pope hat. We laugh together for a while.

"Man, McGinn, it's good to see you haven't changed."

"You're lucky you caught me. I had a gig in Roxbury tonight, but it wrapped up early." McGinn's a trumpeter, a great one.

"I'm glad you're still playing. I heard some rumors about a bank job and I got scared."

"They're true, but I try to keep trumpeting. Believe me, I'm no fan of the bank job either, but I like eating every day."

I lose track of the bar while I get caught up with my friend from the old neighborhood. Minutes go by before a commotion outside tunes me back in. I look up through the window to see John and Chris being sent away by security. I turn to Band-Aid Man, who is flanked by girls I don't recognize, "What's that all about?"

"Well, Ames, either we can disregard all the Boston Yard local advice those two gave us, or we can take it and accept that the best way to pick up women in Boston is to call them fucking cunts." He puts his arms over the girls' shoulders and adds, "Never, never call a woman a cunt. Those boys need an education in southern style."

"They sure do," a girl chirps.

"Well, what happened?"

"I went to the restroom," Band-Aid explains, "and John came in there, slipped, fell, almost killed himself, and I came back out, all of a sudden security was standing there ushering those two guys out the doors, and me totally dismayed as to what happened. I asked the girls, 'Hey, uh... what happened? what went wrong?' I come to find out that John called this girl a fucking cunt. Girls totally distraught."

"Wow. What a turn of events."

"Never, never, ever call a girl a cunt," Band-Aid emphasizes again to the girls. "Bush or bitch or whore, fine, but not cunt."

The girls leave. I introduce my two friends to each other and we move on to a bar called Daisy Buchanan's. Band-Aid keeps throwing quick, uncertain glances at McGinn, and I can tell he's wondering when our new host is going to lose the pope hat. Daisy's is nice.

"This is Bush Gardens!" Band-Aid exclaims happily, skipping down the short staircase. He runs his hand over his hair, tightens his tie, gives the lapels on his jacket a good tug, and rubs the adhesive bandage on his earlobe between his thumb and forefinger as a final systems check. There are women everywhere. "Hey!" he shouts suddenly, "There's John and Chris!" He steps swiftly toward them and I hear him begin a lecture: "Never, ever, *ever* call a ..."

McGinn grabs us some beers at the bar. This is going to be an alcohol abuse evening, I can see it. McGinn's just starting and I already can't think straight. We start catching up on each other and we're meeting people. It's fun this way, because other people are asking my high school friend questions I want to ask.

Band-Aid, seminar in southern style wrapped up, joins us at the bar. There are three fun girls around us and Band-Aid wastes no time in charming them. McGinn interrupts suddenly, "This man is related to George S. Patton, but he's still getting out of the Army!" He's pointing at me while he says this. The group is all at once confused. Heads turning, foreheads creasing, shoulders rising. Band-Aid tries to swing the momentum back, but McGinn keeps pressing the George Patton thing. Pretty soon, the girls leave.

Band-Aid glares at McGinn. "What the fuck was that, Mit?" he demands. Wow, that's a memory. Mit was an Army lieutenant who invoked the wrath of The Band-Aid Man in a bar in Kaprun, Austria, two years ago. That bar had been full of women too, but Mit kept cornering Band-Aid and telling him Army stories, even though he knew Band-Aid had already been kicked out. Finally, Band-Aid Man exploded, "Listen, Mit! I don't give a fuck about your Army career! Shut your mouth unless you want to tell me about alcohol or bush, or trying to get either one!" And for the first time since that freezing night in the Austrian Alps, Band-Aid Man believes that someone else is worthy of the Mit title. So be it.

Mit delivers an unsatisfactory explanation, grinning all the while.

"Listen, Mit! I don't give a fuck how popular you say George Patton is around here, obviously he's not a big hit with the chicks tonight, so I don't want to hear about him!"

Mit grins wildly under his pope hat.

"Take us someplace else!" orders a frustrated Band-Aid Man.

"What happened to Bush Gardens?"

"Well, it was, until Mit put a *mojo* on my ass."

We're downstairs in a place called The Pour House and Mit's at the bar grabbing some more beers. It's now plain that Band-Aid is going to get another chance, the girls in here are pretty and forward.

"God damn, Ames, the chicks are even checking you out in here. Look! That one blew a kiss at you."

"Cool."

"What do you mean, cool? She wants you, do something. This might be the night we both get laid together. Come on, Ames, make my dream come true."

"It has come true, you just don't remember. And you're not gonna remember tonight, either."

Band-Aid drops the idea, leaning in closer to confide, "Ames, when I first came downstairs, those biker guys were pointing at Mit, calling him a fucking geek."

"You're imagining things, Band-Aid." Two girls come up to us and start talking. I'm still doing that trick with my Saints cap, but they both look good from the nose down. Suddenly, Mit's here to pass out beers.

"Hey, this man is related to George S. Patton."

The girls excuse themselves. I look at The Band-Aid Man's crestfallen expression and I start laughing uncontrollably. I'm laughing so hard my sides are hurting. Mit is on a roll. This whole scene is so mad, with Mit's pope hat, George S. Patton, the fleeing girls, and the wind being sucked out of Band-Aid Man's sails.

Band-Aid's stomping up the steps to leave and we follow him. He hasn't said a word to Mit this time and I think I know why. I met Mit in my junior year of high school and I respected him right away. There's a genius to him, one that would never show up on a test. It's a genius that eludes the five senses, but is unmistakably there, lurking. Something in Mit's grin says, "Go ahead, give me your best shot. I'll top it." Band-Aid's got his own genius for living large, normally he's unflappable. But Mit's gotten inside the wall. I'm drunk right now, but that's what I'm thinking, and I'm thinking Band-Aid's scared.

We go to the Cactus Club and my mind's spinning. I see Band-Aid pull the E bottle out of his jacket and I make him give me some. I ask for three this time. This place is kind of a blur, I've got to rein it in. Got to hold on to my beer, don't want to drop it, can't forget it's in my hand. There are more girls here with us. Nice nose mine has, she's trying to say something to me. I can't talk, honey, I'm just gonna ride this. I have to tilt my head sideways to see The Band-Aid Man and still shield my eyes from the girls, otherwise the game will be over. Mit's telling them I'm related to George S. Patton. They're leaving.

Band-Aid slams his beer on the table and runs. He barely touched his beer. I'd better drink it, don't want to waste. I hit the bathroom. I find them outside on the street. I'm getting better now. Band-Aid Man is appealing to Mit, asking him please not to mention George S. Patton again. Mit grins under his pope hat, but this time he says okay and he looks different. Maybe he means it.

We're upstairs in the Crossroads and Mit and I are drinking at the bar. I'm drunk, but I'm under control. The E's kicking in and it's offsetting the alcohol a little bit. The Band-Aid Man has gone off on his own to meet females while Mit and I talk and drink. Mit's a character and he's still being a character, but he's decided to leave The Band-Aid Man alone. The bartender announces last call and we get our final beers and finish them. I can see Band-Aid at the other side of the bar, talking with a tall girl. She's not pretty, but he doesn't really care what a female looks like. She's touching him while she talks. Mit suggests we wait for Band-Aid outside where he and I can sit on some steps and rap the way we used to in the city. So we walk toward Band-Aid to tell him.

The Band-Aid Man looks up and sees us. He sees Mit's pope hat slicing through the crowd like a shark fin and his eyes register fear. He knows the curse the pope hat brings, he's terrified. But he'll breathe a huge sigh of relief when we tell him we're just going to wait for him outside. He's trying to say something to the tall girl when we arrive, but he starts stammering. He turns to Mit and exclaims, "Don't fucking say anything about fucking George S. Patton!"

"No, we're just —"

Band-Aid shakes his head crazily, "This Mit fucker's been telling people all night that Ames is related to George S. Patton. He's just been saying it for no fucking reason — 'Hey, this man is related to George S.

Patton.' George Patton! Ge-ooorge! Pat-tooooon!"

The girl leaves. Band-Aid reaches toward her, he calls, nothing. His face drops, he appears close to tears.

"Anyone else hungry?" I ask.

"IHOP's open," Mit says, so we head that way. The International House of Pancakes seems to be the place to go at this time, it's jam-packed. We slide into a table when another crew leaves and I accidentally make eye-contact with a gorgeous Hispanic chick next to me. Her friend's hot too, but she's got the beautiful eyes, wow! I'm doing the brim thing now, so I can't see the eyes anymore, but they're burnt into my memory. I can see them inside my head. The girls start talking with us. They don't have any food either, there's not a waiter in sight. The girls ask us where we're staying tonight. They ask us what we're doing. "We're trying to demilitarize our friend," Band-Aid's talking for the males. He reaches under the table and pulls my pen out of my pocket. He jots a secret note on a napkin and slides it to me: "If Mit doesn't fuck this one up, my dream's coming true. I won't black out. Love, BAM."

"Let me see your eyes." Oh, that's the beautiful one. I don't move or speak, I'll let Band-Aid handle it.

"Ames, show her your eyes."

"Come on, I think they're hot." Let her think that. If bloodshot is hot, I guess she's right. I don't show them. "You're an asshole."

"Quiet type," her friend picks up. "Is he in the military or something?"

"Goddamn," Band-Aid drawls miserably. "That's what we're trying to get him out of. He's in reset mode now. Out with the military Ames, in with the civilian Ames. You've met him at the most critical stage of his life."

The first girl, with the eyes, gives me another shot, "Well, talk to me. What do you do?"

"Right now we're just art thieves," I answer, brim low. "But I have bigger dreams. I don't feel that's really what I am."

She nods understandingly, now I ask her, "What do *you* do?"

"For right now, I repair desks at a high school."

I remember Band-Aid's words about always being on the lookout for job possibilities. "Wow, desk repair... how did you break into that field?"

"I was right, you're an asshole," she curses. Oh, no, she's mistaken my genuine interest in her desk-repair job for sarcasm. I can't think of a good way to explain that she's wrong. The beautiful-eyed Latina pulls her friend out of a conversation with The Band-Aid Man and both ladies leave the International House of Pancakes.

We wait five more minutes and no waiter ever shows, so we leave too, stomachs growling. We drift over near Fenway Park. The Pizza Pad is closing up, but they've got one more pepperoni on the rack. "How much you want for it?" Band-Aid asks.

"Eight dollars."

"Too much," Mit shoos me and Band-Aid Man away. "Go outside, I'll take care of this."

Band-Aid and I are out on the sidewalk. Thirty feet away, through the pizza shop window, Mit is wheeling and dealing with the employees in a scene that comes off as a silent security-camera short from our angle. In a few minutes, he steps from the brightly lit business and becomes a silhouette of a man with a pizza box on his forearm. He approaches us and I take the box. I pleasure in its weight and heat, I savor its smell.

"What'd you bring 'em down to?"

"Eight bucks."

"What!" Band-Aid shrieks. "You wasted all that time, we're starving out here, and didn't bring the price down a penny? You fucked up my whole night and then, to cap it off, you fuck up the pizza, too!" The Band-Aid Man's arms are flying about, his hands swooping in rage and anguish, he's pacing and pivoting on the sidewalk like a man with nothing in the world. "Fuck you, Mit! I'm in the easiest town to get laid in in the USA, north of Dallas and east of California, women checking us out left and right, and doing it very noticeably, so we can make a move – say, 'Hi, fucking cunt!' in the local tradition – and you sabotage every aspect of pussy obtaining whatsoever. I set myself up with good bush in five places and you shut me down five times in a row. 'This man is related to George S. Patton! This man is related to George S. Patton!' Patton S. George! Pope Mit the Shithead!" He's falling apart now, blathering, visibly shaking.

Mit squares off and fires back, "If all I have to do is mention the name of Ames's relative and the girls scurry, then you never had 'em in the first place. You blew it solo most of the time. What was that breakdown in the Crossroads with the tall chick? I didn't even mention Patton and wasn't going to, and you scared her away all by yourself –"

"Sure, I already had your mojo on my ass. I was doomed as soon as I met you, fucking Mit."

"And I didn't say a word in IHOP. Ames chased that girl out and you never got mad at him."

"Ames can't help himself. That's just Ames being Ames. Plus at least that fucker has the excuse of trying to become a civilian. But, you! Mit, you went out of your way to cockblock me, you ruined me!" He raises his flat hand to hold off further protest. His chest is heaving from the intensity of his emotion. He looks down and tries to compose himself. He lifts his head and stares deeply into Mit's eyes to deliver a controlled closing statement: "Thank you, Mit, for my low point of this discharge."

Mit says nothing in return. Band-Aid's a broken man and words are useless now. Band-Aid can let off all the steam he wants. There's no harm in it and it's probably good for him. Both of my friends walk over to the pizza box in my hand. Band-Aid lifts the top.

"Half a pizza? God damn, Mit, you fucked up even worse than I thought. They were gonna give us the whole thing for eight bucks before you got involved."

"I thought it was the whole thing. I'm getting our money," Mit starts for the Pizza Pad, but the place is locked up now, lights out.

"Fucking Mit," Band-Aid sighs and shakes his head.

Actually, I ate half the pizza while they were yelling at each other. I wasn't thinking about it really, just enjoying my pizza with the show. I'll let Mit take the fall, Band-Aid already hates him anyway. No sense in creating any new bad blood.

Mit's apartment is close by, we all pour in. The Band-Aid Man stretches out in a chair and picks up a Cosmopolitan magazine.

"'How to Have a Better Orgasm.' Why am I reading this when I should be acting it out?"

"Hey, Band-Aid, try some of this Jameson," Mit says, pouring us each a glass.

"Hey, this is good. Almost as smooth as Crown."

"It's smoother than Crown. Irish whiskey, you gotta go Irish."

We talk and drink until the bottle's empty. The Jameson was definitely a hit.

"That's good whiskey."

"I told you, go Irish."

"Thanks for breaking it out. You've almost redeemed yourself, Mit. Almost." With that, The Band-Aid Man closes his eyes and falls asleep. I realize we haven't been up close with any prostitutes in days, and this all at once allays my old fears that hookers would be an unshakable theme of my civilian life. Mit opens another bottle of something else. We throw some memories out and laugh together. I enjoy my old friend's unique sense of humor. The clock's moving, he's got that bank job.

I wake up to find Band-Aid Man already showered and on a mission. "I think Mit's shampoo fucked up my hair," he mentions sadly before jumping to business. "Let's get some ice right away," he urges. A few blocks short of the freeway there's a liquor store, so Band-Aid puts two tires over the curb. An extremely dirty man with greasy red hair splits us as we enter.

"Get out of here, you son of a piper!" the grizzled storeowner inside shouts past us at the dirty man. The storeowner's holding an axe handle, trembling with fury.

We carry out five bags of ice, and Band-Aid strains out the old water and repacks the coolers there on the sidewalk. The greasy man walks up to Band-Aid Man and shakes his head.

"What!" Band-Aid demands.

The redhead delivers a muddled condemnation of people who park on the sidewalk. His voice is phlegm-filled and disgusting.

"We're leaving in two…" The Band-Aid man stops himself. "Why am I even defending myself to you? You're a fucking bum!"

The bum dances around in anger, greasy hair flying.

"Easy, Red," I offer consolingly. "Don't worry about Poncho. He ain't had his breakfast. He gets grumpy when he ain't had his breakfast." I snatch a Miller from the small cooler and finger-roll it to the dirty man who opens it immediately.

"I will smash your lights out!"

I spin around to see the issuer of that exclamation and my eyes fall on the trembling figure of the storeowner, axe handle in hand.

"These gutter tramps are bad enough as it is. The last thing I need is a couple of red-hot pipers like you giving out beers, convincing 'em this is a good corner! I'm gonna smash your car!"

"Leave the Cadillac out of this!" Band-Aid Man runs around to the driver's side.

The storeowner starts twirling the axe handle like a propeller and advancing on the car.

"Smash Red's kneecaps instead!" Band-Aid pleads, double-starting the engine in panic and accelerating off the curb with two doors open. The storeowner runs after him with surprising speed.

The red-haired bum rubs his fingers together in front of my face. He keeps gargling requests for money. I reach into my back pocket and feel the wad of paper. No money there, just napkins, matchbook covers, and slips of stationery.

"Here you go, friend. You don't have to live like that. These are numbers of people who can help you. Feel free to call collect."

The Cadillac is gone, so I walk in the direction I saw it heading.

There I was, Sisi, roaming the streets of Boston, imagining that my mission to turn into a civilian was going pretty well so far. At the very least, I was content in the cloud of reasonable human understanding that the military and I were on two separate vectors, moving ever further apart. And, though Band-Aid Man and I might have to visit bases to keep our road trip going, any contact we'd have with the military from then on would be our choice. And despite my sharp and unremitting awareness that there was no telling how my metamorphosis would play out, with all the mysteries on the horizon yet unrevealed, a thought that never even came close to crossing my mind was that one day, eleven years later, the Army machine would reenter my life and tell me that I had never left.

The Hostile Buffalo Cabbie and the German Limbo King

Almost a week of checking my mailbox for the *mobi-pack* that Major Horse-pelt had promised me, and it finally arrived by FedEx. The FedEx driver was chatty, a real nice guy, but I'm sure I came off as a jerk because I couldn't pay attention to a word he said. No sooner had the driver spun back toward his truck than I tore into the envelope.

I flipped through every one of the dozens of pages therein, my eyes scanning rabidly for all usable data to feed to my information-starved mind. I was in urgent need of enlightenment. And at the end of my furious speed-read, my mind was as starved as before. Apart from my precise report date, 24 days later, Major Horse-pelt's mobi-pack contained no answers whatsoever. I felt my mood nosedive, sad at the absence of answers and stinging from anger at myself for having expected any more from the military machine. I *knew* the Army better than that. Nothing I'd ever experienced in my time in uniform had given me any reason to hope that their mobi-pack would be useful. This worthless pile of garbage should have been exactly what I'd expected.

I pulled out a random sheet and studied the child-appropriate travel tips that filled the page. "Always use your safety belt!" was typical of the included guidance that shouldn't need to be given to adult professionals. Then again, maybe this was the answer to why the Pentagon was calling up guys like me: Too many actual servicemembers were flying through their windshields on the way to report. Aside from life-saving advice of that caliber, the mobi-pack was loaded with jarring checklists that reinforced exactly how unprepared I was for anything like this. "*REPORT WITH THESE ITEMS,*" one flyer commanded, "*Class B Uniform, US Army ID Tags, 2 pr. Combat Boots…*" I had none of it. I was not a sentimental veteran who hung onto uniforms or mementoes. The single piece of equipment from my Army days I hadn't thrown away was my rucksack, which I'd kept around for its general utility. I was feeling a sliver of relief that I'd at least hung onto that, until I saw the list of prohibited items on the next page: "*WARNING! DO NOT BRING – Rucksack...*" Everything was wrong.

It took me a long time to even breathe properly after I set the mobi-pack down. If these guys – Major Horse-pelt, Major Bivens, any of them – could have seen my discharge and grasped what I'd done to become a civilian, they would have stopped this insanity.

But *you* see this, don't you Sisi? You see it all, right?

The bathroom door swings inward and The Band-Aid Man emerges dramatically in a cloud of steam, shirtless for the moment to highlight his new look. A wet razor dangles in his hand. Upon his handsome face is an old-fashioned goatee. It's black as coal, every edge pointed and sharp.

"My God, Satan!"

He grins excitedly, "Do you think the babes will like it?"

"They'll give you their souls as soon as they lay eyes on it." I am envious. Not of his beauty, which suits Band-Aid Man's personality and would certainly throw mine off. But I'm definitely envious that he looks like such a civilian. No member of any branch of the military – not the guys with shaving profiles, nor the Squids who have more license with facial hair, and especially not the Special Forces operators with their Stonewall Jackson combat beards – sport anything half as civilian as what's etched around Band-Aid's smile here in Buffalo. I don't even bother to look at myself in the hotel mirror. I know I still look too much like a soldier, and I can't go out like this with him tonight. "This calls for a countermeasure!"

My eyes hunt the room and arrive at the head of our king-sized bed, home to an enticing double-deck of spongey pillows. I calmly reach for the most swollen pillow of the litter and stuff it in the front of my red sweatshirt. "Since you are the handsome and diabolical Prince of Darkness, I have no choice but to be Mavis the Angel."

"Take that out, you're gonna fuck up our bush," Band-Aid insists.

But I hold fast. "We need balance, Satan," I spring into the hallway bellyfirst.

Multiple neighborhoods, live music shows, and acquaintances later, somewhere on Elmwood Avenue in Buffalo, Band-Aid decides we should return to his favorite bar we hit on this strip tonight. We weave back toward it, one of those drunken marches that seems to take a long time and no time at all.

"Here it is, Fatboy!" he gestures kitty-corner to the club.

Still bellyfirst, I'm making the diagonal cross to follow Band-Aid into the doorway. Four hours earlier, this was a female bonanza. Now we walk in and find it completely deserted. Crickets chirping... wind howling... zero patrons. The Band-Aid Man's bartender is here, however, and she explains that the whole crowd was college girls and now they're all at sorority parties.

"That's wild, I didn't see one sorority sweatshirt."

"You weren't looking at the ugly girls," the bartender playfully punches my belly and I double over in pretend pain. It's a routine I've been performing all night. "Those are the ones who always wear the sorority letters, much to the shame of their sisters."

"Sounds like an experienced opinion."

"Yeah, I'm a sorority girl."

The Band-Aid Man smiles at her and asks, "Well, are you going home with me tonight, or what?"

She giggles, "Ssshh! That's my boyfriend right behind me." There's a guy in a baseball cap carrying liquor into the back storeroom.

"You work in the same bar as your boyfriend?"

"That's how we met."

"Can't you tell him I'm an old friend or something?"

"No, but I'm talking to you. I bet you wouldn't talk to me if I met you in San Antonio with your girlfriend."

"I'd work something out."

"You would?"

"Why don't you come visit me and see for yourself?" He gives her his Miller Beer card which she takes and tucks away in her jeans.

"Come here, I want to tell you something." He leans in and she pulls her face close and whispers, "I can't tell you with my boyfriend there. Tell me right when he goes into the back."

Band-Aid watches around her head and says, "Now."

She doesn't tell him anything. She closes her eyes, opens her mouth, and kisses him passionately for twenty seconds. When she releases him, she says, "You're sweet."

The Band-Aid Man is beaming, large smile bracketed by sinister goatee. Me, meanwhile, off to the side... regarded with pity... no friends... no job... huge belly... drunken fool... rock bottom. I look down my stomach and laugh at myself. I walk outside. The place across the street is empty too. This whole strip cleared out in four short hours.

My partner puts his arm over my shoulders and he pulls out his silver flask. We both take a gulp.

"Ames, my brother, thanks for saving my life in Italy."

"We're family, Band-Aid. Stop saying that."

"Have I said it before?"

"Every time you drink more than fifteen beers."

"That often?"

A cab almost runs us over in the middle of the street, so Band-Aid opens the door and orders: "Take us to the college." The Band-Aid Man picks up strains of music in the air and navigates us to a full-on house party. He smacks the driver on the shoulder, "You're coming in with us."

"I can't," the driver protests. He's a young guy, even looks like a college student.

"What do you mean you can't? Who the fuck are you going to pick up at this hour?"

"No one, it's just that I quit drinking a month ago."

"Well, just come in and don't drink."

"Yeah," I second. "Then we can go to bed together naked, but we won't have sex."

"Hey! Don't listen to this dickhead," Band-Aid stops the driver as he's about to pull away. "I got your cover. Let's go."

The driver locks his cab and follows us up the walk and through the door. It's a chaotic scene in here, live band and hard-rocking college students on two stories. I peel off to hit a bathroom. When I come out, I spot Band-Aid and the taxi driver cutting through the crowd. I head after them, but a blond guy intercepts me and starts talking.

"You were at the disco, yeah?" Holy cow, I'll always recognize that accent. This guy's a German.

"I don't think so."

"Yeah, I saw you."

"All right, maybe I was."

"When I saw you I was on the phone. I had to make urgently this phone call to my friend. But it is long distance. I'm only twenty miles away and it is long distance." Here he does that condescending chuckle that Germans do when talking about America's ills. "Well, of course you know how shitty the American phone system is. It's really shit."

"What? America's got the best phone system in the world."

"Are you kidding me?" Condescending chuckle.

"No, I'm not kidding you. What happened to the Deutscher standard American put-downs? Tell me we killed more Indians than Hitler killed Jews, say we're behind Romania in Math and behind *Germany* in *English*. Say something with some truth, but don't tell me our phones don't work."

"I couldn't call long distance because I didn't have enough change. It took me an hour to get the change."

"Call collect next time, we have that luxury here. American phones can do anything, we invented the telephone."

Chuckle. "I think you need to go back to school. The telephone was invented by Germany."

"What? I just left Germany last week and your phones still weighed ten pounds apiece and nobody had heard of touch tone yet. America invented the telephone, Germany invented mind control rallies – get your history of communications straight." I leave that guy. I've typically been entertained when Germans really start going off on the USA, but they have to have their facts straight. It is fun to laugh at the top dog's faults, but this guy was just making stuff up. He was baiting me back into my American soldier persona when I need to leave that behind.

I find The Band-Aid Man and our cabdriver near the keg. "The important thing is that you proved you could quit for a month," Band-Aid reassures. They both drain their cups in single gulps and go back for more. The cabdriver's eyes are orange like fire. Band-Aid puts an arm over his shoulder, "That's something nobody can take away from you."

"Fucking A! These bitches aren't taking shit away from me!"

A few girls come by to refill and we talk for a little while. Band-Aid is flirting playfully and they're intrigued. Suddenly the trio dashes away together.

I turn to our driver and see his hostile stare.

"Bitches!" he shouts threateningly. "They're trying to take what's mine."

"Dude, I think you got the wrong idea," Band-Aid counsels.

"Oh, if the idea is that some bitches are going to get what's coming, then I got the right idea." The cabdriver surveys the room hatefully, his eyes throwing flaming stakes.

I whistle like a cuckoo clock and from out of nowhere I get bumped in the hip. Oh Lord, it's the German. He bumps me several more times to the music.

"You said you were in Bayern, yeah? Hop to it, buddy, let's show these Americans how to make party, München-style." He smiles at me and grabs a nearby lamp connected to an extension cord. It's a tall model lamp, flat base and a six-foot pole running up to an exposed bulb. The German turns the lamp horizontal, pointing the light straight out. "Limbo! Party people! Limbo!"

I cut back into the keg line. I'm going to escape somehow, even if it's just into wasted oblivion. I fill my cup to the top and try to let some of the foam settle when the cabdriver butts through to yank the hose out of my hand. He glares at me challengingly while he fills his cup, downs it, and fills it again. It's clear that in his mind I'm one of the bitches who's come to take what's his.

When I find The Band-Aid Man, he's ducking under the limbo lamp in front of a cheering crowd. "How loooow can you go!" the German shouts. Band-Aid leans back super far and shimmies his way under, he makes it all the way to his chin before he crashes on his back. The crowd groans.

I lift my partner off the floor and the next dancer shakes his way up. The German catches my eye and yells, "Americans don't know how to make party!" Then he says something to me in German and laughs boldly.

"That fucker lowered the pole midway," Band-Aid reports in anger.

I wave that whole scene off. "That Molotov you brought to the party is freaking everybody out."

"The cabdriver? He's all right."

"No he's not. He was staring me down at the keg."

"You?" Band-Aid sighs. "When will people realize that Ames' enemies are my enemies?"

"He'll explode if we don't do something."

"Mean drunks are easy. You just make 'em drink themselves out."

The limbo crowd roars as another contestant slides under the lamp. Band-Aid Man stares suspiciously at the German, "Did you see him lower the pole on me?"

"I put nothing past him."

"You don't lower the pole while someone is limboing," Band-Aid states sorely. "Watch that blond fucker, figure out his tricks. I've got to go find the hard shit."

I creep closer to this ghastly limbo scene. The annoying German is on top of the world, all the cuties in the room shuffling with his every limbo cry. Even the band is going along with it, playing a rocking jam with the chorus of "Limbo Now!" I'm about to dismiss my partner's instructions and just get out of here, maybe run upstairs.

Band-Aid Man arrives swiftly and hands me a beer. "See him lower the pole on anybody?"

"No."

He nods as if he knew it all along, "Motherfucker was singling me out."

The crowd screams again as another dancer falls. The German sets the lamp upright. "Intermission," he announces, smiling broadly. "Nature calls. Even master of ceremony has to take a ..." he points to his crotch and makes a hissing sound. The audience applauds as he walks off. Band-Aid tracks him warily out of the corners of his eyes. My partner is flexing his jaw, still stinging from the cheating he perceives was at the root of his limbo elimination. I've got to help him move on.

"How's our driver?"

"Good. I introduced him to Everclear."

"Where is he?" I start to search when a woman's shriek pierces through every other noise in the house.

We run toward the keg and nearly trip over our cabdriver. He's facedown on the carpet. A river of vomit is surging from his mouth into an expanding lake of vomit around his head. Stunned spectators are crowding and murmuring, asking what happened. I shudder when I see the convulsions start.

A girl announces, "Someone gave him a big cup and he drank it really fast."

"A cup of what?"

"Who gave it to him?"

While the crowd hunts for answers I look toward the front door.

"It's electric shock," declares The Band-Aid Man, just another voice in the crowd. "That blond dude zapped his ass with the electric limbo rod."

Blood starts rushing to my head, Band-Aid's about to get us both killed. My buzz is instantly gone and I realize we don't belong anywhere near here.

"It's plugged into an extension cord," comes a voice from the rear. I turn around to see a stringy-haired youth holding the limbo lamp in the air.

"Put that down!" comes a terrified cry.

"Unplug it!"

A frantic student up front with me asks, "How do you treat electric shock?"

"I already called the ambulance," someone replies quickly.

The wails of the limbo king drift into the scene. "I didn't know! I'm sorry." Four husky bruisers carry him past me in a joint-cracking gang press. The German looks right at me – his tight face crowned in newborn yellow hair – and whimpers: "I was only trying to show them how to make party."

Good God. I have to admire Band-Aid's having taken out two adversaries with one move at a house party, but everybody's whole night is collateral damage. We need to go.

Red lights flash through the windows. I grab my partner and pull him outside, we cross paths with the EMT's on the lawn. The paramedics are seconds away from recognizing alcohol poisoning – not electric shock – and we need to march off in the cold before the bruisers plow us into the frozen earth exactly the way they have that German.

Sisi, even more than I had wanted *not* to talk to that German back in Buffalo, I wanted desperately to talk to the Army during my recall crisis.

From the day I tore into the mobi-pack and found maddening nonsense instead of answers, I started firing e-mails at Personnel Command and calling them around the clock. But Horse-pelt wasn't responding, and it seemed the entire Pentagon was too busy to acknowledge, much less enlighten me. I was completely cut off. All I had was a list of uniforms and equipment I was required to report with, but didn't own, and a rapidly approaching report date, now less than three weeks away.

My situation was bleak, Sisi, but I wasn't in this alone. Word of my recall was splashing across fifty states. Even as I tumbled deeper into the Army abyss, friends of mine rallied overtime with rescue in mind. My inbox exploded with e-mails. Some offered schemes; others, lawyers; and more still, outpourings of kind words. And there were a couple that completely defied category. The very first friend Band-Aid and I encountered on the discharge road trip transmitted one of the most memorable e-mails in the deluge. It was composed in a flamboyant specialized font known as "Curlz MT" that my computer is not capable of, Sisi, but it may help if you imagine flowers and rainbows:

From: "Jammer"
To: 'Ames Holbrook'
Subject: DO NOT GO!!!!!!

Ames, I have heard this horrible news and I urge you YOU CAN'T GO! Don't fight the imperialists' war for oil! Do not play a part in the evil business of resource hoarding and world domination.
GO UNDERGROUND! The Pink Slip Movement is growing stronger. I have some pamphlets I am going to send you that will help you understand the evil plan that the rulers want to make you their pawn in. I'll let you know when you can pick them up at the Amtrak station. READ THEM!!!
Magical love,
Jammer

You can't predict the twists and turns your old Army buddies' lives will take over the years. There are friends who disappear right off the middle of your radar screen, and there are guys like Jammer, who willfully out-fly the radar, but keep in contact with *only you.* Somewhere between now and the night I'd spent with him in D.C. to kick off the discharge, Jammer had been busted at Heathrow International Airport for attempting to smuggle a pound of ecstasy through London to New York. Before he was sentenced, I bought a ticket I couldn't really afford, flew to England, and made an on-the-stand plea for the court's leniency. Amid the white-wigged U.K. barristers, I proclaimed that Jammer was the one-in-a-thousand case and who would turn his life around. He could've gotten ten years, the judge wound up giving him four, which Jammer served aboard the notorious British prison ship, HMP Weare.

While Jammer's latest e-mail convinced me that he had not yet taken any major steps to change the direction of his life, part of me couldn't help looking forward to the pledged pamphlets. I knew that if any pamphlets did arrive, they would immediately prove no more useful than Horse-pelt's mobi-pack, but I was highly intrigued by the delivery system. Prior to Jammer's e-mail, I had never considered Amtrak as a way to transport goods. Then again, maybe Amtrak didn't officially ship anything. Jammer was just as likely to be using some bottom-rung courier network, or even operatives in the Pink Slip Movement carrying things for each other on railroads and Greyhounds.

It should give you an idea of my general condition, Sisi, when I say Jammer's e-mail was a bright spot.

The Canadian Border Guard and the 170-Foot Dangle

A roll of the die tells us to drive to Chicago, but it would be criminal to get out of Buffalo without hitting Niagara Falls, so we make a quick stop on the American side to be impressed by nature's raw power.

Back in the Cadillac, we're still talking about it, "That was incredible."

"If it was a little warmer, we could try to go down it."

"Band-Aid, I'm constantly amazed that you're not dead already."

"It said a seven year-old kid went over the edge in a life preserver and he lived."

"By accident, and we heard about it because it's a miracle."

"Let's check out the Canadian side."

"Naw, let's not." Art thieves crossing the border doesn't strike me as a smart idea.

Band-Aid pushes, "Here, have a shot of Crown... How'd that taste?"

"Great, of course."

"Crown Royal comes from Canada, dude. We owe it to 'em to go over there. More importantly, we're trying to make a civilian out of you and Canada's the most civilian place on earth. American draft dodgers from the Vietnam era have been populating this country for decades. They say twenty percent of the country is now American draft dodgers and their descendants."

I laugh, "All right. Let's go see my new people."

He wheels us to the border checkpoint and the unsmiling agent peers in, "Good morning."

"Good morning, sir."

"Why are you coming into Canada?"

"We're dodging the draft," Band-Aid offers. I'd be more comfortable, what with the stolen dog painting and all, if my partner would start playing this straight – especially considering the agent has revealed no glimmer of a sense of humor.

"I'll ask you again. For what purpose are you entering Canada?"

"Oh, we figured we'd come see the falls, rent some barrels."

"Do you have any firearms in your vehicle?"

"No."

"Any other self-defense products such as knives or pepper spray?"

Sisi, this is going to seem ridiculous to you, now that pepper spray is a household word, but the discharge took place on the side of the millennium when pepper spray was known to few outside law enforcement and criminal circles. Crossing that border was the first time Band-Aid and I had ever heard of it.

"*Pepper* spray? No."

The inspector misreads Band-Aid's confusion as dishonesty. "If I were to search your car for pepper spray now, I wouldn't find any. That's what you're telling me?"

"No."

"*No*, we would not find pepper spray? or *No*, you're not telling me that I wouldn't find any pepper spray?"

I gnash my teeth on the passenger side. I'm already foreseeing the search of our Cadillac, me and Band-Aid sitting with our hands cuffed on the edge of the bridge, numerous stolen paintings leaning against the Cadillac fenders.

"Uh… Officer, I don't even know what pepper spray is."

"That's not what I'm asking. I'm asking a simple yes or no question: is there pepper spray in your car?"

"No. Pepper spray? Is that for salads?"

"How long will you be in Canada?"

"Sir, as soon as we figure out what pepper spray is, we're leaving."

I lean across and blurt, "Just an hour." My sole contribution.

The inspector looks at me. Finally, he says, "Good bye."

"Pepper spraaaaaaaaaaaaaay!" The Band-Aid Man cries as he flattens the accelerator. The muffler problem is getting worse and now the car is screaming like a cigarette boat. Here we are in a brand new, icy cold land. We park in a lot and bail.

Now that my border anxiety has washed away, I have to credit Band-Aid Man for his good call in coming into Canada. This view is spectacular. Even more than the view, the sound is overwhelming. It's constant surf, like the sound of a wave crashing over your head and just not stopping. All those thousands of gallons of white water dropping off the edge every second and exploding 160 feet below, it's the kind of thing that makes you respect nature. I peer over the rail at that frothing, leaping, drownpool at the bottom and it seems to be alive and hungry. It's ripping and slashing at itself, rolling over, turning inside out. It's a beast and it scares me.

"Hey, Ames, you see that rock ledge sticking out over the falls?"

I lean over the rail. The ledge actually starts about fifteen feet below us and extends out in a finger, 170 feet above the froth. "Yeah."

"I wonder if anyone's ever gone out there."

"Yeah, a seven-year-old in a life preserver."

"We should do it."

I grab my friend by the shoulder and march him away from the rail. This seems like a good time to get something to eat. Inside I'll be free to ask my friend a few questions that will give me a better understanding of his disease. The lodge is big, I guess in the summer it's full of tourists. It's got souvenir stands, gift shops, restaurants, and information counters, and The Band-Aid Man is asking the staff of each where we can rent barrels. He's kidding about that, but he was completely serious about going out on that rock finger of doom. I assume that's something we'd be arrested for trying, but of course a humiliating Canadian jail stay is one of the best outcomes we could hope for. I've got to make him forget the idea in a hurry. Got to find some girls. I'm looking...

looking... come on, where are you ladies? Where'd you run to? Here we go. Two right there, working at the snack counter at the end of the building.

"Hey, Band-Aid, let's get a hot dog." So we do. We order two hot dogs and a large Coke, the girls tell us we can't get any barrels, we chat with them a little bit, we pull the hot dogs out of their wrappers. We bite into the hot dogs.

"Holy fuck!"

"Oh no," I sputter. "What is this?"

The Band-Aid Man furiously throws his hot dog in the garbage can, I abandon mine on the counter. We run outside at top speed to spit our bites into the grass.

"That was the worst fucking hot dog I've ever tasted!" Band-Aid gasps. He sticks out his tongue and begins washing it with Crown Royal.

I've already sucked down the entire Coke, "Canada's a different world. Mexico doesn't have this problem, I devoured those Tijuana hot dogs every time I went down there. How in the world did Canada get it wrong?"

It suddenly dawns on Band-Aid: "South of the Canadian border they treat all hot dogs with pepper spray. Canada won't cooperate."

We've somehow made our way out to the falls again, the rail's right in front of us. I stare down into that boiling drownpool and I see white demons lunging out, springing suddenly alive, reaching and clawing for something, anything, to bring under. And still grabbing as they fall. To my left, I see a place where the rail doesn't extend because a rock is there. It's a big rock, a part of the same cliff the water is spilling over in front of me. The rock has kind of a flat area about five feet down from the path we're standing on. If a person were to climb over the rail there, that person could jump down onto that flat part of the rock, drop down again, walk down a narrow shelf to the ledge, and then crawl out to the end of the finger. The Band-Aid Man and I are sliding down the rail in the direction of that rock. The mix is roaring at us from way below.

I've played in the surf before. I spent a lot of time at the beach in Hawaii, and I know what it's like to get beaten by the water. I've been somersaulted at Waimea. I've been dropped on my head by the ruthless Sandy's shorebreak. Dragged on coral at Diamond Head. Clubbed with my own board at Sunset. Stung by Portuguese men-of-war at Bellows. I can't count the times I've been dragged under and pounded into the sand, so dizzy I don't know which way is up, for so long that my lungs are on fire, blind and crying on the ocean floor, hanging onto an ounce of hope that I would draw another breath. That hope is what made me survive. Here, next to these monstrous falls, I have no hope. If I fell off that perch, I wouldn't even bother to draw a breath. I wouldn't brace myself, try to land feet first, nothing. As soon as I started slipping, I would count myself gone. Better to be shot dead at that moment by a Mountie who mistakenly thought I'd smuggled in pepper spray than to live that six-second tumble into the foaming jaws below.

We're at the rock now.

"Hey, Ames, I think I see a –"

"Yeah, I see it too, you maniac."

"Are you ready?"

I answer his question by vaulting the rail and he's in the air at the same time. I put my Montecristo on the sidewalk and drop onto the flat part of the rock. I drop again. We're running down the narrow ledge and we're flat on the finger. He pulls out his panoramic camera, we roll onto our backs.

"Slide out further."

"Further?"

"Stick your head over the edge, your whole head."

He's got his arm around my shoulder and his other hand is holding the camera. It's a trademark Band-Aid Man photo, even if we are horizontal with our heads dangling 170 feet above the deadly pool. Click!

We roll toward safety, run, climb the rock, put our cigars in our mouths, and spring back over the rail. No police are waiting to arrest us, our welcoming party consists of only a dozen murmuring spectators and some impressed children nodding and smiling. I think our composure kept us from getting in any trouble. We must have looked very professional. My heart's pounding. "That was civilian, huh?" I ask Band-Aid.

He nods, "That was civilian as fuck."

One wild-eyed teenager in a black leather jacket tells his girlfriend, "We should do that," and, for the first time this trip, I feel like a role model. The idea that I'm becoming not only a civilian, but a shining example for other civilians to aspire to, really convinces me that things are going right.

Sisi, moments of exhilaration and joy were all over that road trip, but I don't want you to think they were exclusive to the discharge. Believe it or not, there were highs during the recall eleven years later. Granted, such moments were rarer, but they happened.

Very luckily for me, not all my old Army buddies had forsaken the military to join the Pink Slip Nation. The next e-mail in line was from Rusty Spray, my ace partner in the ROTC days and now head of operations for an infantry brigade in the Hawaii National Guard.

A Hawaiian local boy, Rusty had been a leader among leaders in my earliest training grounds, taking charge of exercises with a combination of personal magnetism and military grandiosity so winning that our actual instructors usually smiled when he stepped on their toes. Aware of his rocketing military stardom, Rusty had worked around the clock to ensure his out-of-uniform legend always eclipsed it. As the Army commendations rolled in, so multiplied the kegs, girls, brawls, beach parties, and the rest of the after-hours pursuits. I'd gravitated to him in those dreamy tropical days when, despite his endless self-competition, he'd found time to be an awesome friend. This decade-plus later I was about to learn that friends of Rusty's rare caliber remain awesome for life.

114

From: Rusty Spray
To: Ames Holbrook
Subject: Reunion
Okay, I heard the timing couldn't be any more fucked for you, but all
seriousness.
Ames, if you're getting mobilized anyway, come with me. Suzanne Vares is
the BDE S2. Chez Moriyama is the PA, and I am the BDE S3. Paul Takata is
the Information Officer in my section. Let's do it, UH reunion in Baghdad.
When we get back from Iraq, I promise to discharge you and erase you from
the database completely.
Let me know by Friday.

And with that, my world opened. What was this message from my
Hawaiian running partner, but a ticket out of the lunacy? I was stepping
from "*fully automated*" straight into reason, from the jaws of the machine
to the arms of a true brother – who happened to be a standout military
leader with a mission. I replied immediately and told Rusty I was with
him. I suddenly felt I was getting close to where I ought to be. It was
the same feeling I'd had eleven years earlier as I rolled out of Canada, my
goal of being a full-on civilian so close I could taste it in the Niagara-
sprayed air.

My heart is beating in a good way now, high from survival, and Band-
Aid's on his best behavior during our border crossing back into the
United States. He even volunteers that we're officers, which produces a
pleasant smile on the face of the customs agent who waves us by.

"Ames, what's our cash situation?"

"We'll make it tonight, probably."

"Your card's still fucked."

"Yeah."

"All right, back to the well tomorrow, then. We'll find another base and write checks."

I sigh at the prospect. I don't like that he keeps having to write hot checks, or that we have to keep swinging into Army bases while on a mission to outrun the Army.

Band-Aid senses my anxiety, "Don't worry about that shit. Visiting a base doesn't make you military. Just like if you walk in on a circle jerk and guys cum all over you it doesn't make you a circle jerker."

"Thank you."

"We've got a lot of driving to make Chi-town. Do you think we'll make it by eight?"

"Easily. We buy an hour at Hudson Lake, Indiana."

"Yeah. Well you try to get some rest now, and I'll make us some time."

He hits scan on the radio to find a good station while I drop the seat back and close my eyes. I haven't been able to sleep in the car since this trip began. The road excites me too much. I know there are all kinds of wonders flying by me, wonders I haven't seen in years or never at all. If I sleep, I'll miss them. This is tied into the mood I share with every other discharged vet – the feeling that we need to catch up with the real world and we'll have to work hard just to get to where the rest of these civilians already are. But I also know Band-Aid and I are splitting a long drive today, and we'll go all night in Chicago, so sleep would be smart. I let myself drift.

I might be asleep or I might not when The Band-Aid Man says, "Ames, they got us."

"What?" I open my eyes and sit up.

"We're busted. We got lucky, though – I was going a lot faster, but I saw him ahead and I slowed down." We stop on the shoulder. I drop my jacket over the Crown bottle, and the pink-faced patrolman comes to the driver window slowly. He's got a partner back in the car.

His voice is terrible, high and grating: "Do you have any idea how fast you were going?"

"No, sir, this speedometer only goes up to eighty-five."

"You were going ninety-three miles an hour! The speed limit on the New York State Thruway is fifty-five." Yes, it is a good thing Band-Aid slowed down so much. "Let me have your registration and insurance."

"Here's the registration. I think you're doing a good job, officer."

"I still need proof of insurance."

"Oh, I thought you said *assurance*."

"Why isn't your name on the registration?"

"It's rented to my brother, sir," Montecristo smoking in mouth.

"Is that your brother?" pointing to me.

"No, sir, it isn't."

"Neither one of you is registered to drive this car. I could have this Cadillac seized and make you get out and walk. This insurance isn't even valid for you. What's that on the floor?" I follow the officer's gaze to a half-full green bottle between my feet. It must have slid forward when Band-Aid braked.

"That's Jägermeister, sir."

"Oh! I suppose you've been drinking!"

"No, sir. Nobody drinks warm Jägermeister."

I break my silence, "That was from six days ago. We thought we lost it."

"We were celebrating because Ames just got out of the Army from overseas. We're making a civilian out of him, but we still have a ways to go."

"Let me see your ID," meaning mine.

He scrutinizes my info with mounting dissatisfaction, "Where is Bob Brown?"

"My brother's in the hospital, sir. We have to bring this car back for him."

"This rental agreement says this car isn't allowed outside the state of Texas."

"Well, that has to do with my brother's sickness. He gets

117

disoriented."

For a strange moment, that seems to calm the officer. But then something in the paperwork catches his eye. "Waaait a minute. This here says Bob Brown only rented the car through the fourteenth. That's last Sunday."

"I know, sir, I phoned in an extension. The company knows."

"How do I know?"

"You don't really have to know, sir."

"Oh, yes I do. I'll know, all right. You're going to send me a fax."

"A fax of what."

"A fax of the rental extension form."

"There is no rental extension form, sir. It's just in the computer."

"If it's in the computer, it can be faxed. I'll write my fax number on your ticket, and as soon as you get to a city of any size, you send me the fax."

"That sounds complicated, sir. Can't you just call the rental company?"

"I've been New York State Police for several years now, and I've learned to trust my instincts. My instincts don't trust voices, they trust hard copy."

"Yes, sir."

"Another thing. When I see a big car with a big trunk, it makes me suspicious ..."

Oh, God, exactly what I didn't want to happen – the cop must have picked up my vibe. This stolen art will be our undoing.

"Why does a big trunk on a big car make you suspicious?" Band-Aid Man challenges, to my mounting unease. I swear I hear the painted dog howling for rescue behind us. Band-Aid's right, but it's so obvious to me that rational argument isn't going to help us here. I sigh helplessly as my partner continues to make his point to the cop, "If you see a *small* car with a specially-built big trunk, I can understand you being suspicious, or even a big car with a small trunk, but not a big car with a big trunk.

That's how it should be."

"Whoa! Now you're talking crazy stuff. Why don't you unlock the trunk and let me take a look at what you have in there."

"All right, but I can't take responsibility for my brother's possessions. He's eccentric."

I close my eyes and wait in agony for the stolen art to be discovered. Since I'm not officially out of the Army till the end of this month, my participation in the interstate transport of priceless stolen military art would render me subject to the Uniform Code of Military Justice. The worst thing in the world I can imagine right now is being arrested for a criminal act during this discharge, and, just when I'm supposed to be leaving the military behind, to instead have my Army career extended by a bid in Leavenworth.

But in less than a minute, I hear the trunk slam shut. The pink-faced cop comes back to the window and hands the ticket over with our IDs and registration. "I'll tell you right now: you're heading into Pennsylvania. If you keep driving like that, they'll throw your ass in jail."

"Thank you, sir." We pull out slowly and The Band-Aid Man drives the speed limit for a few miles. "We lost some time, but at least we found the Jägermeister. Bury it in the ice chest and we'll drink it when we get to town."

"Cool. And keep an eye out for a fax machine."

"Yeah, right. Weird shit always happens around the border, dude, but things will start getting more normal real soon."

Rusty Spray and the University of Hawaii Reunion in Baghdad

At a gas station in Indiana, Band-Aid announces, "We should call Sweets."

Sounds like a great idea. Sweetser is a friend of ours in Milwaukee who was kicked out of the Army by that same Tony Whorlander paranoid who threw out The Band-Aid Man. My partner drives half an inch from a pay phone, enabling me to dial from the car as he dictates numbers out of his address book. A female voice answers.

"Hey, this is Ames, is Sweetser there?"

"Just a minute."

"Ames!"

"Yeah, man."

"Great, sorry about the screen – bill collectors, you know. Tell me the deal!"

"We're in Gary, Indiana, and we want to meet you in Chicago."

"Meet me at the Rock & Roll McDonald's at nine-thirty."

"Did you say *Rock & Roll McDonald's*?"

"You'll find it." Click.

I take another gulp of my Power Master while the dial tone hums in my ear. Band-Aid Man steps on the accelerator so the phone pops out of my hand, through the window, and strikes back at the coin box like a cobra. I have good feelings about tonight.

Sweetser and The Band-Aid Man are two-thirds of my cashiered lieutenant buddies from Italy. The third, my roommate Darryl, was such an amazing screw-up that my unit got calls for him from customs officials, MPs, and Italian Carabinieri for a year after he left. Darryl is a shifty drifter who cuts ties. Tonight's as close as I'll get to a bad-lieutenant reunion.

"Fill me up, bro." Band-Aid's tapping the lid of his half-drunk McDonald's Coke, indicating it's ready for a dose of Crown Royal.

He always wants to start drinking hard when we roll into town, and I've got to keep him in check. While he's watching the road, I shake a few drops of Crown Royal into the Coke and then I pull out his straw and lower it into the bottle. Now I put my thumb over the top of the straw and carefully lift it, full of Crown Royal, and lower it back into his cup. "Here you go."

He takes the cup, "I hope this isn't too weak."

"Try it."

He sucks the straw. "God damn! It definitely ain't weak."

"Told you." That first sip is the only one that matters, because after that, the drinker just thinks he's used to it.

"I can't believe we're seeing Sweetser after all these years."

"Yeah, the guy who predicted to me that you'd get kicked out of the Army."

"He did?"

"Yeah, I never told you? One night while I was on duty and he had about two weeks left, he pulled me aside and said, 'Ames, I've got to tell you, The Band-Aid Man isn't going to make it. I hung out with the guy in Monterey and the guy's a maniac. It won't be too long before he gets Whorlander's fiancée pregnant, or runs an Italian general off the road, or something. It is going to happen. The guy is out of control.'"

"Fucking psychic, dude. He briefed me on you, too."

"Oh yeah?"

"He told me: 'A lot of officers are going to tell you that Ames is fucked up and you shouldn't hang around him. But when you ask any of the soldiers over there who they'd want to go to war with, they'll tell you Ames. He's made his team the best in the unit.' And then Sweets goes, 'He still shouldn't be in the Army, though. The problem with Ames is the guy has no respect for authority.'"

"No respect for...? Well, at least he was right about you."

"Yeah, right. Just about me."

From a distance Chicago is an awesome-looking city at night, glittering and huge. It looks untouchable, but we're shooting right into it. We're under the skyscrapers now, in town. It's busy, people everywhere.

We find a hotel, do three or four Jäger shots, and rush right back out into the active city. We're on Division Street and it's hopping, lined with bars and full of people. We get drinks at a couple of places, The Band-Aid Man's head is spinning, there are a lot of pretty women around. It's ten after nine, we've got to move. There's a cab outside.

"Do you have a stereo?"

"Yeah."

"Let's hear some rock & roll on the way to the Rock & Roll McDonald's."

No questions from the cabbie, he knows where to go and he gets us there in a hurry. The Band-Aid Man and I find ourselves walking in with ten minutes to spare.

"Fifty-nine 'Vette," Band-Aid identifies the candy-red car on the floor to our right. In the front seat, two eerie wax figures smile cruelly while enjoying a plastic McDonald's meal. That is only the first in a series of ghoulish decorations that assault my eyes. At the front counter a primitive fake jukebox sporting horrible fast-food rock & roll selections like: "Johnny B. Hamburger, by Chuck McNugget." Crazily jumbled musical symbols on the walls and windows. A cardboard cutout of Mayor McCheese in purple rock & roll zoot suit playing the drums. It's all so terrible. Sweets must be getting a pretty good laugh knowing we're waiting for him in this chamber of horrors.

"Ames, check this shit out."

I face the direction that The Band-Aid Man is facing and I make the most shocking discovery yet. The rock & roll tunes that I thought were pre-recorded and piped in through the McDonald's sound system are actually coming from a live band at the other end of the restaurant.

Ronald McDonald in red and yellow clown outfit jamming on electric guitar. Hamburglar banging keyboards. No other band members. Drum machine beating wildly. No fans. We walk in that direction.

"Yeah! Rockin Ronald!" The Band-Aid Man shouts from twenty feet away. Ronald smiles and his eyes light up at the recognition. "Rock & roll!" Band-Aid shouts again, and Ronald turns to him and performs a special guitar solo in his honor. "Yeah! Chi-town rock & roll!" The Band-Aid Man is really getting into this.

Ronald and the Hamburglar apparently haven't had this kind of crowd response all day, because now they're going crazy. They're not singing anything, I don't think there's a microphone. But, boy, they are playing hard. Ronald is cranking the guitar. He's leaning way back and the portable amplifier is screaming. Hamburglar is pounding those keys like crazy, sweat streaming down his face. It amazes me even more when I remember that Ronald McDonald and the Hamburglar are mortal enemies, like the Crips and the Bloods. Not today, though – today we're witnessing rock & roll's power to bring people together, no doubt what this restaurant's founders had in mind.

"Yeah, rockin!" Band-Aid Man shouts excitedly. He's standing right next to Ronald now, slapping him on the back and urging him on. "Hear that rock & roll fly!"

I wonder if The Band-Aid Man is going to join the band for a number, but he starts dancing away from them. He grabs a lady's hand and pulls her out of her chair and the two dance wildly together while Ronald McDonald and the Hamburglar deliver the performance of their lives.

It's a beautiful scene, and when the number ends and Band-Aid Man escorts the lady back to her seat and walks toward the front counter with a series of fist pumps and a cry of, "Rock & roll!" I know the people are sorry to see him go. Ronald McDonald may miss Band-Aid too, but he's loving life too much to let it bring him down. I've never seen a more euphoric clown.

Sisi, if you can imagine the opposite end of the emotional spectrum from Ronald McDonald at that moment, you have a good idea of my mental state eleven years later when my Fort Sill report date loomed less than two weeks away. I was in my bedroom when the phone rang, and I recoiled. It didn't matter that only days earlier I'd been trying to call them and on some level I actually *wanted* to talk to them – I was frightened either way. Ever since Horse-pelt's first alarm, I imagined every telephone peal was the U.S. Army transmitting yet another strike of devastating news.

This time, Sisi, I was right, and I was wrong.

"Bruddah Ames," a voice gushed into the phone, "You didn't get my e-mail?"

I recognized at once it was Rusty Spray, my University of Hawaii classmate. Now his island pidgin was coming in so dense, complete with offbeat accents, I just knew he was piling it on to mess with me. "If you have to go, brah, why you don' come wit us?"

"Yes I got your e-mail!" I exclaimed. "I replied to it, like five times. I'm in."

"They already plan one Persian Gulf mission, see you can still get up on da board. We get UH reunion in Baghdad."

"Can you make it happen?"

"Shoots, what you tink? Have one captain slot fo' your name."

"Me, a *captain*? Man." Rusty's promoting me gave me an initial jolt of surprise, before I realized that it was no more absurd than any other component of my recall.

"Iraq dat's no joke, brah, we get plenty blood, but wit who you raddah go? We been beefin in da sand since forevahs. Best of all da down time – guaran's presidential suites. Dubai liquor connect, wahines from Bahrain…"

Rusty was on the money – if I had to put on the uniform, these were the boys to do it with. Not only would I fight alongside my old island playmates and crack-of-dawn surfing partners, but I was joining a light infantry brigade of rocked-up Samoans, Tongans, and true-blood Hawaiians. The Gods of War would have our backs the whole time.

I told Rusty all there was to tell: "Thank you."

Sometimes life works out. Major Horse-pelt and Major Bivens had told me I'd be randomly assigned to a National Guard unit, and here was a National Guard unit that needed me. Even if my Rip Van Winkle recall still defied explanation and I was headed back to an employee-company relationship that had been mutually confounding, I could count on Rusty to place me where I'd do some good, which was worlds better than what might have happened had my fate been left entirely in the hands of the U.S. Army.

The first person I shared the news with was my wife.

I'd met Soraya 14 years ago, when I was in the military. How I met her was a fluke, really. I was assigned to artillery school in Fort Sill, with follow-on orders to the "First to Fight" 24th Infantry Division. In the months that followed, the 24th lived up to its motto and hit the sand in the Middle East before almost everybody else, as part of a rapid deployment force. By the time the dust had settled a year later, the 24th Infantry Division had overcome some of the fiercest resistance in the Gulf War and had been roundly commended for their critical role in that successful American campaign. I had nothing to do with it.

Back at Fort Sill, our gunnery instruction had been interrupted one morning so my whole class could take something called the Defense Language Aptitude Battery, a nearly nonsensical exam that the military believed gauged a soldier's ability to learn a foreign language. Out of more than a hundred students in my class, I got the top score. My orders to the 24th ID were canceled, and I was quickly issued replacement orders for the Southern European Task Force – specifically to a Top Secret special weapons unit in Italy. On my way there, the Army sent me to a basic Italian course at the Defense Language Institute in Monterey, California. The Italian course was a low-pressure affair. In severe contrast to the 70-hour-plus weeks that characterized every other Army assignment I experienced, students at the Italian course in Monterey were dismissed at three o'clock, Monday through Friday. Weekends and all holidays were wide open. So, while the parallel-universe virtual Ames was in the desert sand of Saudi Arabia, gearing up for the savage war march into Iraq and the Euphrates River valley, the actual Ames was in the beach sand of the Golden State, touring my Monte Carlo up and down 101, from San Diego to my hometown San Francisco, having the time of my life. And I also met the *love* of my life.

On one of those wide-open weekends, I dropped into the ocean in Santa Cruz, and there I caught a vision of this bronze surfer radiating light as she rode the face of a smooth Pacific curl. She creased the wave with her hand as she slid across, and her fingers left gilded trails in the sunlit ocean, there for a moment, until the curl closed out and erased it all. If I had to describe who Soraya is, even now in the modern day, the best way I could do it would be to point to those sunlit trails on that sublime Pacific wave. The way her hand creased the ocean describes her better than I could in any arrangement of words.

It turned out that this Bangkok-born surfer chick, whose mother had pulled her from Thai royal society to raise her in America, had actually gone to my same high school, although she'd just graduated, a young eighteen, so we hadn't been at San Francisco's Lowell High at the same time. We spent all our free time together beginning that summer.

More than a dozen summers later, when the Pentagon recalled me, Soraya was understandably having trouble with the entire concept. Although she had known me for a few of those years when I was a soldier, she'd known me as a civilian for a lot longer – living with me for almost a decade of it – and she was less than satisfied with the possibility that she wouldn't be able to see her husband for the next year-and-a-half because the Army wanted me back in.

But, at last I had good news for her. When I told her about Rusty's phone call and the University of Hawaii reunion in Baghdad, my queen smiled wide enough to flash out my field of vision.

"Really? *Rusty?*" Soraya took a run at me and I felt my ribs compress from the force of her hug. "Oh, baby, I'm so happy."

"Me too. It's a borderline miracle."

Soraya couldn't stop squeezing me, "I know it's going to be dangerous and all, but now I know whatever you do in the Army is gonna be okay. If you're working for Rusty, I'm not worried anymore."

Now I was euphoric like Rockin Ronald McDonald.

Sweetser and the Baby Possibly Getting Killed

The Band-Aid Man and I get some Rock & Roll Big Macs and sit by the Corvette. We're almost to our last bites when Sweetser drops into the booth. "What's up, guys?"

"All right, Sweets!"

He takes a sip of Band-Aid Man's Coke. "Yes! Crown Royal, you haven't changed."

Band-Aid smiles and flashes his silver flask in response.

"Well, let's go, guys."

"It was pretty rowdy on Division Street."

"What about Rush Street?"

"No," Sweets dismisses those ideas. "The downtown party scene is overrated. If we're turning Ames into a civilian, we're doing it the local way, northeast."

"You still have the 'Stang?"

"Yeah, look at this." The old 5.0 Mustang is sitting in the lot, still jet black with the windows highly smoked. He lifts the trunk to reveal the Armed Forces International license plates he used to carry in Italy and a stack of about thirty parking tickets. "I kept my AFI plates on until last month, and I parked wherever the hell I wanted for two-and-a-half years."

"It won't trace?"

"No way, I was never even registered before. Now I've got Wisconsin plates and a new record."

He takes us to a club called Cubbies across the street from Wrigley Field. This place is huge and I like it right off. Clothes and skin tones run the spectrum. We grab three beers at the bar and Band-Aid is the first to spot the bachelorette party. We ask the handsome bartender to make a tray of virgin shots, each glass topped with pure lime juice and accompanied by a cut lemon. He serves the tray to the bachelorette crew with flourish. The girls gulp the shots, and then bite into their lemons, extending the citrus rush. They glare at us through helplessly squinted eyes like a nest of sourpusses. I really want them to answer by sending us some drinks back, but they just keep shaking their heads ungratefully.

Sweets shows us he lost half his nose when a cargo sled ran it over on an airborne jump. After Sweets got kicked out of the officer corps, he rejoined the Army as an enlisted reservist. Now he's a sergeant in a Special Forces unit, doing all kinds of crazy missions. He flips a Kool into his mouth and asks for a light from a tailor-dressed tall guy who acts very inconvenienced before handing over a book of matches. "It's my last book," the tall guy stresses, as if the matches are a treasure.

"The Pack takes on the Chiefs," Band-Aid Man reads a Budweiser poster on the wall announcing this Monday Night Football contest between Green Bay and Kansas City. Sweets sets the whole book of matches on fire and casually lights his cigarette with the giant flame. He slowly shakes it out and hands the smoking book back to the tailor-dressed guy while Band-Aid asks, "Ames, Where's your buddy Kai live?"

"Minneapolis."

"How far is that from K.C.?"

"Under 500 miles."

"We're gonna be on TV."

There's a long line into the bathroom and there are only two stalls inside, so Band-Aid is urging people to use the sink. The guy at the head of the line now is refusing to use the sink, so Band-Aid rushes in and uses it himself. The guy follows him in and before too long they reemerge. There must have been some words exchanged in the bathroom, because now the guy is having a fit.

"You have a baby bladder!" the guy accuses. "A little tiny bladder so small it's a shame." This insult brings deep laughter from all of us, and now the guy reacts the only way he knows how, with more bladder insults: "You all have little baby bladders! In fact, your bladders would all fit in the bladder of a newborn baby!" We laugh wildly. Suddenly security comes and breaks up the whole scene. They don't kick us out, but the crowd has soured on us and we make our way to the door.

We drop by a place called the Smart Bar. "Five dollar cover," says the doorman.

The Band-Aid Man flashes his wholesaler's license. "I work for Miller Beer."

The guy nods and we head in for free. Band-Aid Man begins scouring low and high for eligible ladies, while Sweets and I drink beers and swap stories. I set another empty bottle down and Band-Aid Man pulls me and Sweets off our stools and pushes us out into the crowd. "That's enough of you two sitting there like lovebirds who are too lazy to suck each other's dicks. There's bush to be had in this town. Sweets, take these, you need 'em. They'll make your hair tingle when you take a piss." He straightens his tie and runs into the crowd.

Extremely drunk Sweets chews the tablets without a word. I notice he's wearing Gargoyle sunglasses in this extremely dark club, don't remember if he's had those on the whole time. He's got one hand on the bar, rocking like a cabin boy on high seas. Sweets's storytelling skills have been deteriorating for hours, and his latest outpouring is a barely coherent date-rape narrative from his perspective as a victimized male. Fortunately, he keeps forgetting where he was and starting over at the beginning, but I don't know how long it will take me to shake the disturbing picture of his miserable Gargoyle eyeballs while he softly moans, "She sat on my face and took advantage, Ames. She defied me!" I'll keep my distance for now and wait for those four E he swallowed to pick him up.

"Hi," a voice comes from my left. I turn to see a leather-jacket-clad, short, spacey girl with lots of make-up looking up at me. "Do you want to dance?"

"Aww, nuts, I'd love to, but I lost a bet and now I'm not allowed to dance at all."

"That sucks," she moves closer and we talk more. I see The Band-Aid Man out dancing on the floor like a monster crushing a city and swatting planes out of the air. Sweets stumbles toward me, grinning dizzily. He's lost but mending well.

"Hey, Sweets, I'm gonna grab another beer. Gladys, this is Sweetser. You two have a lot in common." Gladys's eyes light up, she obviously considers Sweets a major upgrade from me. I hit the bar and get Millers for me and Band-Aid. Sweets is already holding two beer bottles, drinking out of one and spitting tobacco into the other. I thread Band-Aid Man's beer under the arms of his two female dance partners and I decide to check this place out. I start to walk and I hear a voice.

"You're actually a friend of his?" asks a pretty brown-haired girl, flipping her eyes toward The Band-Aid Man. She's wearing red lipstick and no other makeup and her eyes are a beautiful green.

"More like his brother."

"That's what he said too."

"You know him, then."

"I know he's a cheeseball. He asked me to show him my bush."

"Did you?"

"I'm sorry, I didn't take eighteen hours of feminist literature classes so I could show some frat-boy asshole my body."

"Hey," I defend, "Band-Aid was never in a fraternity."

"I'm Shannon, may I buy you a beer?" We go to the bar on the side and I listen while she tells me about herself. I take my eyes off hers for a second and I see Sweets with his lips smashed into the face of the spacey girl. They're kissing hard and non-stop, no other thought in their minds.

"I wonder," Shannon says, "about drinking while going to school. Alcohol impairs the mind, yet I'm paying to enrich my mind in class. I learn all day and then set myself back all night."

"But that's the time to drink, when you're in an environment that works your mind. Drink takes away, but school puts it back. When I was in the Army drinking, that was cause for worry, because in the Army it's the environment that shrinks your brain. I'd have to consume enough alcohol to tear my pancreas asunder before I could equal the brain damage done by a single meeting with my commanding officer."

She laughs beautifully and she's not wearing a bra. Her red lips are moving while her voice sings the benefits of one-night stands. She's a buzz-chasing intellectual and her hand's running across my chest. "I've said a lot about me," she speaks. "What about you?"

"There's nothing you don't see."

"Would I see more if you came home with me?"

"I don't know."

"Is that too hard? How about just: Will you come home with me right now?"

"Can my friends come too?"

"No."

"Then I can't either."

"Why not?"

"Does there have to be an explanation?"

"There can be no explanation. You defy reason."

"I'm gay."

"No you're not. Homosexuals are good-looking."

"I'm serious. My father hasn't talked to me since I came out of the closet." Shannon's eyes express a momentary concern for me, and I go on, "Well, it wasn't so much *that* I came out, it was *how* – I woke him up by smoking his pole."

Shannon cough-sprays her beer, "You are off."

"How about if you give me your number and I come over next time I'm in town?"

"Now or never. We want each other, it's obvious, let's go."

"Thanks, but… tonight won't work. These brothers of mine… we have a history. One was my partner on the night The Band-Aid Man was born. The other is The Band-Aid Man himself, who called in every favor he ever had so he could stock a rented Cadillac like a bar and drive more than sixteen-hundred miles to meet me, and he's since taken two weeks off from work, one without pay, risked losing his job, arranged the transport of priceless stolen military art, hung hot checks and racked up speeding tickets just to turn me into a civilian."

"That's touching," Shannon says, getting nasty. "Look at your friends now." My eyes find Sweets in the same spot, Gargoyles askew as he continues to kiss the made-up girl unrelentingly. The music's stopped and Band-Aid is still on the floor, alternately squeezing both his female partners – maybe one slightly more excited than the other. Shannon goes on, "They're really thinking about you now, Ames. Do you think they wouldn't go home with me? That meathead stud who asked me to *show him my bush* would ditch you in a second if he could get laid."

"You're wrong, but that's not even the point," I say. "I just spent the first half of my twenties serving my country. Now I'm free and alive and in love, and these guys are a part of it. I had forgotten how amazing this country is. I had forgotten about Rockin Ronald McDonald, I had forgotten about bikers, yuppies, blacks and whites and everybody else under the same roof, listening to each other's music. I'd forgotten about beautiful straight-shooting women like you. Man, I—"

"He'd forgotten about predatory females sitting on their victims faces with all their weight, smothering their cries for help!" Sweets interrupts despairingly, Gargoyle eyes in force. Just as quickly as he arrived, he moves away.

I try to resume as if there was no Sweetser, "Man, I like you a lot, Shannon, but when my friends are ready to leave this place, I'm going to go with them because that's what I feel like doing. It's a new civilian world I'm in. Randomness wins."

Her eyes sparkle and her tongue pushes through her teeth and withdraws. She says, "Randomness would be going home with me."

Sweets circles back, he's looking better. Next to him comes Band-

Aid, trying to check his hair in the reflection of a bottle.

Shannon smiles and she's stepping on my toe. "You can have the rain check," she says. "But you can't have my number. It'll have to be random. If we ever see each other again, we'll have our night no matter who's with us. All right?"

"*FIDO.*"

"Excuse me? Are you saying I'm a dog? You're out of line with the general population."

"No! W—"

"You must have reverse-beer goggles!" she yells, but I can tell she's not offended. She's confident enough to be amused by her mistaken impression that I just had the nerve to assail her looks. A helpless smile spreads across her face. I think she likes me more now.

I hold out my hand, "Nice to have met you, Shannon." She grabs it and yanks me close, her wet lips are almost touching mine. The Band-Aid Man and Sweetser are right behind me and the tide is pulling. Band-Aid says three ladies are meeting us out on the street, I draw back, and Shannon's not letting go of my hand. I slide out, break away, and we all three crash outside.

It's a crystal clear night and we're on the sidewalk. Whatever ladies Band-Aid thought he had lined up are nowhere to be found, but a 300-pound woman pulls us all into her orbit and we hang with her until the bar closes.

We hop in Sweetser's Mustang and he roars us back to the hotel, windows down. He says he has to leave. Our hotel inside matches the out – strikingly run-down yet somehow formal, with a couple of uniformed employees floating around the periphery like ghosts. It's less expensive than I was imagining a downtown Chicago hotel would be, so I ride the elevator up with that as a consolation. Band-Aid and I brush our teeth together in the room sink and dive into the king-sized.

A minute later the door flies open and a guy wearing a pearl-colored hotel uniform, shoes to cap, steps inside. Band-Aid Man sits up straight in the bed and stares expectantly.

"Security," the intruder states. "I thought I heard a baby crying."

"There's no baby in here," Band-Aid says.

"Sounded like one."

"Tonight we learned we have baby bladders," I offer. "That may be part of the confusion."

"What's that?" the man's tone conveys mounting suspicion.

"No, Ames, he's talking about an actual baby crying," Band-Aid explains, as if I didn't understand the premise. He turns back to the man in the pearl uniform, "It was probably from three rooms down. Your walls are made of goddamn crackers."

"Sounded like someone was hitting a baby. It was screaming."

"Well, you've gotta barge into all the rooms till you find it. Start with the premium suites," Band-Aid stresses. The man exits and Band-Aid Man gets up and double-bolts the door. "Sorry perdente excuse for security."

I drift into a sleep that's interrupted when the door swings into the wall. The lights flick on to reveal the uniformed man.

"What now?" Band-Aid shouts desperately.

"Where's the baby?" he tucks his skeleton key in a pocket and scouts the premises. "I'm sure I heard it crying."

"Okay, I need to call your manager."

"He's the one who sent me, sir. This is one thing that's more serious than sleep. We're talking about a baby possibly getting killed."

"Fine, just prop the door open so you don't wake my ass up every time."

"Can't do that," the man says. "Lawsuits." He backs into the hallway and pulls the door shut.

Band-Aid lunges out of bed and kills the lights, "Lawsuits? That's what motivates these dickheads?" He cracks the door and yells down the hall: "Hey, security! We've got the baby behind the door – we just taped a dart to his fucking head."

"What!" The security man and I gasp together.

"You heard me. If you open our door a millimeter it'll pierce his skull."

Band-Aid slams the door and jumps into bed. I hear footsteps bear down on our room.

"Careful," Band-Aid Man warns from the bed. "Open the door, kill the baby. We'll sue your ass off!"

"No you won't," comes the trembling voice from the hall. "It's on you."

"Bullshit. We served you notice."

The footsteps retreat at a high clip until I can't hear them at all.

I glance through the room window, seeing only darkness outside, and then I turn back to my partner in time to catch his head sinking into the pillow with a contented sigh. While he plunges into dreamland, I take stock of the near future. My bank card is still broken and, up till a few minutes ago, I regarded that as our most pressing problem. But now that my mentor has made us suspects in a crime involving a baby, the concept of our jaunting onto Army bases to get cash doesn't seem like a big deal at all. I glance toward the window again, briefly. The Band-Aid Man works in mysterious ways. His snore fills the room, he won't be spelling it out for me – but the moral is there for my taking. I can *feel* the moral better than I can put it into words: how, as civilians, we can overcome any problem the world gives us by replacing it with a worse problem of our own creation. That power is in our hands.

If this is what civilian life is going to be like, I might as well get comfortable with it. Before I drift off with my brother, I take a last look through the window I expect to hear SWAT personnel crashing through sometime before dawn.

Kai and the Bitches in a Limo

"Aaah. I wanted to do that french-fry babe at Hardee's."

"I wouldn't call her a babe."

"Still, I'd do her."

"Yes, Band-Aid, I know you'd do her. You'd do every woman in the world."

"Just about. You should start thinking that way too."

"I wish I could."

"Ames, that's the Army talking. Standards are a military concept. Civilians don't have goddamn standards – they go down on anything that moves."

"It's just not my nature."

"Fuck your nature. At some point during this trip, you will lose your standards and at least hold hands with an ugly dumb bitch, and preferably fuck her. Until then, you can't be a civilian."

"All right, tell me when."

"So, what's this guy, Kai, like? Is he gonna set me up with some Minneapolis bush?"

"I doubt it, he's not that kind of guy."

"What, is he gay?"

"No, he isn't. I'll tell you a story about that in a minute, though. He came from a super liberal family. When I met him in the eighth grade, he was circulating a petition saying we should give all convicted killers a thousand dollars. Something about the thousand dollars would give the murderers a new start on life and it would show them that human life is valuable."

"Fuck, he'll give murderers a grand and he won't even let me fuck any of his girlfriends. I thought those hippies were supposed to be into free love and shit."

"Well, he's changed a lot. He was one of the most sexually active guys in my high school, girls couldn't get enough of Kai. Then somewhere between high school and college he made up his mind that his womanizing lifestyle was at odds with his liberal identity."

"Weird, dude. What was that gay story you were gonna tell me about him?"

"Oh yeah. I heard a lot of this stuff from guys he went to college with, but… apparently while he was at UCLA he announced he was gay. It was some point he was trying to prove, like: 'I'm so liberal, I'm gay.' He tried to make it work, I think he even gave a guy a hand job –"

"God damn!"

"But in the end he couldn't bring himself to kiss a man. He was born straight and he couldn't do anything about it. He was disgusted by the thought of another man's tongue in his mouth, that was his curse."

"What a fucking curse. Wake me up when we get to town, dude." He drops his seat back electrically and I continue to jet us through the frozen Wisconsin countryside all the way to Minnesota.

I find a pay phone and give Kai a call. He's expecting me, I called him soon after I landed in America. He also knows a little about The Band-Aid Man.

"Hello." His voice is very soft and warm, even answering a phone.

"Kai!"

"Hey, Ames, did you make it?"

"Sure did, I'm in front of the Hubert H. Humphrey Metrodome."

"Good, I'm not far."

"Band-Aid Man wants to know if you've got any bush lined up for him."

"Busch beer? I do have beer for you in the refrigerator."

"I think he means females."

"That's what I was afraid of. I can't even imagine using such a

138

degrading term. Ames, I hope you told him about my roommate. She's a very respectable older woman and it would be unthinkable for The Band-Aid Man to hit on her."

"I'll tell him, but he might not listen. He's out of control. I was driving into Boston and he grabbed the steering wheel out of my hand, that's the kind of thing he does."

"Oh no! Well, I'm glad you're here, Ames. But I don't think of women like that."

"Like what? Are you gay again?"

"Yes."

"Well, that's cool. You and Band-Aid Man are as opposite as two people can be."

"I hope so!" He gives me the directions to his house and I tell him we'll be right there. I take the last gulp of my Colt 45 and see that The Band-Aid Man is already behind the wheel. We're off.

"So, what did he say about the bush?"

"Nothing planned. And he doesn't want you to mess with the woman who lives in his house."

"His girlfriend?"

"No, she just lives there."

"Oh, it's a commune kind of deal?"

"Yeah, I think so. Kai also said he's gay."

"And he still can't set us up with any whores? All the gay dudes I know have bitches all over them. What the fuck?"

"Maybe he hasn't been gay long enough. If he touches you in a way that makes you uncomfortable, just ask him to stop."

"Is he gonna grab my cazzo?"

"There's no telling. Hey, by the way, Kai and Mit were two of Juanvig's conquests."

"Get the fuck out of here! Mit?"

"Yep."

"Don't even mention that guy. I'd rather you bring me to an

ungenerous homo any night, at least Kai won't cockblock me. Hey, why doesn't Kai call up Juanvig and get her to Juanvig me?"

"Wrong state, or I'd introduce you myself."

"Is this it? Hennepin?"

"Yeah, to 36th." He's cruising Hennepin and I pour a shot of Crown. Suddenly, the Crown Royal bottle tips over completely and I'm thrown against my door with such force that my Montecristo, caught between my jaws and the window, disintegrates completely in a fiery shower of sparks. I understand immediately that The Band-Aid Man has just performed a very sudden and tight U-turn. But as I pull my face from the glass and survey the losses – one fresh Montecristo and four ounces of Crown Royal, beloved treasures to my partner – I have to ask, "Why?"

"Bitches in a limo!" replies The Band-Aid Man. I look over and see his glazed eyes and determined scowl, and I know all I can do is shut up and make sure my seatbelt is buckled. There is a long, white Lincoln limousine ahead. It was a distant pair of red tail-lights way down Hennepin when I first saw it, but now the gap between us is two blocks and dropping fast. We're running red lights in the bus lane to catch up. We get alongside and Band-Aid plays a winning serenade on the Cadillac horn. This results in one girl dropping her window in back and another jumping through the top, and both shouting, "Meet us at CC!" A third girl does a handstand inside, poking a lovely pair of stockinged legs through the sunroof while the Lincoln turns away at the intersection.

"Hey, Ames, there's 36th street right there. Those bitches turned us in the right direction."

"Good job, Band-Aid. We'll have to thank them at Club Susie."

"It was CC, don't fuck with me. Just thinking of those legs makes me hungry."

We make it to Kai's place and it's great to see him. Still the same brown-eyed, brown-haired, handsome guy with a permanent case of the sniffles I've known since we went to San Francisco's Marina Middle School together. Growing up an Army brat, you get used to moving and never seeing your friends again, but I keep seeing Kai. He goes back further than any other friend I have. Kai helps us bring our stuff in, tells us to bring our clothes and do laundry, and shows us our bedroom upstairs. I find myself alone in the room for a minute, so I take the opportunity to do my pushups. I get to 60.

I catch up with the guys and we meet Kai's lady roommate in the living room. She's with her boyfriend, possibly on Kai's recommendation, and Band-Aid makes no wild advances.

Kai volunteers to drive to give us a break, so we pack into his Honda. Most American liberals won't drive cars made in imperialist America. Instead, they drive cars from other historically imperialist nations. Kai and Band-Aid Man are exchanging words cautiously. I'm stretched out in the back and I'm enjoying the uneasy front-seat conversation you might expect between new acquaintances when the passenger believes the driver might casually reach over and rub his crotch and the driver is expecting the passenger to wrench the steering wheel out of his hand at any moment.

The place Kai takes us to turns out to be the very CC club. No limousine out front, though. We rush the icy ten yards from the car to the door and the teenage doorman hassles us for ID.

"I can't look that young," complains Band-Aid Man, approaching the bar and returning his wallet to his pocket. "I haven't been carded in years."

"They're like that here. If it makes you feel any better, they got him too," Kai says.

"God damn!" Band-Aid exclaims, looking back at the door where a cloudy-eyed man in a USS Arizona baseball cap has leaned his cane against the doorframe and is now grimacing as he fumbles slowly in his pocket for identification.

It's nice and warm in here, we grab a table and a pitcher.

"Damn, those limo bitches aren't here."

"They probably came and left."

We drink a little bit, and I think Kai is slowly understanding that Band-Aid is at least human. I see a chalkboard on the wall that advertises spicy chicken wings. I flag the waitress, "Are you the wings girl too?"

"Yes, I am," she says cheerfully. "Do you want an order?"

"We'll take two, please."

The server heads off with our order and Kai lectures me gravely, "I think she would have preferred 'wings person.' Women don't like to be called girls."

"So, you noticed she was a woman," Band-Aid Man puts his arm over Kai's shoulder. "You were looking down her shirt too, huh?"

"What? No."

Band-Aid gulps down his beer, lowers his glass to the table, and demands, "So Kai, what's the deal? What kind of gay are you?"

I laugh and Kai shakes his head. "I know Ames didn't believe I was gay for a minute. Did he tell you the story that I gave a guy a hand job too?"

"Yes, Ames did."

"All bullshit."

"Well, I'd call it hyperbole," I defend.

"It's just such an immature topic of conversation," Kai turns away from me in disgust and tells Band-Aid, "It shouldn't have made any difference to you if I were gay."

"That depends on what kind of gay you were."

"What do you mean?"

"Well," Band-Aid explains, "There's a difference between gay homo and gay fag."

Kai winces, but Band-Aid does appear to be commanding his full attention for the first time. He's commanding mine too, actually. I've never heard homosexuality broken down this way, and I'm eager to hear the master explain the differences.

Eager is not the word to describe Kai, who is quite obviously bracing himself. His teeth are gritted and he appears locked between powerful urges to protest or flee.

"Take this homo waiter at this restaurant I go to – he's always squeezing my ass when I sit down, and he checks out my dick when I go to take a piss, but I know it stops there. Homos are normal people. The only difference between him and me is he just prefers a hard dick to a soft pussy. But, Kai, fags are the ones who gotta fuck every man they see. You might be minding your own business and all of a sudden they tear a hole in your pants and fuck you in the ass. When Ames told me about your aggressive gay style, I was afraid you might be a fag and I'd wake up tomorrow morning with your dick in my mouth. That's what scared me. Even among guys, no means no, right?"

Kai has no answer, beyond his pained look. His teeth remain gritted because he can't accept the Band-Aid definitions, but he can't exactly reject the no-means-no declaration outright, either. The Band-Aid Man's entire explanation is so far out of bounds that Kai can't even grope for a proper response.

Luckily, our wings arrive. We polish them off quickly, get another pitcher, and my friends begin to get along surprisingly well. What I like best is that neither one of them is softening his act for the benefit of the other. Kai calls our attention to the evils of red meat, even labeling it a drug and lumping it in with cocaine and heroin, and Band-Aid Man tells a story about a woman who begged him to beat her with a bullwhip.

Some girl bumps into my chair for her second time tonight. She can't walk straight, she's high on something. Kai goes to the bathroom and when he comes back, he says, "Band-Aid Man, you must be off tonight. Ames told me you were the big ladies' man, and I haven't seen you go after one yet. I expected you to be on the prowl."

The Band-Aid Man takes a deep breath and begins, "Those two babes over there are hot, but they're with their husbands. She's a lesbian. The fat one didn't hang around long enough..."

I'm enjoying the thorough case-by-case rundown on the CC female situation, when suddenly that freaky girl comes out of nowhere to bang my chair for the third time.

Band-Aid continues, "She's all right, but she has an ear infection and can't keep her balance."

"Ear infection?" We all laugh. "She's on some mind-blowing narcotic."

"Red meat," Band-Aid says.

"That's everybody but the waitperson," says Kai.

"Her name is Nicole. I'm trying."

"All right," Kai nods approvingly. "You did a little work while I was in the bathroom."

"Fuck, Kai, I'm glad I met you. It's been a good stop on the road trip, kind of an intellectual pause."

"What do you mean by that?" Kai reminds me of one of those good schoolteachers, he never lets anything slide.

"I'm paying homage to you for tapping into my mind and not my cazzo. It was meant as a compliment. Forgive me, I'm not p.c., I'm from Texas."

"You know, p.c. isn't even an expression that progressives acknowledge. It was invented by the right to make fun of the left." There he goes again, nothing slides.

"Well, Kai," Band-Aid laughs, "I sure can't imagine a better person to help me turn Ames into a civilian. I feel like you're pushing the Army out of his blood every minute we're with you."

I agree, "Yeah, it's like a transfusion. Out with the military Ames blood, in with the civilian Kai blood. When I come out of this, I'll be voting for fringe candidates in the Hemp Party."

Kai smiles, "Do you guys ever vote at all?"

"Uhhhhh..." Band-Aid blanks.

"I learned not voting from my dad," I offer. "He said he served under the orders of the Commander in Chief, regardless of the President's party."

"Well, now that you're out, you two can start exercising your civic duty. In the next election cycle, I'll give you some recommendations."

"I'm assuming your recommended candidates will make President Clinton look like a right-wing fascist?"

Kai cracks up, "Well, he is."

In the morning we go out for a great breakfast of huge omelets with everything. I write Kai a check for two-fifty and he gets me the cash from his bank. Beautiful, means we don't have to go to a military base today. We drop Kai back off at his house, thank him, and say good bye. We're right next to giant Lake Calhoun, so I start in that direction, figuring I'll drive us around it.

"Hold it!" The Band-Aid Man orders. "Kai was really cool. I've got something for him." I put it in reverse and drive back to the front of Kai's house, and Band-Aid runs up and rings the doorbell.

"Hello. You forget something?"

"No, come on out. Put your shoes on, Kai, I've got something for you."

Kai cooperates, although with eyebrows raised. He's running late for work as it is, and now he's got to make this special trip to the car.

"Kai, before I give this to you, I want you to know that you've always got a home in San Antonio. If you're ever in town for any reason – a protest, peace rally, whatever – you have my number. Call me up, I'll get you laid."

"Thank you." Kai glances quickly at his watch. This second goodbye is eating up time.

"I've got cool neighbors, you can play the tambourine all night." Band-Aid opens the front door of the Cadillac. Aaah, the climax of this special farewell ceremony. The reason we're all gathered out here. "Kai, do you like cigars?"

"No."

If Band-Aid was expecting something like the giddy gleam we witnessed in the eyes of the Indian garage manager in Manhattan when Band-Aid offered him Cuban cigars as payment, there is nothing like that in Kai's expression now. Kai's brown eyes appear flat, nearer to annoyance than joy.

"Well, I've got a little something for you." Band-Aid reaches into the cigar box and pulls a fresh, uncut Montecristo off the top of the stack. "It's Cuban, Kai. I want you to take this as a token of our appreciation for last night." I admire the way he's sticking with his original plan. The Band-Aid Man has made up his mind to award our host a top Cuban cigar, and he won't be discouraged by something as silly as Kai's not liking cigars.

Kai takes the cigar and runs into the house. Band-Aid Man buckles up and I drive toward the lake. Monday Night Football in Kansas City tonight. We have no tickets, we don't know anyone in town, and Arrowhead Stadium isn't on our map. The Band-Aid Man says he'll get us in to watch the game.

You may be surprised to hear this, Sisi, but a decade later, when the Army was coming after me and the e-mails from friends were streaming in, my favorite of all of the bulletins came from Kai.

From: "Kai"
To: 'Ames Holbrook'
Subject: Hey
Ames (and Soraya if this is a shared email account),
Got the word about your call-up. I'm sure you can imagine my horror upon finding out, and anger at Bush, et al. I'll spare you the rest of my vitriol about those villains who are sending you there. I mainly just wanted to let you know that we're all thinking of two/three of you. Please let Soraya know that if there's anything we can do while you're away, anything at all, we'll do it. As much as I don't want you to go (and if I thought there was a 1 in a million chance that you would consider not reporting I would try to convince you) I have to tell you that knowing you'll be one of the folks over there makes me feel just a smidgen better about the whole goddamn operation.
Peace out,
Kai

To this day I still rank that as the coolest thing a genetic anti-war radical ever said to a veteran.

The Leavenworth Hitchhiker and the Breaching of Arrowhead Stadium

A late sign informs us this is the turnoff for Fort Leavenworth. Feels like a bad omen, but Band-Aid and I already decided to exit here for gas and snacks, and our egos keep us from chickening out. I feel a pall cloak the Cadillac as we pull off. The very proximity to the notorious military prison is enough to make us both uneasy. Just being here makes it too convenient for authorities to throw us into the stockade for any reason.

To reassure us both, I bring up the fact that my grandfather is from Leavenworth. That has to give us some kind of positive communion with the land. Before he went to West Point, Willard A. Holbrook, Jr., graduated from Leavenworth High School. That's where he got his nickname, in fact. "Hunk" Holbrook led the 11th Armored Division in World War II. Fought in the Battle of Ardennes and the Battle of the Bulge; Silver Star, Bronze Star. The man was solid, but I witnessed his edge. Once, he told me – and a room full of other folks – that the Holbrooks first entered the Army "to kill people in all accordance with the law." I loved the guy. In the arena of knockout résumé bullets, Hunk has one of the greatest: *Took the surrender of Linz, Austria, from the Nazis.* He personally raised the American flag over the city.

Brigadier General "Hunk" Holbrook is yet another family battlefield legend to make my own military experience laughable by comparison. After volunteering for every conflict from Iraq to Somalia, I tossed a Hail Mary when the Balkans were blowing up. I was in Europe, and meanwhile a million Europeans were homeless from ethnic cleansing, tens of thousands dying by the month, and the Army decided to send me to a big parade to be an usher. I wrote Combat Command once again,

148

and I told them I was a highly trained artilleryman who maxed the Army's physical fitness test and would bring special weapons experience and other valuable skills to the fight. This time Personnel Command actually wrote me back. It was so rare for them to give me more than a quick phone call that I kept the letter, even though the colonel who sent it declined my offer. On behalf of the Army, he wrote, "I encourage you to do well in your present assignment (big parade)."

Sisi, when it comes to your path in the military, you lose control the minute you sign up. If you're lucky, you can choose your specialty at the start, the way I chose artillery, but from there the Pentagon pulls you on a leash. Once I read that letter from Personnel Command, I couldn't delude myself any longer – I knew in my bones that I was not slated for the battlefield greatness of my ancestors.

The winning energy of my grandfather's Leavenworth connection gets Band-Aid and me through our quick fuel stop. We roll out with potato chips and a full tank of gas. I'm about to merge back onto the freeway when I notice the hitchhiker. We haven't had one of those yet, so I slow down.

"You've got to be fucking kidding me. Ames, do not stop this car."

The man picks up his hobo sack and ambles toward us, looking dejectedly at the ground.

"Ames, I'm not bullshitting. This motherfucker is not getting in here," Band-Aid hits the automatic door lock button on his side.

I roll down his window and flick a switch to cut off his control. The hitchhiker's almost to the door now, he's wearing a camouflage jacket. "Look, he's an Army man too. You guys can swap stories."

"Fuck you. Drive the car."

The hitchhiker leans in Band-Aid's window, yellow beard blowing like a wind sock, "I'm going to Topeka."

"Will Kansas City do?"

"Yes it will."

Suddenly The Band-Aid Man speaks, "You looking to join the team?"

He downs his Miller rabidly and his eyes zero in on those of the hitchhiker. "'Cause we need a team player."

"Uh... yeah, I guess so."

"You don't sound so sure," The Band-Aid Man says, smashing his bottle over the right-side mirror and glaring menacingly.

"I'm not sure."

"I think you five-O. Ames, does he look like a cop to you?"

"I'm not a cop!"

"It's your choice then. Our operation's gotten too big," Band-Aid Man explains, waving his broken bottle. "We need someone to take care of the shit details."

"I don't know."

"Nickel and dime shit, you know. You know goddamn well!"

The hitchhiker's eyes widen and his beard appears to leap back with surprise. "You go... you go on. I'll wait."

"Wait for what? The authorities? Are you wearing a goddamn wire!"

The hitchhiker backpedals away from the door and The Band-Aid Man leans way out his window, slashing the air with his bottle. "If I cut your Army jacket open and find a wire, you're finished! I promise you, snitch! I will personally..."

I race a Mercedes and merge in front of it on I-29 South and Band-Aid finally ducks back inside. I flick the switch giving him control of his window, and he raises it. He glares at me, "Ames, I don't want to see any more of your crazy shit."

"Mine?"

"Yeah, fucker, yours. What's the idea trying to pick up a criminal?"

"Criminal? That man was a soldier."

He laughs finally, "Yeah, right, more like he just stole a jacket off some drunk GI who he hit over the head. Which he also would've done to me if we would've let him in."

"It's cold out there, Band-Aid. That guy's on your conscience."

"Conscience? Dude, I saved our lives. Look, we don't need any more passengers in the Cadillac unless it's cool bush. And we especially don't need to pick up anyone with a yellow beard in the vicinity of Leavenworth Prison."

He's got a point there. Until we've got a hundred miles between us and that yellow beard, we should trust no one.

In half an hour, we're barely moving at all, "Is this game traffic or rush hour?"

"Fuck if I know."

We're crawling. I-29 was getting bad and I was hoping I-435 would be an improvement, but it's worse if anything. I relax my body and let myself sink back into the blue leather. I've got one finger touching the bottom of the steering wheel, my foot resting on the brake, my seat's back, stereo on, windows up, outside sound minimal, inside temperature is 73 degrees. If you have to get stuck in traffic, Cadillac's the car to do it in.

As we inch toward Arrowhead Stadium in Kansas City, it occurs to me that getting into this Monday Night Football game is the only concrete mission we've established on this trip. The all-encompassing purpose of turning me into a civilian goes without saying, but, under that umbrella, whim and die rolls have mapped most of our jags. This game is different. The only other mission carved into our agenda is that grand Band-Aid Man caper he's hailed from the beginning: the return of Reveille. Discussion of our turning in the priceless stolen art has always made me nervous, but right now I welcome my nervousness about that event in our relatively distant future to help distract me from my nervousness about that event in our immediate future that is sneaking into the football stadium. The competing anxiety brings me a kind of comfort.

Out of respect, I've tried to stop calling it The Dog Painting. At this moment I don't even think of Reveille that way, because as the Cadillac odometer continues to accumulate miles, Band-Aid makes the long freeway spans my own A&M campus while he lectures me on the history of the painting, its artist, and its canine subject. It's the morsels on the dog that most captivate me. I learn Reveille was a *she*. She was a rescue mutt taken in by Aggie band members who found her injured and whimpering on the side of the road. She got her name the next morning when the Corps bugler played "Reveille" and the dog started barking to the bugle. She even appeared in a World War II movie, "We've Never Been Licked," that was filmed on A&M campus. As a student in this speeding Cadillac classroom, I'm completely won over. There used to be a piece of my character that rebelled against tradition. But now is different, I can feel The Band-Aid Man's and A&M's respect for the legacies rubbing off.

We eat chips and drink beer until we've crawled all the way there. A hotel, the Drury Inn, is right across the street from the stadium. Turns out they have one room, it's ours.

Inside room 225 we start drinking hard and Band-Aid calls out the gameplan. We'll go in through the service entrance and pose as Miller Beer representatives. He'll do the talking from start to finish.

We each make barely understandable calls to our friends and families to tell them we'll be on television. We continue drinking and we forget the gameplan. It'll come back to us when we need it.

It's 7:30 and we're walking across Blue Ridge Cutoff. Ahead, white light is shooting out the top of Arrowhead Stadium. We walk across the freeway exit and run down a steep, grassy slope into the parking lot below. Most of the tailgaters are inside already, but some guys in a red Ford pickup call out to us. There are five of them, we shake hands all around. Band-Aid and I finish our own beers we brought from the hotel.

"Throw those empties back here." The truckbed's full of them. We sail ours in with the rest of the aluminum, shake up the pile with a clatter. "Here's a couple more, we've got plenty of beer." We're enjoying talking with these locals, we're getting hammered on the beers they keep handing us. There's a little television on the lowered tailgate, tuned to the game channel. Kickoff's getting closer.

"There's gonna be an A-10 fly-by."

"Cool," says Band-Aid.

"Yeah, they're gonna fly right over the stadium. Should be right about now." We all stare up into the black sky for a minute, waiting for the jets to streak across. Coincidentally, a small, slow plane hums over us instead.

"Cessna one-fifty fly-by," Band-Aid remarks.

"Are you all going in?" I ask.

"The stadium? No, we don't have tickets."

"Monday Night in Arrowhead? You can forget it."

"This game was sold out before us folks had a chance."

"We'll be watching on this, right here, getting drunk."

"What about you two?"

"We're sneaking in," Band-Aid says confidently. There is an outburst of good-natured laughter all the way around. Our new friends are greatly amused by the idea.

"Ho boy, heh heh, that's all right, have another beer. Hoo hoooo!"

"How... he he... are you two going to do that? Heeeaagh ha ha!"

Some seconds go by while The Band-Aid Man thinks. At last he says, "I forgot. It has something to do with the service entrance."

"Whooooo hoooo!"

"Haaagh... service en.... haaaa haaa ha!"

"Heeeeeeeeeeeeeeeeeeeeeee!"

I don't know how their laughter doesn't demoralize us into giving up, but we thank them all and head toward the ramp. "Service Only," reads the sign that we pass. Down underground it's hectic. Most of the employees have badges and Band-Aid is trying to find out where we can get some. One office sends him to another office and that office sends him back to the first one. My baby bladder's full, so I hit the employee locker room and find a urinal. I'm washing my hands when Band-Aid comes in. He's in a stall and I notice a vendor's smock balled up on top of the hand dryer. When he comes out, he sees me trying it on.

"No, you dumbfuck, you don't need a costume, that's why I lent you my jacket. We're Miller Beer reps."

"Oh yeah," I return the red and white striped smock to the dryer. I'm wearing his light-blue Miller Lite jacket with no stitching.

"Listen," he says. "This place is so fucked up and confused that we should be able to march right in from here. I think the hard part is supposed to be getting in from outside, which we've already done."

While he's talking I'm overcome by a feeling this is going too fast, "Wait, wait. Let's think about this."

"No," Band-Aid orders. "Remember the quote from your great uncle, George S. Patton."

"Which quote?"

"*A good plan violently executed now is better than a perfect plan executed next week.* Let's go."

We head out of the locker room and follow the flow of employees down the hallway. This is it. The only reason we came to this city is to get into this game. So much depends on what happens next. Are we for real? This is a pride thing, and it's also winning versus losing. Sneaking into the game is a decisive civilian act. If we succeed, it means I'm that much closer.

A whim was born in a Chicago bar. I can still hear Band-Aid reading the poster, I can see in slow motion Sweets relaxedly shaking the matchbook fire in his hand. The fire died, the whim survived. An idea carried for a thousand miles is coming down to this next sixty seconds. It's Judgment Night in Arrowhead, we take a left down another corridor. A defeat here would set a tone I can't imagine. Our hearts are beating wildly, no one's saying a word.

I'm thinking about that third week. If we get into this game, The Band-Aid Man will take a third week off. I won't even have to remind him, he'll do it by himself. If we don't get in, then our peak's behind us, and tonight is just the lead plunge in a depressing spiral into the dungeons of alcohol and ephedrine despair. Oh, these final five nights will be interesting, but they'll be a hellish black and blue sludgecrawl through the gutters of humanity, marked by violent self-abuse and the darkest humor.

We're looking good, looking real good. There's a security guard at a desk with a TV. We're walking toward him, closer, his desk is on our left, he's tapping his thumb on the desk surface, we're walking past him. We are past him. Yes.

"Hold it! You two, where are you going?"

Oh, no. We halt.

"I work for Miller Beer, we're going to check on our supply." Band-Aid flips out his wholesaler's license and his business card to the blond security guy who's in his thirties.

"And how about you?"

"I work for Miller too," I say, pointing to the Lite logo over my left breast.

"Sometimes during big events like this, they let supplies run too low. We're just going to make sure everything's all right."

"How do I know you won't watch the game?"

"Well, we probably will watch a little of it while we're up there."

The security guard looks at both of us silently. He keeps looking at us. He shakes his head and says, "Don't ever do this again."

"Thank you," Band-Aid Man says and we both round the corner and head straight up into the star-white stadium light. We're here! Among the fans!

We find a pair of seats up high, just right for the high life we're living. The game's underway and the audience is energized. What we might've spent on tickets, we spend on beer, and we're lit. Midway through the third quarter, Band-Aid Man notices that we're sitting right next to the camera booth. He bangs on the door and offers bribes to any camera operator who will film us, but no one will, and Band-Aid soon settles back down with his beers.

At the fourth quarter my friend shoots to his feet. "Give me your pen!" he cries. "Stand up and take off the jacket." I comply and suddenly he tears the pen cap off in his teeth and begins scrawling frantically on my white T-shirt. The pen's a Bic Metaltip, and Band-Aid's got it overhand in his fist like a madwoman lunging out with a dagger. He's carving block letters into my chest, running the Metaltip back and forth over each line of every letter to make it stand out. This is no less painful than a tattoo, but I'm excited about my partner's supreme inspiration.

"There it is!" he shrieks happily. I pull my shirt out at the bottom to read the message more easily. It says: "4K MILES FOR MNF ON ABC!" It's certainly cryptic and, even in my drunken state, I am fully aware of just how primitive and shabby our bulletin will appear to the general public. But I also know that this is the kind of design you have to roll with. In seconds, I am on the shoulders of The Band-Aid Man and we are ranting crazily and directly into the camera. The red light is on.

The cameraman leans out the door, "I got it, but the heads didn't take it. There are a lot of cameras and we all send film in."

Well, we gave it a try and this is a lot of fun anyway, we get back in our seats and keep cheering. The cameraman opens the door and tells us to do it again, so I'm on Band-Aid's shoulders and we never stop screaming. The red light on top of the camera goes on again, and this time a guy next to us taps us and tells us to look at the big screen over the end zone. And there we are! We're cheering up on the screen, our heads as big as mattresses, our wide-open mouths like manhole covers. And between our giant heads – the shirt I'm wearing, a freeway billboard tipped on its end, the stadium's most daring cryptic banner. The crowd in our seating section roars in support and we receive numerous slaps on our hands and backs. The cameraman leans out again, "They took it, you're nationwide."

"Damn right we are!" The Band-Aid Man shouts. We give an extra cheer of thanks to the cameraman and I drop back down.

A girl a few rows ahead smiles and does a dance for The Band-Aid Man, and her grumpy boyfriend scolds us, "Do you guys think you're special?"

"Yes!" Band-Aid Man shouts. Nothing can take us off this high, and grumpy boyfriend only makes us higher. Our exhilaration is like a powerful fire now, the kind that swallows arsonists and uses them for fuel. It's a runaway game for our runaway high, the local team on top and out of reach. The mood of the entire city will soar tonight in an H-bomb wave rolling out in a spreading circle from this stadium, and we will ride it all the way.

Some things lift you up like that, Sisi. When Rusty pledged to snatch me from my random assignment and get me into his unit, Soraya and I couldn't be knocked out of our good mood. The glow lasted for days.

I didn't hear back from Rusty as soon as I thought I would, but I still had more than a week before I had to report to Fort Sill on the original recall orders. I figured that was more than enough time for Rusty to take military ownership of me. Doubt didn't even start to seep in until his next e-mail hit.

From: Rusty Spray
To: Ames Holbrook
Subject: Re: Reunion

Ames, your buddy Major Horse-pelt is a total dick. I'm going over his head, but it's taking time. If you talk to anybody at Branch more reasonable than that asshole, give them my number (808) — —. Tell them to ask for Major Spray, which is the same name I use when I make porn movies. Say we're cutting out the middleman.

Any idea why Horse-pelt is trying to fuck you? Was he your commander when you were on active duty? If so, I understand.

Good luck with what you have going on at home.

I tried to stay upbeat. As long as I'd known Rusty, he was a person who made things happen. All the wild feats Rusty pulled off were part of what made him a legend. I told Soraya about the time Rusty drove our mutual buddy's car onto an aircraft on the mainland and rolled it off the tailgate in Hawaii, no paper trail, like magic. I told Soraya more Rusty stories of a similar stripe, but I didn't tell her about that e-mail from Rusty. And I certainly didn't tell her about the communication that came next, when Horse-pelt finally broke his silence to hit me with a shot that shook me to my core.

The Fireworks Vendor and the Plague

We're almost out of Kansas. I'm going west on I-70 and I can see a long way. There's a turnoff ahead and there's a brown sign staked into the ground right next to the standard green sign that says exit. The brown sign is unfinished fiberboard with orange letters spray-painted across it. The orange letters spell: "Fireworks."

I drift right and soon the Cadillac tires are on a dusty unlined road. It's a good thing my belly's full, because there's nothing to eat around here. There's a brown-powder wind blowing across the hood and I see only one building. It's a big building with an exterior of tall metal panels. It has a yellow roof and on this roof are huge black letters spelling: "Fireworks." The surrounding ground is a patchwork mix of chipped concrete and asphalt. I pull around to the front door which is closed, but not all the way. Whoever's in there must get a ride to work, because this Cadillac is the only car in sight.

I put it in park and kill the engine. I'll just head in here for a minute. No need to wake up The Band-Aid Man.

It's one huge room inside, full of shelves full of fireworks, a small counter with a phone up front, and a man with a beard sitting behind it. "How are you today?"

I know right away that the scrawny vendor is my kind of guy. And I know in the same instant that few others feel the same. I speculate that he's likely been called a *beardo*, perhaps more than once in the past twenty-four hours. "I'm just fine, how about you?"

"Oh, can't complain. Uh, can I help you with somethin?"

There's a sign on the wall informing customers that all fireworks purchased here may not be legal outside of Kansas. "Just looking around, thanks."

"Well, lookin around is a great start. That's the best way to go about it, yes it is, lookin around. Lookin around, lookin around. That's what he's doin..."

Leaving him in his own world, I start walking through the aisles, seeing what's interesting. There's a lot to choose from, it's exciting. All kinds of different effects, cool colors, great names. After the first three rows, I've got my arms full. I go up to the counter and set everything down.

"Well, you like the powerful ones, do ya?"

"I guess so. I'm gonna rattle some cages."

"Rattle cages, huh? Hear what he said? Rattle cages, that's all right. I like that."

"Thank you."

"Well... uh... you're gonna be shootin 'em off around here, are ya?"

"No, I'm leaving Kansas."

"Oh... you're leavin, ya say. Leavin Kansas... I think I might have somethin ya might wanna take a look at."

"Oh yeah?"

"Aaah... right over at that aisle there... yeah, if you walk over one more, that's it... and go down a little bit, and lift that curtain, you see the big package with the plastic broken? It says 'Power Pack?'"

I grab it and lift it high. It's about four feet long, three feet wide, seven inches deep, and heavy. I bring it to the counter.

"Yessir, that's the one. You can see how the plastic's broken, so I'll give it to you for twenty dollars. It's got a lot of powerful stuff. When you said, 'Rattle some cages,' that's what I thought of right off. It's a lot better than all that stuff you got individually..."

"Thanks, I'll put these things back." I pick up everything except for the package and two Black Cat Cannons I can't bring myself to shelve, and I walk back into the aisles. The door opens and the bearded man reaches suddenly for the package, but when he sees The Band-Aid Man, he withdraws his trembling hands. Band-Aid asks the man if he can use the phone to make a free call and I try to put everything in its proper place.

I get back up to the counter just as Band-Aid is hanging up the phone. I'm pretty sure I know what his call was about, and I'm dying to hear the report from Band-Aid, but this transaction requires all my focus. The bearded man looks around nervously as he takes my payment for the package, which he's already wrapped securely in plain brown shipping paper. "Oh, you wanted the Black Cat Cannons too, didn't you? Well, that's all right, we'll just ring those up separate. This is just between you, me, and the fencepost, of course, 'cause I'm givin you such a big discount."

"I understand," I nod as I accept my change for the Black Cat Cannons in the second transaction.

"You aren't plannin on goin up thataway, tellin them people up there?" he jabs his thumb behind him. Whoever those people up there are, they must be very far away, because, again, there wasn't anything within eyesight of this building when I pulled up.

"No, I'm getting right back on the freeway. Thanks for the deal." I see that there's a purchase log on the counter and this box has not been entered.

"Yeah, back on the freeway... that's good. If those people up there found out, it'd be a real wrench in the monkeyworks."

"Don't worry," I say on my way to the door. "Remember, I've got cages to rattle."

"He hee hee! Rattlin cages!" he cackles as the door closes behind me.

Band-Aid's waiting, leaning on the Caddy. "What the fuck did you get?"

"Fireworks, man."

"No shit. What kind?"

"Two Black Cat Cannons and a package with a lot of stuff." I drop the whole load on top of the trunk.

"What kind of stuff?"

"I don't really know. He wrapped it up before I had a chance to look at it."

"You didn't see anything?"

"It was a lot."

"Well, open it up!" He knocks the Black Cat Cannons aside and eagerly tears through the brown paper. In seconds, the package is naked and staring at us. And we're staring back, still and speechless. I think we both realize that we are involved in something very big. Our hands jump through the cellophane to hold and feel the individual samples. We're still not talking, but our hands are scrambling, our minds are racing, our eyes are reading and inspecting, our grins are growing wide.

There's a reason the cellophane was broken. Nothing in here is fitting into any of the package's slots. The box does read, "Power Pack," but clearly the original Power Pack items have gone elsewhere to be replaced with these very different substitutes. There are some colorful fireworks here, but a third of the items are either pale brown or olive drab. Most of these have Chinese writing on them, and a few have illustrations of uniformed Chinese soldiers in combat poses.

I'm trying to figure this out, but it's going to take a while. I'll try to start by putting them into categories, and the way I see it right now, there are three. The first category is small unnamed fireworks in sealed clear plastic bags. There is nothing unusual in the appearance of these fireworks, and if these ten clear baggies hadn't come as a part of this particular package, I would have no reason to believe they were anything but normal firecrackers, whistlers, jumping jacks, and bottle rockets.

The second category is a unique one. These fireworks are larger, like those in the third category, but these are brightly and beautifully jacketed in all different colors. Also, most of these fireworks have English names, and some even list English instructions like: "Light and Run Away," or "This Side toward Enemy." If the instructions are some kind of tip-off, the real eye-opener is the names. "Ghost Attack" is probably the friendliest name of the bunch, but two that stick in my head are "Yankee Gone to Seed" and "White Bastard," and these names are far more typical.

This brings us to the third category, the plain brown and olive drab ones. How these things got to Kansas and why they wound up in our Power Pack are both mysteries. They may blow the trunk open while we're driving down the freeway, I'm not even sure they're stable. All I know is that China walked into Tibet with these in 1950 and this is the twenty buck bargain of the century.

It is The Band-Aid Man who speaks first. "God damn! This shit can't be legal!"

"It's legal. Probably some of it's been recalled."

"Recalled? This shit is banned! Did you see this one?"

"The Plague? Yeah, freaky."

"Freaky ain't the word, dude, read this shit: 'The Plague. Colorless! Odorless! Noiseless!' What the fuck does it do, then? What the fuck kind of firecracker is that!"

"Good question." I unlock the trunk and force in the whole package minus The Plague which Band-Aid's still got in his hand. It's shaped like a flat rectangle, roughly the dimensions of a stack of ten postcards.

"Where's my blue-flame lighter?"

I move around to the driver door. "Forget it, man! Let's go!"

Suddenly he runs up and starts digging in the glove compartment. He's got the lighter, I start the engine. The Plague's got a fuse, same as the rest of them. "Get out and look at this! I didn't ask you to stop here, this is your responsibility!"

I stand up and he sets it down ten feet in front of our grill and lights it. He runs back and we're both watching it from behind our doors like cops in a gunfight. The fuse burns down and the rectangle appears to turn instantly into liquid. It bubbles like boiling water and then disappears, either evaporating into the air or sinking into the earth. It's gone, the whole operation lasted ten seconds. We dive back into the car at the same time and I jam it in reverse for five feet before dropping into drive. The change of direction slams both doors shut like thunder and I point us at the freeway and gun. "The Plaaaaaaaaaaaaaaaague!" screams The Band-Aid Man. He's jabbering all kinds of things, but I am silent for some time.

"It was colorless, odorless, and noiseless," Band-Aid pronounces. "No false advertising."

I try to shake The Plague off as I merge us back onto the freeway, "Did I tell you about my most disappointing experience with false advertising?"

"No."

"We were in Thailand—"

"With Soraya?"

"Yeah, but a bunch of us, walking down Bangla Road in Phuket. This local guy kept trying to steer us into his club, yelling, 'Pussy blow fire!' over and over. There was this big sign on the front of the club with 'Pussy Blow Fire' written in English. And here was this Thai guy, putting his hands on our backs, pushing us toward the door, 'Pussy blow fire! Pussy blow fire!'"

"You went in?" Band-Aid asks.

"Yeah, we fell for it. As soon as we got inside, these girls were all over us, trying to rope us into more than we'd signed up for, but I held firm. I announced to the whole house, 'Hey, we're here to see pussy blow fire, and then we're leaving.'"

"What'd they do?"

"One girl lit a candle and then put a paper cone in her vagina and pointed the cone at the candle flame, and then she contracted her vaginal muscles so air puffed through the cone and it blew out the candle."

"What?"

"Yeah, total false advertising. It should have been Pussy Blow *Out* Fire."

"Did you get a refund?"

"No, there's no recourse in Thailand. It was like three dollars apiece, down the tubes."

"Shit." Band-Aid's quiet for a while, then he casually reports, "Ames, I got the third week."

"Awesome, man! I love it! How can you even make an announcement like that without two shots of Crown on the dash?"

"Fuck, I don't know. My boss was drunk."

"What do you mean?"

"He's a big-time alcoholic and he always goes home after work and gets shitfaced. That's why I called him when I did, 'cause I knew he'd give me the third week. But when he gets sober and figures out what he did, he's gonna want my ass back, driving that beer truck."

"Then it's a good thing he won't be able to reach you." Band-Aid's cold feet aren't spreading to me. I'm thrilled about all we'll be able to do with a third week, and frankly I welcome any postponement of the Reveille painting return, which is clearly going to be the riskiest sortie of this entire campaign.

"My girlfriend's going to be pissed off too."

"What girlfriend? You have a girlfriend now?"

"Fuck yeah," he says dejectedly. "She's gonna be pissed I left her for three weeks, touring the whole country with you, and she and I haven't even been on a real date."

"You haven't been on a date, but she's suddenly your girlfriend?"

"She's a bartender. We were both working Fiesta and hooked up, and ever since then we've been working our asses off so all we've had time to do is go to each other's apartments and bang each other before we get up and go back to work."

I'm still staggered to just be hearing about his girlfriend now. We've had more than a week of road time, during which we've engaged in completely frivolous conversations like best and worst zombie movies, and a "Would you?" game where appealing females have body parts from completely unappealing donors, e.g. Would you kiss Vanessa Williams if she had Muammar Gaddafi's lips and moustache. We were discussing *Pussy Blow Fire*, for Pete's sake, and Band-Aid didn't figure that was worth pushing aside to tell me he has a girlfriend? "What's her name?"

"Lori Kafanek."

"God, that sounds just like Laura Coffeecake. Did you start liking her for her name?"

"No, it's not the same at all."

"Can I call her Laura Bananas, so I don't get her mixed up with your crazy A&M girlfriend?"

"Fuck no, Laura Bananas makes her sound crazy too. Why don't you just call her Lori, since that's her name, and since it's a totally different name from Laura Coffeecake?"

"How could you get in a serious relationship with a girl who has the same name? You obviously didn't take any of your friends' feelings into consideration."

"I took everyone's feelings into consideration except yours, since you're the only dumbfuck who would think Lori is the same as Laura. It's like saying Ames is the same as Ahmed."

"Well, let's at least toast to your new girlfriend. Pour us a couple shots so we can cheers to Laura Bananas."

Ten minutes later, Band Aid's quiet and he still hasn't poured any Crown Royal, so I know he's still not feeling right. There's something more at play than the third week, and I need to figure it out, because we can't come into Colorado Springs with him like this. The only reason we're going there is to see some old friend of his, Buck, who's an alleged party animal. Buck was his running partner at the artillery course in Oklahoma and he's stationed at Ft. Carson now. A sad-sack Band-Aid Man will ruin the reunion and I won't let that happen.

Daylight disappears, it's black out. I pull off at Limon, Colorado, and get us away from the main drag. "Hey, Band-Aid, let's fire off a few of these things. I'll feel better when I know The Plague was a one-of-a-kind deal."

He steps out of the car with me, "Ames, you had my dream and you walked away."

Oh, no. It all comes to me, I've heard this before.

"I got thrown out of the Army. That's all I ever wanted to be. But I couldn't. Then you come along with your Regular Army commission, and you walk away. You ask the Army to send you to combat a few times, they don't do it, so you just fucking *quit*."

He's usually drunk when this comes up, but his leading my discharge is taking a toll. This Army-exorcism odyssey has released thoughts he'd buried for a while. He doesn't have tears rolling down his face the way he did in Italy when he got kicked out, when the Army sliced his tether suddenly, in coldest possible blood, hurling him into desolate midnight space where he freefell alone with his thoughts that fed him the impulse to push his exit beyond a departure from just the Army and all the way to a departure from the world itself. I kidnaped him to Rome to show him how infinitely beautiful life outside the military could be, and he saw it, and since then he's thanked me for saving his life – even though I acted only selfishly, not wanting to lose a friend, not wanting our world to be deprived of The Band-Aid Man. American veterans kill themselves at a rate far in excess of those who have never served, and the tragic suicides are not exclusive to the heroes who have been washed in the blood of the dead. God knows those are the best of us, but every discharged vet has a hole that will never again be filled. My brother Band-Aid is not in that hole now, thankfully. Then again, he's not that far from it. His eyes are wet.

"You can't think like that anymore, Band-Aid."

"Why can't I? The Army wouldn't let me live my life's purpose." I feel for Band-Aid Man, his path's not having gone the way he planned it. You grow up dreaming of yourself as a battlefield commander, courageous leader of your people in your country's times of need, and one day that dream has slipped away, and you're driving a beer truck on a vector that's taking you further and further away. I feel his pain, but I know my brother's thinking the wrong way. For 99% of us, life doesn't go the way we thought it would. As an American civilian, though, there's always possibility. There are dreams out there we haven't even considered, some more sublime than our imaginations can hatch. We'll just have to stick around long enough to see them for ourselves. I don't know anything better than that.

"Band-Aid, stop!" I step to my mentor and give him a hug. "The Army made a mistake and let you go – you win. You're a living god. You do your life your way. You have friends and girls from coast to coast. You fit more fun in your life than most people can dream of. You're my civilian idol here – who do you think gave me the courage to do this?"

Band-Aid hugs me back, "I did that?"

"Of course."

His chest heaves a couple times from emotion before we let each other go. At the same time, standing next to our Cadillac, both of us remember our cargo.

We go into the trunk, scoop random samples out of the package and drop them on the roof. We've both got Montecristos going, so we just start setting things down and lighting them. It's a beautiful scene full of the most spectacular flashes and wonderful noises and it just keeps going. The sky is a million brilliant colors. The bangs, hisses, and whistles overlap like an orchestra. Our nostrils thrill on the smell of burning powder. The Plague is a joke from the distant past, this is the real deal.

Some fireworks race head to head down the empty road before destructing. Many lift off their stands and fly right at us like filled but untied balloons that have been let go. Surprise ones explode above us in a cute flower, then drop harmful pellets that rock the earth and blow our eardrums out. Little ones from a plastic baggie are super bright eye-burners, way brighter than a welder's torch. Band-Aid brings out the Crown midway and the taste goes great with the smell of firework smoke. The fog is settling. The concert is over. In addition to making me forget The Plague, the fireworks show had exactly the effect I'd hoped it would on Band-Aid Man. He's now grinning from ear to ear and prancing happily, Cuban crop fire clenched in his teeth with blazing self-assurance. I've handed over the Cadillac keys and they're bouncing in his palm to a joyful rhythm.

Sisi, I appreciated the chance to rescue The Band-Aid Man from himself once in a while. Eleven years later, it was I who was in desperate need of rescue. After Rusty's last downer e-mail about how Horse-pelt was trying to block him, I kept checking to see if my friend had found a way around. Imagine my surprise when I saw a new e-mail not from Rusty, but from Horse-pelt. The major been too busy to answer my phone calls or e-mails up to now, but my old nemesis finally found the time to transmit a bulletin of ruin.

From: "Horse-pelt, Monticello, HRC-St. Louis"
To: 'Ames Holbrook'
Subject: Thin Ice
1LT Holbrook
In the past week I have been contacted by two of your
friends who wish to discuss your mobilization. I do not
have the time or responsibility of explaining the details
to your friends. Consequently, I will not respond to such
inquiries.
As you are currently on mobilization orders you cannot
change your status by joining the National Guard. Let me
caution you that we have had some soldiers enlist in the
National Guard to avoid their mobilization tour. We
prosecute these soldiers to the full extent of the law.
Major Horse-pelt

I stared at his e-mail for at least thirty seconds in shock. And then I roared.

In its determination to ruin me, the Army had derailed my University of Hawaii Baghdad reunion, thereby killing not just my best plan, but the most effective military option.

There was no way to fight the madness of the machine.

The future flashed before me, and in it I was guarding Fort Sill's tennis courts.

How in the world had it come to this! In spite of my participation in the most definitive conversion of a soldier into a civilian that the world had ever witnessed, I was nonetheless caught in the machine, facing a *report-or-MP's-will-haul-you-to-Leavenworth* recall straight into the Army's gunpowder guts.

Sisi, I've mentioned Ft. Leavenworth more than once, in connection with both the Reveille painting and the Army's having classified me a deserter, so maybe I owe you a little background. I realize the famed military prison can take on kind of a mythical quality to those who have never served, but I assure you that to those personally acquainted with the military, the United States Disciplinary Barracks at Ft. Leavenworth, Kansas, is real. At the time Major Horse-pelt threatened to prosecute me, I'd already had two close friends who'd found themselves in the military penal system.

My friend Tyrone wound up in a red violent-offender jumpsuit in the Philadelphia Naval Shipyard stockade, at the time Leavenworth's way station for personnel accused of crimes in the Northeastern United States and the Mediterranean. Tyrone's crime was beating down a white man who'd pulled a knife on him, only to have Tyrone teach him the age-old lesson that a stick beats a knife. Tyrone went on to become both a federal law enforcement officer and a standout Reserve NCO who attained the rank of sergeant major, which tells you all you need to know about the legitimacy of his imprisonment.

For the social activist in you, Sisi, yes, both the guys I'm telling you about here are Black and both were innocent. Another friend of mine, Wally, defied his redneck commander and refused to accept a no-time deal for a minor offense he hadn't committed, which led the spiteful commander to hand Wally the maximum punishment. Honored recipient of the Bronze Star for valor he displayed in the desert, Wally now found himself walled in at Leavenworth. His was a very short sentence, and he would have been out before we knew it, but unfortunately, he was jumped by a fellow inmate who tried to rape Wally: "Give it up – you know what this is!" Wally got the upper hand, and the shank, "NO! *You* know what this is!" and left his attacker well ventilated on the cellblock floor. While the authorities did not deny that Wally had defended himself from a sexual assault, they decided he had stabbed his attacker excessively, and they extended Wally's initial short sentence into 45 months hard time.

Wally spent the last weekend before his initial verdict – what turned out to be his last weekend of freedom for almost four years – with me and my other main running partner from the 3rd Infantry Division, the three of us converging in New Orleans for a big blowout because there was nothing else to do. Wally said, "You know, if this were a civilian trial, I wouldn't have a thing to worry about. I didn't do it, and there's no evidence that I did." Sisi, nothing sums it up better than that. The Uniform Code of Military Justice bears little resemblance to the justice system we know in America. When you're in the military, the machine owns you and the machine decides your fate.

Not surprisingly, Wally had a ton of wild stories from inside, but the one that always stuck with me was when he rattled off a bunch of sensational crimes, "You remember the sergeant whose wife was cheating on him so he put her lover's head in the mailbox? How about that pilot who sliced the gondola cable in Italy and killed 20 people? And the asshole who threw the grenades..." And I kept nodding, "Yeah. Yeah. Yeah..." I remembered them, pretty much all of us who served would. And Wally said, "I sat at the dining hall table with every one of 'em. I played a lot of cards with the head-in-the-mailbox guy."

Leavenworth is not mythical, Sisi. Military prison is a real consideration for everyone in uniform, and when senior officers threaten to prosecute, you take notice.

When I read Horse-pelt's message, I wanted to dive through the screen and choke the major. For a long interval, I furiously shadowboxed and kicked the air from room to room in my house. When I returned to my e-mail, I was still shaking, but I was just composed enough to type a reply. I fired it off to Horse-pelt with a High Priority tag.

If I'd been a smarter man, I would have waited until I'd completely cooled down.

Buck and the Insubordinate E-Mail

Band-Aid downshifts suddenly, "Fucker, make up your mind! Stop or go!" He blasts the horn as he swings around a bend. I don't see a car anywhere.

"Who are you talking to?"

He looks around, squinting and blinking. "Oh, fuck, I thought it was brakelights. I've got all kinds of weird afterimages burnt into my eyes from those fireworks."

"Yeah, me too. Those little ones are like looking at the sun. But worse for me is my ears. I keep hearing echoes and whistles and beeps. I hope this stuff wears off before we have to interact with other people."

"No shit," says The Band-Aid Man, still driving about seventy on a two-lane highway and wildly clicking his brights at other imagined vehicles.

We make it to Colorado Springs, home of the United States Air Force Academy, which I came very close to attending. The school actually accepted me, and I went out the spring before to visit the campus. My visit didn't sell me on the place, all the cadets in pressed uniforms marching off every turn at a right angle, but what really made me rule it out was a conversation with my uncle, Major General George S. Patton.

George Patton, son and namesake of "Old Blood and Guts," was himself a legendary military leader who served in the Korean War and three tours in Vietnam, famously survived multiple helicopter crashes, and picked up two Distinguished Service Crosses and two Silver Stars among numerous other commendations for bravery along the way. He was a force of nature, and he was something to see at family reunions, where I had the privilege of watching him in social settings and

173

benefitting from his advice.

When I told him I was thinking about going to the Air Force Academy, he let me know immediately that it was a terrible idea. Dashing my dreams of rescuing downed pilots in the mountains or securing airfields behind enemy lines, he lectured, "Ames, why the hell would you join the Air Force? Your eyes aren't good enough to be a pilot, and if you're not a pilot, you're a goddamn second-class citizen as far as the Air Force is concerned. If you insist on going a different path from the Army, then try the Navy. You can be a nuke sub commander and then you're king of the world. But really, from what you're saying you want to do with the Air Force, running around in the bush in hostile territory like that, I think you need to take another look at the Army."

Looking back now, it's pretty obvious I was paying attention to my Uncle George.

Band-Aid pulls us into a Loaf 'n Jug for some Swisher Sweets cigars to light our fireworks. We can't sacrifice valuable Montecristos every time we want to blow something up. I've got big plans for our greeting of Buck. Ever since Boston, I've been hearing Band-Aid Man's complaints about how my friends aren't partiers and they didn't set us up with any bush. Well, I'm not going to cut his buddy any slack either.

We pull into Buck's apartment complex and park next to a dumpster. Our Swishers are glowing and when the trunk pops I go right for the Red Army stuff.

"Come on, Ames, that's too much."

"But he's a wildman."

"His roommate's got a fiancée, all right? You can't just be blowing up shit when fiancées are involved. That's a commitment... love. This is like the early stages where everything's kinda fragile. You start blowing up all kinds of pyrotechnics and that could fuck up some shit. And I'm not talking about physical buildings or whatever, I'm talking about romantic shit." The Band-Aid Man delivers this lecture with such seriousness of tone and expression that I actually feel guilty. I put the plain brown and olive drab items back and we walk toward the apartment with only the two Black Cat Cannons and a large double-chain of firecrackers wrapped in thin red paper.

The plan is that Band-Aid will ring the doorbell, I'll light the Black Cat Cannons, he'll light the firecracker chain, and we'll both run and hide behind the bushes. I take a long drag on my Swisher Sweet, he pushes the bell, and fuses are hissing. We're behind the bushes and things are going off loud and bright. The powerful firecracker chain knocks one Black Cat Cannon on its side so it's shooting exploding fireballs right into the door. If they open it, it'll be perfect. But after about a minute, the fireworks stop and they still haven't opened the door. There are some faces pressed to windows in other apartments, but nothing from Buck's.

We go to the door and Band-Aid Man starts knocking. The door opens about a foot to reveal a frightened white youth with a quivering smile. "Yes?"

"I'm The Band-Aid Man. You must be Kip."

The door comes open all the way. "Oh, heh heh, yes. That was you guys?" We barge in and Kip sits sheepishly on the couch with an arm around his girlfriend. The television is on and Kip keeps his eyes on the screen.

"Where's Buck?"

"He should be here soon," Kip says hopefully.

"I'm The Band-Aid Man," he offers his hand to Kip's girlfriend who shakes it mechanically with uncertain smile. The phone rings and I'm the closest to it, so I pick it up. It's Buck, he's on the way. I set down my empty Red Bull malt liquor and walk into the kitchen where The Band-Aid Man is cracking liquor bottles and mixing some drinks.

Band-Aid starts banging ice trays on the counter. Things are falling over, a dial falls off the oven and bounces across the tile. Kip and girlfriend retreat to their bedroom. The front door swings open, it's Buck. He's blond, about five-nine with a pot belly, and he's smiling.

Band-Aid puts a drink in his hand and asks him where the bush is.

"Aww, you guys came on a bad night. If you stay tomorrow night, we can get something going, but Tuesday is a bad scene."

"Dude, I didn't come out here to hear any excuses, we're going out."

"Everybody's got Thursday off for a training holiday. Tomorrow's gonna be a lot better."

"Fine, we'll stay tomorrow, too, but at least show us around tonight. There's bush out there that wants my cazzo."

We get the Cadillac while Buck changes out of his uniform. The parking spaces are in the center of the complex, but there's a fire lane circling the whole thing, so we drive that to pick Buck up at his front door. When we pull around, he gets in and asks, "What did you guys do to Kip? He's all stressing about getting his rent deposit back, told me to keep you in line."

"Deposit? He's moving out soon?" I ask.

"Yeah, on the fifteenth."

"Probably isn't us, then. Kip just has the moving-out jitters."

"Yeah," Band-Aid agrees. "I could tell he was a jittery fucker."

The first place Buck directs us to is closed, and here Buck restates his pitch about the deadness of Tuesdays. Then he asks, "Did I tell you about the Korean whore?"

"No."

"On my last night in Korea, I treated myself to my last Korean whore and it was like midnight and I went down on her and I was munching that box and sucking it and drinking it for hours, it was great. Then the next day on the plane home I was thinking about how it was the end of the night and that whore must've fucked a dozen guys that day and I was eating her pussy."

"God damn!"

"Yeah, I got a problem, man."

"I'll say." Band-Aid wasn't kidding, this Buck is a wild cat.

The Band-Aid Man stares at the dark bar and scowls, "Is anywhere open?"

"I can take us to one place, but I might not be allowed in because last time I walked in naked and they threw me out."

We get in with no problem. Not only has Buck been forgiven, but all the waitresses like him. They give us a free pitcher after Band-Aid tells them how far he's driven to come to their bar. He and I order something called Volcano Wings. Turn out to be tender chicken, but the things are hot. The Band-Aid Man begins complaining of a strange feeling in his stomach. He suggests we go drink at Buck's place so we won't have to bother with a taxi or coming back to pick up the Cadillac in the morning. We're rolling home and suddenly a black cat leaps out in front of us. It's too late to stop, there's a car behind us, and Band-Aid Man keeps going.

"Aww God, dude. You killed a black cat!" Buck cries with alarm.

"What was I supposed to do? It ran right out in the middle of the road."

"Aww, dude, that ain't good. I hope you killed it all the way, it better not be still alive."

"Are you afraid it got our plates?" I ask.

"Dude, this is serious. That's a black cat! Black cats are no joke."

"Fuck, man, it came out of nowhere. The thing's black, I just saw two glowing yellow eyes all of a sudden." Band-Aid's voice rises, Buck's panic is rubbing off on him, "I can't just hit the brakes with a car right on my tail, I got explosive shit in the trunk."

"Well, drive slower, dude. You can't just run over black cats like it's nothing. That's a terrifying thing to happen."

"I got some fucked-up visions in my eyes – tell him, Ames, from the fireworks. We're still hearing whistles and shit. I was being careful and it just appeared."

"It doesn't matter, dude, you can't hit a black cat. That has some consequences."

"What's gonna happen?"

"I don't know, but it's scary. Everybody knows not to mess with black cats. We're in a scary situation."

Sisi, for the record, I'm really sorry about that cat. I was immune to the black cat superstitions that were freaking out Band-Aid and Buck, but I did feel genuinely bad about the death of one of nature's creatures.

And, speaking of genuine emotion, Sisi, I still have to show you that dispatch I fired off to Horse-pelt in a fit of real rage:

From: "Ames Holbrook"
To: 'Horse-pelt, Monticello, HRC-St. Louis'
Subject: Re: Thin Ice
Dear ~~Cyclops~~ Major Horse-pelt,
Thank you for the e-mail, it's good to have this on record.
The National Guard unit that needs me is a fighting infantry unit with orders for the combat zone, as opposed to the undoubtedly useless assignment I will receive under the "fully automated" system you cited. In case you hadn't noticed, I've been trying to do the right thing, even though any claim the Army had to me expired last century. Check your facts. If I interrupt my life and report to Fort Sill because of a bureaucrat's negligence, I will prosecute those responsible to the fullest extent of the law.
True love always,
Ames

The e-mail was irretrievable. No taking it back, even if I'd wanted to. There was going to be some reaction to my words, I just didn't know how severe. I was in too deep now to worry about that. Honestly, Sisi, my backlash e-mail was some salve for my soul, but my world was still crashing. My liberty was at stake, with it the value of the sacrifices made by every serviceman and servicewoman pulling duty out there in order that free Americans could remain so. If I allowed the Army to take me against my will, then those warriors' sacrifices would be wasted. I could not let that happen.

Sisi, I don't need you to stand up right now and declare that America is the greatest country in the world. I mean, it is to *me*, but I certainly welcome other opinions. I know you have two passports, after all, and your life experience is so different. But, surely you would agree with me that whatever America is, good and bad, it is *its own beast*. America is still unique. Here we have the freedom to succeed or fail spectacularly at whatever we choose to be. And as long as we have the greatest military in the world defending us, then Americans will continue to have that freedom. But, Sisi, what happens when the greatest military in the world malfunctions?

Doesn't that turn everything on its head?

The Junkie and the Tempting Impostor Proposal

The countdown clock to my insane recall was ticking down. My Army orders said I had to be at Fort Sill in six days, reporting for duty in a uniform I'd cast off more than a decade ago.

Out of nowhere, I was summoned outside by a heavy undercarriage scrape at my driveway and the bleat of a powerful horn. In the bright daylight I squinted to identify the vehicle: it was a stylish Cadillac, albeit an old one, probably off a used car lot.

The driver door swung open and The Band-Aid Man emerged. "Dude, what's this about the Army being just like the Mob – you can never get out?"

I laughed and hugged his six-foot-five frame, then stepped back and took in his face with his pale-blue eyes, brilliant smile, and perfect hair. "What are you doing here?"

"I'm driving you to Oklahoma. And back."

"My God. Who knows when *back* will be?"

"Oh, it'll be soon," Band-Aid stated. "Almost immediately." He opened the Cadillac's passenger door and gestured toward a body stretched across the seat. "Introducing our secret weapon."

I had trouble reconciling Band-Aid Man's confident smile with the limp form on the bench. It was nearly still enough to be mistaken for a corpse, but on close inspection I saw the head begin a slight, enduring nod. The watery eyes, treated to sunlight after so long behind the Cadillac's heavy tint, blinked nervously. I cringed at the sight of the black veins, the mucous. "This man is obviously a junkie."

"He's *you*," said The Band-Aid Man.

For an instant, as turned around as I was, it struck me that I was standing before the same Cadillac we'd rented a decade ago and that junkie on the pavement *was* me – my friend was showing me an alternate reality where that discharge road trip had never ended.

Band-Aid clarified, "When we get to Fort Sill, this dude's gonna report in as you. He'll piss so hot on the drug test that you'll be kicked out on the spot."

I smiled. The brazen impostor scheme was hard to resist – one last prank on the Army for old times. But the flaws were too apparent. "Band-Aid, they'll try to treat me. I'll spend six months in some Army rehab center."

"Those things are co-ed," Band-Aid reminisced fondly. "For full salary you play spades all afternoon with real Army addicts who make your own problems seem tiny, then at night you wander the dorms in search of cold-turkey whores who need other releases. The chow's great."

"Wait a minute," I corrected. "*I* won't be in the program."

We examined the form at our feet.

"You'll be doing this fucker a service," The Band-Aid Man gushed. "Everybody wins."

I began to shake my head.

"Stop!" Band-Aid ordered. "Don't just reject this without thinking about it. You owe me at least a full minute of consideration. Just shut your mouth and close your eyes for one goddamn minute, all right?"

I let out a breath and squeezed my eyelids shut.

"Thank you, Ames. Now just clear your mind, forget about everything else, and ponder deeply on the genius of my plan."

I waited in silence for what felt like sixty seconds. When I lifted my lids, I found my friend's blue eyes only inches away from mine, drilling into my brain. I stepped back and sputtered apologetically, "I can't. This is my problem."

Band-Aid cursed. He shut the man back in the Cadillac and retrieved two large shot-glasses and a bottle of Crown Royal from the driver's side. "How can the Army do this to you, Ames? Have you told them about your situation? Do they know about Soraya's a—."

"My situation's irrelevant to the Army, Band-Aid. Lots of soldiers have situations, and they're all irrelevant."

"You hear what you said? Lots of *soldiers* have situations. You don't look like no soldier to me, not since your greatest, bush-getting friend took you on a certain legendary road trip that turned your ass civilian."

"Band-Aid Man, it's starting to look as if we took that trip into a parallel universe, and you and I are the only ones in this world who know it happened."

"Bullshit. We had witnesses."

"Individual legs don't count. Those are just sightings. No one who wasn't there for the whole trip can grasp the totality of the discharge."

"True. Then, dude, I'm going to ask you one last time – will you at least *tell* the Army about Soraya?"

"No. I'm not trying to get out of this sideways. No excuses, not my wife needs me or I'm a junkie. If I'm going to win against the U.S. Army, I want to win because it's *right*."

Band-Aid filled our glasses on the hot hood. "You gonna answer the question everyone's asking?"

"Let's hear it."

"*Why*? Dude, this is your life. The Army made a mistake. Why don't you just tear up your orders and let the brass come get you if they're so sure you have a commitment?"

I answered: "Dad." I thought about my father, now 70 and banged up in retirement. He'd served a rough thirty years as an airborne infantryman, his name continuously coming up for combat deployments – including Vietnam three times. Dad had never failed to answer his country's call.

"Oh, yeah," Band-Aid Man said. "You don't want to let your father down."

"I'm not worried about letting him down. But this thing's such a mess, if I don't show, I think they might recall Dad next."

Band-Aid threw his big arm across my back. "You know you're an idiot, right?"

"I never deny that."

He smiled wearily, "Give me the number of the office that cut your orders. I'm gonna tell 'em I want to go back in with you on the buddy system."

"Band-Aid, that's crazy."

"No, dude, it'd be the only part of the whole thing that makes sense. I had almost the same Army career as you did – no reason they should want you and not me."

The Band-Aid Man handed me my shot from the Cadillac hood. He lifted his own and we drank to whatever came next.

Nitro Harris and the Colorado Black Cat Explosion

I take us on Ft. Carson where we write checks, get gas and ice, and repack both coolers. Band-Aid says the big one will come into play tonight. I leave post and we're heading for Pikes Peak in the Rocky Mountains. As much as I dread all on-post excursions, I have to admit this trip was pretty painless. I think that, as I'm becoming more civilian, the military machine is becoming more separate from me and consequently easier to live with.

"Hey, stop right here."

I hit the brakes, "What's up?"

"This is where I hit that black cat last night." Band-Aid hops out and starts looking around. He drops below my sight, I guess he's peering under parked cars. He doesn't say anything for a while. I put on the hazards, get out on my side, and walk around. When I find my partner he's crouched over a dead black cat. "This is the one, Ames."

"So what, man? Some rats will eat it, let's go."

"Ames, we can't take that chance. This is a black cat."

"Man, you're really letting Buck's ridiculous superstitions get to you."

"Buck didn't invent black cat superstitions, the whole world knows you can't fuck with black cats."

"It's dead."

"It's still intact. If it came back alive it could kill us all."

"Are you serious? It's got a hole in its neck the size of a tennis ball, that right arm's held on by cheese."

"I'd feel a lot better if we threw it off Pikes Peak."

This confirms it, last night's drunken distress is over, he's no longer the least bit scared of this black cat. Now he's only seized by the impulse to throw a cat off the top of a mountain three miles high. I'll play along. "All right, Band-Aid, let's do it." He picks the cat up carefully in his arms and walks to his door. "Band-Aid, I know you're not going to put that cat in the Cadillac."

"I'll keep it in my lap."

"No you won't either. That thing is not going in the car or the trunk."

"Fine," he says. He sets the cat on the hood, with its throat on the Cadillac ornament. There are some hand and arm movements on his part that give me the feeling, for at least a moment, that The Band-Aid Man is up to something. I walk around front to see his work head-on – what a gruesome sight. The cat's mouth is open all the way, fangs bared in a frozen death scream, and both ears are sticking straight up. The left eye is wide open, but on the more damaged right side, the eye is either closed or missing. Its long tail is stretched out toward the windshield and both front paws are dangling over the front of the grill. From five feet or closer, viewed sideways from the right, the gaping wound in the cat's neck and shoulder is apparent and the cat is easily identified as dead. From any other angle, however, or from a greater distance, the animal appears to be a winking, swashbuckling black cat, very much alive and hanging on for dear life to the hood of our Cadillac. And The Band-Aid Man wants me to drive around like this.

I can't do that, not with its face propped up the way it is. I look around for a stick or a flattened aluminum can in the gutter to at least push its chin off the hood ornament. Finding nothing, I take what's left of the Montecristo out of my mouth and try to pry its chin up with that. I pry with the end that was in my mouth, I don't want to set the fur on fire. The thing doesn't budge. "What'd you do, Band-Aid, skewer its throat on the Cadillac crest?" With most hood ornaments, this wouldn't be possible, but the Cadillac's wreaths are two perfect fork tines, and it seems to me that Band-Aid put some weight on the cat's head to secure it.

"I just set it down."

"Well, good job, it's stuck." Worst of all, now my cigar is wedged between the jaws of the cat. The picture is more hideous than ever. I sigh and walk around to my door. I turn off the hazards and drop it into drive. FIDO.

"Fuck! I knew we forgot to do something on post," Band-Aid pounds his fist into the dashboard. "We gotta wash the car, turn around."

I pull a U. "Wait a minute, you just want to take the cat through the car wash."

"The car wash will be closed by the time we get back from Pikes Peak. I'll take it off while the car goes through if you want."

"Yeah, I do want." Good, maybe I'll be able to convince him to leave it off. I'll enjoy Pikes Peak just fine without anybody throwing a cat off it. I get my ID card ready and approach the Ft. Carson gate. The guard's jaw drops and his entire body flinches giantly as I shoot past.

"We're officers!" Band-Aid screams. "This is officer business!"

I don't know if the officer angle is going to save us this time. Driving around post with a swashbuckling cat on your hood is the kind of deviant behavior that makes people dial phones.

"Where's the car wash, Band-Aid?"

"The cigar's still burning."

"You just noticed that?" We haven't had any long stops and the constant air flow against the Montecristo has kept it going. I'm driving exactly twenty-five now and fiery ashes are curling around the cat's head in the breeze.

"The cigar's still burning!" Band-Aid cries with despair.

"How many times do you want to say that? Don't get nervous on me now, man. You put the cat there and you're the one who wanted to come on post."

Bystanders are reacting now. Most appear horrified and some point urgently and shout. Oncoming drivers honk with alarm. Many pedestrians and motorists seem to be trying to call the situation to our attention, as if The Band-Aid Man and I pulled out of the garage this morning with our cat on the hood and we still haven't realized it.

"Why did you leave the cigar there?"

"Man, what's your problem? This is all your doing. Are you going to ask somebody where the car wash is or not?"

He says nothing.

"Look, Band-Aid, if the cat's still creeping you out, I'll stop and you can throw it in a garbage can. I promise it won't come back to life and kill you. We're going to be in a new city tomorrow anyway, cats aren't known for their love of exercise." I pull off at Toyland and I'm crawling through the parking lot at five miles an hour. A lot of Army spouses are here with young children in their arms or walking near. The little boys and girls are looking at the cat and some are smiling and waving. These children are younger than school age, still with imaginations intact. It's wonderful to see people who haven't been conditioned to think a winking, smoking cat on the hood of a car is wrong. There's a nice wind going too, and the tail is rippling and waving cheerfully to the children's delight.

"My God, Ames," The Band-Aid Man whispers. The tone of his voice sends a shiver up my spine. I hear a shrill whistle outside and all at once I feel that something bad is about to happen.

The cat's head explodes in a sudden flash. A powerful blast rocks the lot and the air in front of us is swirling with jets of multicolored sparks. Children are running and crying, parents are stunned. I carefully pull out of the lot.

"No, Ames! Shit! Pussy Blow Fire! Fuck!"

I don't know what to think, I can't figure it out. I hit the rinse button on the wipers to clear my windshield.

"Ames, that's children. We fucked up bad."

"What just happened?"

"I don't know, I don't know."

"You do know." My fingers tremble as I set the cruise control for 25.

"That has The Band-Aid Man written all over it."

"When I found the cat... I had fireworks in my hands... there was a hole in the neck... I don't know what happened."

"What? You did that on purpose!"

"I did not. I didn't light it. What about the cigar?"

"The cigar was an accident. It got stuck in the jaws."

"You know that was no accident, Ames! What kind of stupid shit is that? A cigar accidentally getting stuck in a cat's mouth, yeah, that shit happens every day! You're always saying your schemes are by accident, but mine are on purpose. Bullshit! You had no business parading that cat in front of Toyland in the first place! With Christmas coming up, God damn! That's innocent children. I've seen some fucked-up occurrences, but this takes the cake. Kids don't recover from shit like that!"

He's right, it'll be hard enough for me and him to recover as men in our mid-twenties. And I don't trust either of us right now. This sort of thing can't happen with no intent at all. How much of this did we plan – no spoken conspiracy, but acting in concert just the same? When we started, we had to have aimed for this result, and now, like kids who drop rocks off an overpass and then cry when people actually crash, we're soaked in regret and shock.

"Are you going to ask somebody where a car wash is? We definitely need one now."

"Get off post, dude! We're wanted!"

I get off as directly as I can. We stop once to throw the cat onto a general's lawn. He's a general, he should be able to handle it. On the way to Pikes Peak, we roll through a car wash. We spot a Little Caesars too, so we get some breadsticks and sauce.

Band-Aid wants to drive and I give him the wheel. He's taking our glistening white Cadillac up the mountain's winding trails. Pikes Peak is over 14,000 feet high. We get almost to the top, but a Park Services Ford Explorer is stretched across the path. We leave the Cadillac and start to run up the rest of the way. It's below freezing and there's a forty mile-an-hour wind. We're clawing our way over icy rocks and falling through the snow crust. The air is so thin up here that our lungs are on fire and we're gasping for breath. Finally we drag ourselves to the top and collapse. The wind is so strong that we actually have to hold on so we don't get blown off the edge.

It's a beautiful scene, the white snow and brown jagged rocks up here with us and the creased green hills and blue rivers and lakes way below. It's so beautiful it's hard to leave, and even though our body temperatures are dropping dangerously and we can barely keep our eyes open because of the wind, we stay here for twenty minutes, taking his trademark long-arm snapshots on the panoramic before we go.

He races the Cadillac down the mountain and all the way to Buck's apartment. We both take some E right away. Darkness falls, Buck has already made arrangements for tonight. We pack back into the Caddy and drive to another house.

"These guys are all party animals!" Buck exclaims, two large bottles clutched in his arms.

Band-Aid turns off the lights and pops the trunk while we're coasting up. He and I quietly grab a few fireworks apiece and line them up on the porch. Among the ones I set up is the pyramid-shaped Round-Eye Loses Face. We light the fuses with our Swishers and start running. After an explosive show that is seen and heard for blocks, the party animals come cautiously out of the house telling us that what we did wasn't cool at all. They stress that they can get in a lot of trouble and only after Buck vouches for us do they reluctantly let us inside. Band-Aid and I go back to the trunk and haul the big cooler into the house.

We're introduced all the way around and everybody's an Army lieutenant. There's a fire going in the fireplace, an obscene porno in the player, and drinking games are underway. Stories about infamous past parties are flying through the living room.

Art, the guy whose house this is, asks Band-Aid Man to put out the

189

Swisher. Art's a fast-talking nasal-voiced blond guy who calls everyone *hoss*. Band-Aid throws the cigar in the fire and Art says, "Hey, hold it, hoss, that's a gas fireplace. You can't just throw things in there." Interesting comment from a wild and crazy partier, and I know Art likes to be seen as one. I know all about these guys who embrace the party animal image. They're quick to get drunk and take their clothes off in a bar, but they're the first to stop smiling when things really fly random.

Band-Aid and I get dragged into a game, tops, which is basketball with plastic cup and bottlecap instead of hoop and ball. Every time the other team sinks one, you have to drink a half a cup of Goldschlager, this awful cinnamon syrup with gold flakes in it. It's all drunkenness from here.

The party's first female arrives, a large and loony creature with many masculine features. She begins enjoying the porno feature.

She looks very familiar to me, and Band-Aid is the first to place her. "John Lithgow," he whispers. He and I try to think of any of the dozens of movies or shows John Lithgow has been in, and for some reason we can't come up with one, but we're both nonetheless convinced that she is either Lithgow's daughter or actually the renowned actor himself, pretending to be an Army lieutenant in preparation for a role.

I wander through the house to find a urinal. I'm drunk, I don't bother closing the bathroom door and I hear the phone ring in the bedroom behind me. Somebody picks it up and then yells for Art, the party's host, to come in. "It's Captain Harris," the somebody says, and Art takes over. "Nitro Harris, my favorite and only C.O. What's up, hoss?" Art yells.

Art's half of the rest of the conversation goes like this: "How's Cindy's fever?... Come on over, Nitro, we've got a big bash... Just kiss her good night and say you're coming over to watch a movie... Come on, hoss, they can be without you for a few hours... You better get your shit squared away, I'm telling everybody here that Nitro's pussywhipped... All right, hoss, call me about an hour before so I don't sleep through it...

Out here."

I wait until he's returned to the living room, then I head back there too. Band-Aid calls me to go outside with him. A few other lieutenants follow him without being asked. The Band-Aid Man is such a presence that he regularly pulls people in his wake. Like a hand dragging through water and creating little whirlpools, Band-Aid has whirlpools around him all the time.

The Band-Aid Man pops the trunk and people start freaking over the high explosives with the alcohol backdrop. "Well, shall we light some?" Band-Aid asks.

"Yeah!" a beefy guy exclaims.

"All right, a man who likes his fireworks," Band-Aid Man says, putting a slender stick into the guy's hand. "Here, take the punk and you can set off some shit. I'll light that punk for you."

There's a hissing sound, the punk turns out to be a bottle rocket, the beefy guy screams, and there's a loud explosion very close to all of us. The beefy guy curses and runs inside. Art comes out and tells us, "I'm through playing, hoss. Chill out or get out."

Band-Aid reads the directions on Ghost Attack: "Shoots flaming balls and reports – Light and seek cover," and he decides this is the right time to light it. He grabs a rock from a nearby garden, leans Ghost Attack against this rock, and lights the fuse. It is perfectly aimed and Art is chased back into his house by a barrage of flaming balls and reports. At this point, the whirlpool boys seem to understand that lines have been drawn. Afraid to be a part of the enemy camp, and probably also suspecting The Band-Aid Man might turn his arsenal on them at any moment, the whirlpoolers return to the party all together in a terrified dash.

It's just I, The Band-Aid Man, and John Lithgow. "How do you like my goatee?" Band-Aid asks her, he did just touch it up this morning.

"I think you're very handsome, but I think it's kind of scary," she answers. He looks at her charmingly, and suddenly I realize that he's actually trying to make something happen. My God! I jump into the front of the car to tune some romantic music for them. Good old Band-Aid, she's the only girl at the party and he's going for it. Once again, I have to hand it to him.

Suddenly I wonder, could I do it? That girl is not attractive to me at all. Could I look past that if I had to? Could I kiss her? Following Band-Aid's civilian challenge, it now strikes me as important that I answer yes to all those questions. Before this road trip is over, I'll prove that the answer is yes. I'll pass the challenge. Finding no romantic station, I turn off the stereo and get out of the front seat. I start for the house to leave these two alone, but Band-Aid Man is ahead of me. He's walking across the porch by himself. I turn to the trunk and see the big girl there. She's as tall as I am. She and I are all alone.

"Hi," she says.

"Hi, what happened to The Band-Aid Man?"

"I think I said something that offended him."

"Why are you still here?"

"Maybe the same reason you're still here."

Oh, boy, I doubt that. "What reason would that be?" My God, am I really going to do this? Look at that giant face. I've slept with women when I didn't really want to before, but at least they were physically attractive. I've never kissed anything like John Lithgow.

"What reason do you think?"

"I'm drunk, I'm not thinking tonight." Yeah, right, if she could imagine the internal struggle that's going on between these ears, wow. Come on, Ames, get psyched. Are you a civilian or aren't you?

Suddenly my mind is filled with images of women I've been with, curvy women with full lips, striking eyes, and lots of back. A voice tells me, "Ames, these girls all cut you slack. Imagine if they had the same attitude you have, you'd still be a virgin. Look at yourself, Ames, your face is an abomina—" Enough! I'm tired of that voice.

I grab John Lithgow behind the neck and kiss her recklessly. She pushes me around the corner of the Cadillac and presses against me, sandwiching my body between the right rear door and her big-boned frame. Our mouths still together, she begins to grind. I tear my face away. "That was great!" I declare. "Let's get back to the party." We both jog in and break apart.

I find Band-Aid Man sitting down in a chair. I want to tell him the news, but he won't remember if I tell him now. "Hey, Band-Aid. Let's throw some stuff in the fire."

"What do you mean?"

I show him the fireworks in my jacket pocket. "We'll just casually toss 'em in the fireplace and walk away."

"No, dude, these guys are already uptight. That Art fucker tried to send me home, motherfucker claims I almost killed him."

"So let's throw the fireworks in the fire."

"No, 'cause we all chipped in and rented a big van and it'll be here any minute. We've still got some good partying ahead."

The van does come and we all pile in to make the local club circuit. I stumble out of a bar bathroom and Band-Aid Man runs into me, pushing a few E into my palm. "Don't waste your money on a table dance here," he advises. "Fuck, she wouldn't even let me blow on her asshole. I mean, come on."

"In the Corps, you had *discipline*!"

"God damn righ– Fuck you."

I start to tell Band-Aid that I hadn't even thought about getting a table dance because we're not in a strip club, but he's obviously beyond all understanding now. I'd like to find the innocent bystander whose anus he tried to blow on, just to apologize to her on behalf of all men the world over, but glancing around I see too many scowling candidates to narrow it down.

Someone passes me a bottle of Jim Beam and I consider that I, too, must be teetering on the drunken edge. I take a deep gulp and from here things start to get real hazy.

I open my eyes and look around, our big cooler is on the floor in front of me. It's light outside. I'm on a couch in the living room where the party started last night. I stand up to go to the bathroom and I bang my leg on a table. No one else is up and moving. I walk through the house to the same bathroom I was using last night. Art is out cold in his bed. I cup my hand under the faucet and turn it on. It's barely above freezing, I have to make it warmer to drink it and I drink a lot. On my way back through the bedroom, I grab the phone out of its stand on Art's bedside table. I'll probably need it to call up Buck's place if Band-Aid Man doesn't come by here pretty soon. The Cadillac's still outside, I don't have the keys.

I open the cooler, it's still got plenty in it. Mt. Everest? How'd I miss this? I tried to remove all the malt liquor when I found out this cooler was going to the party, apparently one slipped through the screen. As I set the can back in the cooler, the phone rings in my other hand.

I answer it, "Hello?"

"Artie, you party animal, get your ass in gear. Shit, shower, and grab your racket."

It is mornings like this one, coming hard on the heels of a raging blackout drunk, that a simple city kid sparks like a scientist. Alcohol's muddling properties evaporated, a mad genius emerges.

"Nitro?" I ask in my best nasal Art voice.

"That's a big roger."

"How's Cindy's fever?"

"Normal, I think she's over it. How soon can you be ready?"

"It's gonna take me some time to get my act together today."

"Your shit together?"

"That's a big roger, hoss." Whew, that was close. By using "act together" instead of the accepted military-wide expression, I almost gave myself away.

"About how long?"

"You missed a good one, hoss. This one was different." Talk fast,

Ames, just like Art. "Had some people come in with a shipment, if you know what I mean."

"What?"

"Nitro! You're not hearing me, hoss. I've got friends in town – civilians." The word "civilians" has serious connotations with military personnel. Some can deal with it, but to a captain with a family it carries undercurrents so depraved and frightening that "civilians" and "rioters" are pretty much interchangeable.

"Civilians?" he cries tremblingly.

"That's a very big roger, hoss. Nitro, tell me this. Have you ever done the A-train?"

"I don't know what you mean."

"LSD's what I mean, hoss. I'm talking about being experienced."

"You didn't try LSD last night, did you?" he asks uneasily.

"Try it, hoss? Oh, yeah, I tried it. These guys – the civilians – came in with twenty sheets of the stuff. Some pussies were pulling off little perforated squares, you believe that? I didn't either, I ripped a whole handful of paper out of a sheet and I crammed it in my mouth and I ate it! You know what, Nitro! I am alive!"

"Lieutenant, you're in a lot of trouble," he says in a very nervous voice. He's falling apart. "As your C.O., I have no choice but to report this."

"Sir? I thought you were different. I thought you were one of us."

"I have obligations. You've gone too far..."

"I've got some dirt on you, Nitro. You had better be careful. I'll have your wife filing divorce before you can explain anything."

"No!" he sobs.

"You can't prove any of this, anyway, I'll get witnesses."

"Witnesses?"

"I've got a kid right here in bed with me, thirteen years old. Oh, what we did to this kid, hoss, you couldn't imagine. He'll swear anything I say, just to keep us from doing it again."

"Dear God, please help us... Art, we've got to meet. We've got to talk about this." He's agonizing.

"We've got nothing to talk about, hoss, I'm denying it all. This conversation never happened."

I hang up the phone and turn the ringer off. It would be nice to be there when Art and Nitro meet at work, but you can't have everything.

There's a knock at the door, it's Buck. We carry the big cooler out and drop it in the Cadillac trunk, Power Pack on top. Band-Aid's sitting on the passenger side with a glass of ice water in his lap.

Finally, I can't hold it any longer – I have to tell him what I did.

"Remember that big girl from last night? John Lithgow? I made out with her."

"Good job," says The Band-Aid Man. "You are very close to being a goddamn civilian."

"Aww, dude, you should've fucked her," says Buck.

"I'm proud of you, bro," Band-Aid says. "Next you'll have to eat out an end-of-the-night whore." He suddenly leans out the door and vomits.

"Hey, before you go under, Band-Aid, where are we going?"

"Fuck, I don't know. Just take me somewhere where Goldschlager is illegal."

I open our road atlas to the map of the United States and fold the covers back to show the western half. I know this is risky. Seattle's an option, after all, as are Alaska and Hawaii in little boxes just right for the haphazard stabbings of a sick man. "Point somewhere."

He lifts his eyelids long enough to take a random jab at the book with his index finger.

I grab a Miller out of the back and gulp down half. I offer him the rest, "Hair of the dog, Band-Aid Man."

"There ain't no hair on this dog." His cup slips out of his hands, ice water drenches his crotch, and he doesn't even notice.

The Traffic Vigilante and the Race to Get Off Base

We're flat on our backs broke, rolling in the Cadillac a couple hours south of my hometown San Francisco. I can't go in there with no cash at all. No choice but to make an Army base check run in Monterey, and it's already almost five when Band-Aid and I pull through the gates onto the long straightaway aiming at the traffic light.

"We don't have much time," he says, swallowing an E and flooring it toward to the light. The light turns red and there's another vehicle approaching from our left about a hundred feet away from the intersection. The other car has the green, we have the angle if speeds remain constant. But wait a minute.

"That fucker's speeding up," Band-Aid Man protests. He's right, the other guy wants to cut us off, that's getting more obvious every second. He's too late, though – we've got him. Band-Aid's standing on the accelerator now, and the other guy's not even narrowing the gap. So we'll beat him to the intersection, and we wouldn't even have a problem if we were going straight. Unfortunately, we've got to make a right turn. And even with The Band-Aid Man stamping on the brakes right now, we're still coming into a right angle turn at forty-five.

He hooks us around expertly, our front end sliding across the line and our trunk all the way into the oncoming traffic lane. No one's in that lane – something I'm sure he figured on – but that clown's right on our tail now. It's a Nissan Pathfinder SUV, the high grill in our back window. The driver's honking his horn and gesturing for us to pull over.

The lunatic's lack of mustache convinces me he isn't Military Police, which makes me pretty certain we're dealing with one of those Cro-Magnon traffic vigilantes who get a rush from delivering self-important driving lectures on the shoulders of base roadways.

"I'm losing this fucking psycho!" Band-Aid Man shouts, and he does put some space between us. The problem is that the PX isn't really distant enough to lose anybody along the way. We roll up to the front entrance and the Pathfinder is already next to us by the time I find my checkbook.

The bald vigilante opens his door and leaps out on my side of the car. "I'm Colonel Marc Mann," he announces, thrusting his ID card in my face. "You really screwed the pooch!"

"What?"

"Soldier, you don't know shit from shine-ola!" the colonel stamps his foot.

I look at my watch, "Hey, Band-Aid, the PX closes in five minutes."

"Go write your check. I'll take care of this."

"You'll both stand fast. Driving like a bat out of hell, aren't you?" he demands. I walk away as he crouches down to get a look at The Band-Aid Man.

The PX doors close behind me. There are no customers in here, the lone checkout cashier is closing out the register. I march to the back under white fluorescent lights, I've made it just in time.

I come outside with another hundred-and-fifty dollars and Colonel Mann is standing behind our Cadillac with a notepad in his hand. Band-Aid's behind the wheel and the engine is running.

I take the passenger seat and pull my door closed, "What is happening?"

"The fucker wanted to see our IDs and I said hell no. I told him to buy some Rogaine and now he's taking down our license plates. Total dickhead. He's drunk as hell, too. He's the one who shouldn't be driving."

"You're kidding."

"No, dude. I'm surprised you didn't smell his breath when he got out of his car. The alcoholic fucker nearly fell down when he got his tablet.

Look at his sorry ass."

I look out the back window and the guy can barely keep his balance while he's writing down our numbers. That also explains why he's taking five minutes to perform a five-second chore. "We must've caught him on the way back from the officers' club."

"I don't know where the fuck he came from. Here, dude, check under your seat for any more empties and put 'em in here." He hands me a plastic bag we've been using for trash. It's got a dozen cans and bottles inside and I add two more.

I scan the area around our car, "Is there a garbage can?"

Band-Aid Man shakes his head. "Dump that bag inside his window."

I look at the open Pathfinder window and back at The Band-Aid Man. "Really? Are you serious?"

"Shit yeah. This asshole's trying to fuck with us. He's gonna try to have us arrested at the gate, he said so. Dump it."

I step out, outside the car and sort of outside myself as I perform the exercise as instructed. I hold the trash bag inside the Pathfinder window, and swing it from the bottom. I'm scattering the contents all over the Nissan's light-blue interior. It's a weird feeling, my adrenaline pumping, the cans and bottles bouncing and rolling. Look at all those different brands of beer and malt liquor, all the different colors against the light-blue backdrop. Listen to them roll and collide. Ping! Da da da da da! Taow!

"What the crap is going on here!" the drunken colonel cries. He's lumbering toward me, his pen and pad clenched tight. I jump into the Cadillac and slam the door.

Band-Aid backs up. "We've got to beat him to the gate," he throws it into drive and stomps it.

The Nissan Pathfinder is right behind, the colonel didn't waste any time coming after us. "Go, man! Hurry!"

"We just gotta stay ahead of him. If we beat him out the gate, there's nothing he can do." Suddenly the Nissan roars next to us. The maniac colonel is in the oncoming traffic lane and he's yelling through his passenger window at Band-Aid Man. He's drifting closer. A deft rightward jerk on the wheel and some sudden acceleration by The Band-Aid Man pulls us out in front.

"Asshole almost hit us!" Band-Aid screams. He's focused on the road. We're tearing like a rocket at that stoplight, the colonel can't hang. The Pathfinder is way behind us. But he's still coming. We take the left turn like a slot racer and the gate is straight ahead. We've got it. All we have to do is keep a reasonable speed now – fast enough so the Pathfinder doesn't take us and not so fast that we attract attention. It would be a shame if the gate MP noticed a Cadillac barreling toward him and he pulled his cruiser out to block our exit.

We're both looking behind us – me, over my shoulder, and Band-Aid, in the rearview – and we see the Pathfinder take the turn. It comes fast and I think the colonel's going to lose it, but he keeps it under control. He's coming straight and fast and I know Band-Aid Man and I both realize we counted him out too early.

Then we see the red and blue lights.

Military police car. Normally those lights signal a nuisance or worse. But now they're behind the Nissan Pathfinder. The colonel gives it a burst of gas, denying for a moment that the lights could be for him. But the delusion is temporary. The reality of his own situation is too shocking. He's had. He stops on the shoulder and the lights pull behind him.

Meanwhile, our Cadillac rolls unhindered through the exit gate.

"Yes!" The Band-Aid Man screams. "Fucking yes!" He squeezes the wheel, I pound the dashboard, I slap my hands on his shoulder in a delirious flurry. Our nemesis is ruined. The MPs have him and his rank doesn't mean a thing now. It can't. Not when he's drunk as a wifebeater, driving like a maniac, and the interior of his Pathfinder looks like an alcohol-only recycling bin.

This is pure insurrection. Band-Aid merges us onto the freeway and lets it run in the left lane while I keep looking backward out my window – not at anything I expect to see, but in all-out wonder at what we've just done. It occurs to me that, without exception, this is the most civilian I've ever felt in my life.

San Francisco Sorority Sisters and the Lost Household Goods

I'm coming home with The Band-Aid Man. No sleeping this ride. My partner is grinning like a wild horse, "That started me on a roll, I hope somebody's going to introduce me to some bush in Frisco."

"There'll be plenty." Hugh E M.C. replays in the deck a second time. We cross the city line and the familiar San Francisco atmosphere reclaims me. I peer into the coffeehouses and read the lips of all the high-thinkers as they discuss new piercing options and put down Los Angelenos with unexplainable one-way bitterness.

Band-Aid's looking for a pay phone, a harder find than it used to be, but I guide him into the Fillmore where one of my old favorites still stands. I step into the corner store for a Mountain Dew while he presses the buttons.

I come out to witness Band-Aid slamming the pay phone receiver into the cradle, "Fuck!"

"What's wrong?"

"The Army lost my household goods again. They were supposed to deliver 'em last week and now they can't find them, *again.* I'm out two years and the Army's still fucking me."

"Well, you've done fine without your household goods so far. What's a little more time?"

"Reveille's in my household goods, Ames."

I stare at him for a while, not quite comprehending.

He snorts, "*Reveille,* the priceless painting we were supposed to return to its historic home as one of your great civilian achievements. Now we can't, because the Army can't find my shit."

I'm reeling, "I thought we had Reveille."

"You thought we had it where?" Band-Aid cocks his head at me as if he's talking to an imbecile.

"With us. In the Cadillac. Like, behind the big cooler or something."

"Ames, that painting's every bit of five feet tall. It hasn't been behind something in the goddamn Cadillac."

"Well, thanks for telling me now. That knowledge would've made the numerous police pull-overs a lot more comfortable for me." We both get back in the car, me behind the wheel now to cruise my home turf.

"Fuck," he whimpers again. "Everything was going so great. Look at all you've accomplished: You almost got hired as a nude model, crashed a sold-out Monday Night Football game, dangled a hundred-seventy feet over Niagara Falls, spent the night with Kai: the world's most civilian man, you mugged with John Lithgow in a wig, and ended the career of a dickhead colonel. Shit, everything was all falling into place perfectly, and now we don't have a crowning mission."

"Wait a second, we're not supposed to have a mission," I contradict. "Have you already forgotten what you taught me? We're trying to be civilians now — we can't follow a script. The loss of your household goods was meant to be."

The Band-Aid Man smile comes back out, "Goddamn, Ames, I really am a good teacher."

"The best."

"All right, we'll schedule another road trip to return the painting when the Army finds my shit."

"FIDO."

"Does Soho have something lined up for me?" Soho is Band-Aid Man's favorite nickname for my girlfriend, Soraya.

"Soraya, my sister... between the Asian bombshells and the blond debutantes you'll be dizzy."

"Hey, is your sis still casting movies?"

I roll off Masonic to the top of Geary and pull next to the curb. "Why don't you ask her yourself?"

We walk to the gate, Band-Aid's throwing out some southern gentleman catchphrases for practice. "What's your sister's name?"

"Stefanie."

As his thumb approaches the intercom button, the door buzzes open. They must've seen us from upstairs. We hit the penthouse and crash the door.

There are a lot of females in here. I recognize some of Stefanie's sorority sisters. My sister gives me a big hug. I look over her shoulder and out across the city, she's got a great view. She was living with my parents when I last saw her.

Band-Aid has already introduced himself to everybody and is now banging an ice tray on my sister's tiled counter. "Bacardi-and-Cokes, who wants 'em?"

Everybody lines up. Everybody but me. The car's got to move somehow and I can tell by his eyes he's going over the edge. The self-appointed bartender whips the drinks together in short time. Rum-heavy, as if he wants a tip, but that's how he always does it.

Eyes have been on him from the minute he came in here and zeroed in on the liquor cabinet. He gulps down one Bacardi-and-Coke and chases it with another. The girls are well acquainted with major alcohol consumption by fraternity boys, but watching it outside that framework seems to have them curious. My sister asks me if he's all right. I assure her his actions are intended as compliments, "He's letting the hostess know he's happy."

"That's sweet," my sister says.

The phone rings. Band-Aid picks it up as if he lives here, and walks out onto the balcony. He comes back into the kitchen and starts pulling items out of cabinets and the refrigerator. "We've got everything we need," he announces confidently. "Stefanie, is it all right if I use all your eggs?"

"Of course."

I have to ask, "Eggs for what?"

"Your artist bud Jules had a birthday yesterday, but we're celebrating it at Soho's place tonight. I told her I'd bake the cake."

"You were on the phone with Soraya? She didn't ask to speak with me?"

"I told her you were busy mugging on some sorority bitch," Band-Aid answers, cracking an egg with one hand and pre-heating the oven with the other.

Numerous Bacardi-and-Cokes later Band-Aid puts the last drop of icing on a fine looking birthday cake. A crowd gathers to admire the product and Band-Aid proposes a toast: "Here's to cakes!" Seeing there's no more Coke left, he polishes off the Bacardi. The giant 1.75 liter bottle turned exactly upside down and the rum glug-glugging down his throat, I think the room's fascination with The Band-Aid Man has just now reached a peak.

Stefanie's roommate is the first to speak. "You're an alcoholic," she says.

"No, I'm a drunk. An alcoholic wants to quit."

"Have as much as you want," my sister says hospitably. "There's more in the closet."

Band-Aid could stay here forever, but we have to wish Jules a happy birthday, so I put us back on the road.

Kitten and the Fantastic Return of Mit

I cruise us to my girlfriend's block on Noriega deep in the Avenues. In keeping with her surfing passion, she's a straight shot from Ocean Beach. When we park out front, she's got her second-floor window open and we can see all the partiers inside.

"I hope Jules appreciates what I'm doing for him. I drive into town and bake his cake and give him an awesome fireworks surprise and I've never even met the guy."

"He deserves it."

Band-Aid pops the trunk. "Where's the Chinese shit?"

"We might have used that up. Here's two big ones." I hand him one bright red cone with screaming white faces on it and another tube with wings called The Challenger and shaped roughly like a U.S. space shuttle. I look at my watch, "I thought you said Soraya was supposed to meet us outside."

"Relax, Ames, she'll be here." A quiet squeal of excitement greets my ears. He's right, here comes my girlfriend.

"Soho straight outa Frisco!" The Band-Aid Man exclaims.

Soraya springs up and hugs him, feet in the air. "I get to meet The Band-Aid Man!" Her voice is as feminine and charged as mine is beastly and lethargic. I'm on the street side of the car and slowly she sashays toward me. There should be a slammin hip-hop soundtrack whenever she comes onto a scene like this, when I see her I imagine one anyway. She's closing the distance, five-three, all brown, curvy and strong, her eyes deep like the Mississippi Delta. Bam! Contact. Long black hair around my face, she smells wonderful.

Fireworks explode all around. It is a show fitting for my good friend's birthday and Jules leans out the window to take it in. There are a lot of people leaning out their windows on this block now, they're trying to see whose house is on fire. Band-Aid stands in the middle of the street with his arms folded while the last sparkles of his grand finale settle down.

Soraya's eyes pull me like a dangerous Mississippi current. She takes me by my hand to the staircase and we walk upstairs to meet the crowd.

"Ames!"

"Jules! You look great."

"My brother."

"Ladies and gentlemen: The Band-Aid Man."

It's a good scene, people are enjoying themselves, and I'm hanging with some of my old posse for the first time in a long time.

"I'm drinking Band-Aid Man Beer," announces Jules. He dug up a picture of Band-Aid from Soraya's book and he's got it wrapped around his beer can. It looks funny, as if Band-Aid's face really is on the can, and the whole room's laughing.

Soraya tells me that a comic book publisher hired Jules to draw a new Black superhero in an upcoming issue. It'll be in stores. Jules is downplaying it, but I'm proud. Jules is a veteran himself – of the Marine Corps – and he's also an incredible artist with enough demons in his hard-knock past to inspire a million sketches. I always laugh at his great stories about his final days on drugs, him laid out on the floor of an illegal hotel, all the lights broken, a thieving pimp for a roommate, Jules starving and aching for crystal more than food. I laugh because he's got it all together now. And I laugh about the pimp. If I ever have to hit rock bottom, I hope I hit it all by myself. I hope there's no pimp there trying to take stuff from me even though I don't have anything.

The Band-Aid Man's on the couch now, he's drinking wildly. A bunch of Soraya's girlfriends are here and they're all chatting with Band-Aid. There's a Korean stunner absolutely packing her sweater, and I think she's the one he's going for right now. Hold it, I take that back.

207

Band-Aid could be going for anyone. He won't burn any bridges, that we can count on.

I try to talk with Jules, but every few minutes Band-Aid stands up and exclaims, "Here's to the Birthday Boy!" and he makes Jules do a shot with him. Not only is it a constant interruption, but it's destroying the quality of Jules' conversation. When I first started talking with Jules, he was explaining some of his more complicated artwork. Now he's barely looking at me and he keeps mumbling things like, "Hope we start seeing some titties around here."

Soraya hands me the phone.

"Where'd you get the Eight Ball?" Jules asks.

"The trunk, bro, the trunk has everything," I hand him the Olde English "800," he drinks and passes it back, together we empty the can.

"It's for you, baby," Soraya tells me and I remember I have the phone in my hand. So much is happening, tonight is an overload, this scene is straining circuits in a very beautiful way. I raise the phone to my ear.

"Hello?"

"Lieutenant Holbrook?" Smoky voice.

I step out of the living room into the quieter hallway. "Yes."

"This is General Briggs at the Pentagon, is this a secure line?" Rapid military clip to the words.

"This is a Chinese cordless, General."

"Good, good, I want the whole world to hear this. We're assembling the worst soldiers of the past ten years for a suicide mission and we want you to lead them..."

"McGinn!"

"Aww, man, you guessed. I just talked with your sister, we're all meeting at Pat O'Shea's tonight."

"Wait a minute, did you say, 'We?'"

"I'm in town for the weekend, Ames."

"Awesome, what a surprise! This is—"

"Hey, save your gabbing for the bar."

Soraya waits for me to hang up the phone and she brings out the cake. We all sing Happy Birthday, Jules blows out the candles, and spirits are high. The Band-Aid Man is in heaven — surrounded by women, drunk to the gills, grinning like a fish trying to shake a hook out. I don't know how I'm going to tell him about the phone call I just got. Band-Aid's cut a haphazard, jagged trail across the United States these nine days since Boston, jerking and fishtailing on interstates, city boulevards, and backroads all the way from the Atlantic to the Pacific, sometimes racing like a desert rocket, sometimes inching like a glacier. You can elude a team of crack detectives for decades with behavior like that, but, baby, you can never fight coincidence. And every decision The Band-Aid Man made this trip, however impulsive and random, has added up so that tonight he will see McGinn, the fiend of his nightmares, the man he knows as Mit. To anyone else it's an unexpected intersection in space and time, but what will it be to him?

Convoy to Pat O'Shea's, Band-Aid's next to me in the Cadillac, girls in the back seat are holding sparklers out the windows. I figured if there were ever any dangerous sparklers, they would come with the Power Pack, and I'm not disappointed. These things burn and crackle just like other sparklers, but they drip a waxy, sparking fluid that Band-Aid likened to napalm and which continues to flash and burn after it's dripped off the stick. Fortunately we warned the girls and they were holding them at an angle when they lit them so no hands were seared. But the backfloor carpets burned like the Oakland Hills before the girls rolled their windows down and stuck the sparklers outside.

I switch the stereo to rear speakers only, party music cranking, the backseat crew is in its own world. And I've got something on my mind. I'm bringing The Band-Aid Man straight to Mit and I haven't said a word. I thought about just letting him be surprised, but a shock like that could damage him permanently. "Hey, Band-Aid, I've got some news for you, buddy. I'm trying to figure out how to tell you."

He's got the Crown Royal bottle in two hands and the stuff's pouring out the corners of his mouth, streaming down his neck. He lowers the bottle and gasps crazily before he looks at me and says, "Ames, thanks for saving my life in Italy."

"You're welcome. Are you ready to hear what I have to tell you?" He grunts and I go on. "Mit is in town. He'll be at the bar tonight."

"Cool, maybe he'll bring some Jameson."

My jaw drops. That is not the reaction I was bracing myself for. "The Mit we stayed with in Boston."

"I kinda figured it wasn't the one from Austria."

"You're not upset."

"Why would I be? Maybe he'll set me up with some hot babe."

I don't understand. "Hot babe? You've never talked about Mit this way. You used to say he chased all the hot babes away."

"I don't know why I'd say that, Mit's a good man. He let us stay at his place, gave us plenty of Jameson, he took care of us."

Has he gone into shock to wipe out the news of Mit's arrival? I park right in front of the bar. The backseaters head in the doors, but I clip my partner's shoulder. "Band-Aid," I ask, "are you wasted?"

"No, I'm fine."

"Walk a line." He does, effortlessly. "Lean your head back, lift your foot ..." I talk him through the full sobriety test right here in front of Pat O'Shea's, and he passes with flying colors. I play that hand-slapping game with him and he's smacking my hands with amazing quickness. I should give him the keys. The way he's been drinking tonight I was expecting a Goldschlager repeat, but he's like a robot. "Hey, Band-Aid, what are you going to do inside this bar?"

"Meet some bush."

He's the real Band-Aid Man, we head inside. My sister's crew is dancing by the stage and I head that way. Band-Aid spots Mit first and he races for his table and shakes his hand enthusiastically. Mit's sister is here too, and so is his blonde model-looking wife, coyly sipping a cocktail. Jules is dancing with most of the girls, the band's cranking out some good sound, the drummer's terrific. Band-Aid Man leaps out on the floor and the women are all around him. I've never figured out if Band-Aid is truly a good dancer or if he just thinks he is. I'm not really qualified to judge, not being a dancer myself, but something I'm seeing out there just doesn't ring true. I have no specific complaints about his dancing, and in fact I can't complain at all about a dancing style that, no matter when I see it, brings a smile to my lips. And now my lips are spread wide in true delight as I take in the dancefloor antics of the towering Tyrannosaurus rex with small head and Brontosaurus buttocks. Fists churning in the vicinity of his Adam's apple, high-steppin, knees flyin, chest puffin, elbows jabbin into his own sides, head-bobbin toward the floor, "Whoot-whoots!" blasting from his mouth, eyes squinted downward, sincere, passionate, spectacular. A real crowd-pleaser.

The dancing goes on and on until the band finally quits. The bar's shutting down and they're trying to push us through the doors. I head out to the sidewalk and Jules is out here, he slaps and grips my hand good bye.

My sister and her friends head home, most of Soraya's other friends are gone, but we still somehow have seven people in the Cadillac and we're driving up Geary. The whole lot's gotten drunk, I'm the square who's got to drive everybody home. And we're not going home yet, we're heading to the Lucky Penny restaurant, formerly the Copper Penny, and something else before that. I park it in the lot and watch everybody exit so I can figure out who we've got here. Me and The Band-Aid Man, that doesn't change, Mit, his sister, his wife, Soraya, and Soraya's friend Kitten.

I'm eating my Denver omelet and talking with Mit and his wife. Band-Aid cuts in at least every minute, speaking across the table in Italian. He says he likes Kitten a lot and he asks me what I know about her. Kitten is a chatty girl and that's about all I know. I've never seen her before tonight. She signals Soraya and they both get up to go to the bathroom. She's got a nice figure, full and curvy, I see that as she moves across the floor.

Kitten and Soraya come back and Band-Aid jumps into a conversation with Kitten again. Soraya's next to me, she whispers in my ear that Kitten had a Sicilian boyfriend and she understood everything The Band-Aid Man told me in Italian. That's what the bathroom conference was about. I look at Kitten who is looking very cross right now. She's managed to work herself into a severe mood since she left for the bathroom, but this whole thing is shaky. As fluently as I once gabbed with the Northern Italians, I never understood a Sicilian. They just don't speak the same language. "She's very upset," Soraya adds. Yeah, she's upset at herself for not understanding a word Band-Aid has said. I'll stop him anyway, no sense in letting her be upset for any reason.

"Band-Aid, Kitten understood everything you told me. She had a Sicilian boyfriend." I'm hoping the Sicilian part is enough of a clue for him.

He blushes a little, acts embarrassed, then says, "Well, Kitten, I guess it's no secret, then, that I find you very stimulating and attractive."

Now Kitten blushes a little too, not letting on what a big surprise that news is. I think I even notice a trace of a nod, her square jaw moving up and down. I turn my eyes to The Band-Aid Man to congratulate him telepathically, but he looks as if he's just died of shock. What is going on here? "Hey, Band-Aid, are you all right?" I hate to break the mood, but he looks bad.

He says nothing. His jaw is almost in his plate, his hair has broken the gel's hold and is attempting to stand straight up, and he is perfectly motionless until one eye starts blinking. My god! Just when he'd gotten in with Kitten, something like this happens. This performance is bad enough on a social level, but I'm genuinely concerned for my friend's health. I'm not sure who else has noticed it and who hasn't, but as quickly and as quietly as possible, I move around the table, lift him out of his chair, and walk him to the bathroom. His draping arm supporting his weight on my neck, he continually looks over his other shoulder and exclaims, "Fuck me! Fuck me!" again and again until I throw him through the bathroom door. He collapses on the dirty tile. He's a wreck, trembling and white as a ghost.

"What's wrong, man?"

"Mit!" he cries from the depth of his soul.

I'm trying to help, trying so hard to understand. "Mit? What has he done now?"

"What has he done?" he cries unbelievingly. "He's here. Wake me up!"

"Relax, Band-Aid." An old man hits the hand dryer next to us, shutting down the conversation until he leaves.

"Where are we, Ames?"

"The Copper Skillet... the Lost Penny...some restaurant."

"Boston?"

"San Francisco. What's wrong with you?"

"Mit is at our table," he says softly in panic.

"He's been with us all night. What's the deal here? I was surprised enough four hours ago when you acted as if he were your long lost buddy from the Old Country, and now you flip out all of a sudden. Make up your mind on this one."

"Where's Jules?"

"He didn't even come here, man. He left after Pat O'Shea's."

"What's that? The last thing I remember is doing a shot with Jules at Soho's house."

His quote sinks in and for the first time I begin to understand. I'm completely sympathetic to his breakdown. We're both pathetic blackout drunks long accustomed to piecing together our memories to figure out what happened on previous nights. But as far as I know, up until now, we've both behaved like the fools we were. Tonight, however, The Band-Aid Man drank himself right past intoxication back into sobriety. I remember those coordination tests I gave him earlier, he acted sober, believed he was sober, responded as a sober man would. I've never seen anything like it.

He's sober again now, frightened into a nerve-torn state of super-awareness with on-edge reactions to everything. As he pulls himself together here in the bathroom, I can't help laughing at his account of coming to his senses in the restaurant, eating potatoes he didn't remember ordering, being told by Kitten that he was asking questions twice, and finally noticing Mit at the head of the table. But when I finish laughing, I realize I've been laughing alone. This is not a joke to him, but a horror story. Worse still, an ongoing one.

Eleven years later, I was in my own horror story where nothing made sense. Sisi, despite all the transformation you've witnessed, all the progress I achieved to become a civilian, I remained locked in a fast-approaching reunion with the U.S. Army. There had been no good news from Rusty. There had been no good news from anybody. There was only more chaos.

From: "Horse-pelt, Monticello MAJ, HRC-St. Louis"
To: 'Ames Holbrook'
Subject: RE: Thin Ice
1LT Holbrook,
I find your reply to my last message to be both
unprofessional and disrespectful. If I receive another
message in that tone I will take action to hold you
accountable for your remarks.
I suggest you reexamine my last message to you. In it I
referenced soldiers who enlist in the National Guard in
an attempt to avoid their mobilization. As an officer
you would not be enlisting, so this situation does not
apply to you.
I will no longer be handling your status. MAJ John
Bivens will be managing your mobilization from now on. If

you elect to communicate with him, ensure you do so in a
professional, respectful manner.
Monticello Horse-pelt
MAJ, AR
Operations Officer

Wow! Had I hurt Horse-pelt's feelings? The Army hadn't gotten that soft in a decade, had it? This Major's fragility could not be representative. I suddenly felt like the militarily arrogant Band-Aid Man, thundering: "This man does not belong in my Army!"

Horse-pelt's combination threat and backpedal notwithstanding, the real news here was the Major Bivens handover. A true curveball. Bivens hadn't liked me from the start, and that was *before* I'd gotten him in trouble with Colonel Rosato. Bivens had made it very clear he wasn't excited to see my kind being recalled for action, and now he was the person in charge of my mobilization. The more I thought about it, the harder it was to figure out whether that was a good or bad thing.

Sisi, there really wasn't any time left to find out.

In the San Francisco restaurant bathroom, Band-Aid Man is splashing water in his face and breathing very rapidly. I can see his heart beating in his neck. He looks at himself in the mirror, then shifts his gaze to me. He says nothing, but he's pleading. He may not ever understand tonight, but he is very aware that Mit is on the other side of the door, and he won't make it alone.

"I'm with you, Band-Aid."

"Ames, I like Kitten. I was having fun talking with her and I even thought I was going to sleep with her tonight. It could've been perfect."

"It still will be. Don't give up." I grab him by his collar and pull his head out of the sink. I start pushing him out the door and I notice he still hasn't fixed his hair. I throw some water on it and he slicks it. Perfect. He smiles at himself in the mirror, big teeth gleaming, and his old confidence returns to his blue eyes. This can work, but it's all about momentum.

We rush the table and don't even sit down. I offer to pay the whole bill, but Mit throws down half right away and it's a cool split. I'm looking for the doors when Mit says, "Did you all know Ames is getting out of the Army, even though he's related to George S. Patton?"

The Band-Aid Man looks as if he's been hit in the chest with a railroad tie. I said it was all about momentum and I was wrong. It's all about speed.

I rush my company outside and into the Cadillac. Mit's family lives mere blocks away, right here in the Richmond, which gives me hope. I've got the stereo on loud in the whole car so no one can hear anything. Straight shot down Geary, cut across Clement by the old Coliseum theater, hit California and the brakes. Unload. It's over. I hop out with Mit, his sister, and his wife, and everybody else stays in the car. We talk a little bit while the engine's running, but the women are getting cold and want to go in the house. I give my friend a goodbye hug, it's always great to see McGinn. For me it was an awesome surprise.

We drive through Golden Gate Park to Soraya's house, the girls have a conference and decide they both want to come with us. They run upstairs to get toothbrushes and maybe conference some more. Band-Aid and I are sitting on the Cadillac hood.

"Dude, I have never had a scarier moment in my life than when I realized that was Mit at the table with us."

"Well, Kitten still likes you. That proves you don't have to live in constant fear of Mit."

"I only survived 'cause he had some other woman to cockblock himself on."

I laugh, "That was his wife."

"That fine blonde babe was *Mit's wife*?"

"Yeah, he couldn't cockblock himself on her."

"Mit could do it, I guarantee. His wife could be super wet and be dying for Mit's cazzo and he could still fuck it up somehow. They probably both go to bed frustrated half the time, both wanting to fuck like hell, but not doing anything 'cause Mit cockblocked himself."

We take two cars because the girls have to be back in the city early tomorrow. The scared-sober Band-Aid takes the Cadillac with Kitten shotgun, and Soraya and I follow in her yellow Volkswagen Bug with surf rack. They lose us in the Caddy, the vertical tail lights streaking off to Silicon Valley while we plod along at fifty-five, and So and I are all alone.

"Do you think they'll sleep together?" I ask. I have to ask loudly because the Volkswagen is backfiring and rattling with violence.

"It's up to him. Kitten never does this."

I smile at this ultra-cool wahine behind the wheel. She sticks her tongue out at me and I know she could ruin me the way she's ruined so many other guys. When I went overseas three years ago and hit the ground with Band-Aid Man in Italy, and then continued my run with BT, Sweet-Dick Lew, and Johnny Handsome in Germany and outposts beyond, Soraya was having her own fun with playboys, princes, and other fancies, none of whom left the slightest mark on her. Placeholders, enjoyed and forgotten. Soraya's the one who leaves a mark. She's just not like anybody else. For one thing, Soraya is not a woman you can go after. Soraya is a woman who goes after you, takes your hand and whip-cracks you around the universe, and then sets you down before she moves on again. The look I see in her eyes right now tells me, this many years in, she's still not quite ready to put me down. Odds are that day will come – love passes with time, and all that. Then again, Soraya operates outside of time. You'll never see her checking her watch.

The Volkswagen has stopped its shaking and backfiring, I notice we're coasting and pulling over to the shoulder. "We're out of gas," Soraya says. Apparently, she doesn't check her fuel gauge either. There's an emergency phone right outside, so we call her road club, the guy says half an hour. We get back in the car and my Thai princess kisses me. I briefly remember one of Band-Aid's recent stories that involved his hooking up with some girl in a traffic jam, but it disappears from my mind. Right now Soraya is making me forget everything.

The road service guy comes, his timing's perfect, and he pours enough gas into the Volkswagen tank to get us to my out-of-town friend's house where we're staying. We pull up behind the Cadillac, all the lights inside the house are off. I don't know what's happening with Band-Aid and Kitten, but I'm very curious. I try the first bedroom door quietly, it's locked. I'll have to wait.

I floss and brush my teeth and Soraya does the same. I drop on the bed, "I'm going to sleep." She laughs. She's laughing as if my going to sleep is a funny idea, as if it's not going to happen. She approaches me in her white silk nightie, still laughing.

The sun's barely up and Band-Aid Man and I are on the bed, looking out the upstairs window. We watch our girls get into the yellow Volkswagen and take off.

"Where the fuck were you last night?"

"Soraya ran out of gas."

"Oh, fuck, did you sleep at all?"

"Stop torturing me, man. What happened with you and Kitten?"

He lies down on the bed and I lie next to him. We're both ready to fall asleep as soon as he finishes his story. "It was passionate, dude," begins The Band-Aid Man. "Real passionate."

Soraya and the Unthinkable Pacific Cliff Climb

"I thought this was a double-decker," The Band-Aid Man complains.

"That's the Oakland Bay Bridge, that's the big one. You can see it on our right."

"What are we on this piddly shit for? I wanna take the big one."

"It's out of our way."

"I could do a U-turn right here."

"Don't, man."

"I should, there's no barrier or anything, just these yellow rubber poles." Band-Aid runs over a dozen of them, uprooting several and sending them into the oncoming traffic lane.

"Let's just get across the bridge. There's the rainbow tunnel on the other side, you'll love it. Tell him, So." Soraya doesn't move, she's asleep in the back seat. Soraya can stay awake for days at a time if she's moving, but if she stops she sleeps.

We're across, thank goodness, no U-turn under our belts. We're heading to my parents' place up north on the coast. I mailed them a message the first day of the discharge, "THE EAGLE HAS LANDED" in neat block letters on one of those post office postcards that's pre-stamped and has no picture. So they should be expecting us.

"This is your fucking rainbow tunnel? Painted stripes on the outside, that's it?"

"I knew you'd be excited about it. So's got her camera if you want me to get a shot when we come out."

He laughs, "Fucking rainbow tunnel, I'll have to tell everybody about that. That's some exciting shit."

"It's a sacred site, there's a lot of legend to it. The locals say that if

219

the rainbow gets painted over, everyone in San Francisco will suddenly become less tolerant."

"God damn! Soraya! Wake up! You're missing the rainbow tunnel." He reaches over the seat and pats her knee, her brown eyes open up. "Mornin, darlin. So what did Kitten say about me?"

"She loved you. She said you were a pumpkin."

"A pumpkin? What is that?"

"I don't know but it's good. She said you really took care of her, you made her comfortable."

"It was really passionate. Did she tell you that?"

"I think so."

"I told Kitten I'm gonna sculpt her body, it's that perfect."

The Pacific's on our left, generally, but Highway 1 is so twisted and screwy up here that we face every direction and the ocean can really be anywhere in relation to the Caddy. This is a forty-five mile stretch of narrow ridge driving protected by fifteen feet of guardrail in the least necessary places. Band-Aid comes into one blind curve at forty and stomps on the brakes. The Cadillac's antilocks slow us to a comfortable, shoulder-harnesses-digging-into-chests halt right under the nose of a giant cow. The cow looks through the windshield for a moment, then walks casually off the road. Band-Aid loosens his seatbelt and drives on.

We get to the house, the air is full of the sound of crashing surf. We walk the path to the front door where I'm about to see my parents for the first time since I went overseas.

"Come in, come in," my mom welcomes us inside. I give her a big hug and then I grip my dad's hand. I've been looking forward to my father's getting that seasoned look some men achieve in their elder years, that look of infinite wisdom and hard times weathered, but now my dad looks younger than the last time I saw him. I'll have to live a while to see the seasoned look, he says he'll live to be 108 and I believe him.

Dori, my parents' small dog, is jumping up and down and running all over. My mom's got all kinds of energy too, her life's not winding down at all. She makes daiquiris for everybody but me, I don't drink alcohol around my parents.

I make a powerful fire in the fireplace and we all sit down on the big living room couches. My mom brings us some snacks and Band-Aid tells them where we've been on our trip. He tells them a string of our discharge stories, with some editing. Not enough editing for my comfort, but I guess it's my fault I didn't warn him my parents are not the right audience for fringe material. I try to block out as much of his conversation as I can, but I nonetheless pick up bits like "... I wake up with Ames sleeping next to me naked..." and "... everyone *thinks* the Reveille painting is stolen, but we're going to return it as heroes..." that make me squeeze my eyes shut and try to imagine Band-Aid is talking to someone else. If he heads anywhere near Sugar or her anus, I will cut him off.

I go into the hallway and get down in pushup position. I manage twenty-five good ones and I drop on my face. I pull myself tiredly up the doorframe and reenter the living room where Band-Aid is still holding court. He mentions our fast food diet and my mom interrupts, "You two look as if you've had a lot of fast food. Ames especially, you've put on a lot of fat."

"Not really, mom."

"Well, we could figure it out," says The Band-Aid Man. "We weighed ourselves on the Walgreen scale in D.C."

"We don't believe in scales, we believe in calipers!" my mom booms.

"What are calipers?" I ask nervously.

My mother exits the house for the garage. Soraya mysteriously follows, the dog trails them both.

Soraya and the dog return seconds later, and then my mother with a large pair of tongs. Mom advances on me slowly, primitive device clicking eerily in hands. I shrink back into the couch, frightened into silence as the tongs open and close. She intends to pinch my fat with those things. They weren't meant to be used on humans, those tongs look better suited for picking up ice on the wharves in 19ᵗʰ-century Europe. My mom's eyes are glassy, she says nothing as she brings her fists apart and together. I shoot a desperate glance at my father, he appears unfazed. Soraya and Band-Aid are caught off-guard, I can tell they don't fully understand the barbaric nature of this scene.

"First the neck," my mother says smiling. The tongs are mere inches from my jugular.

"No!" The tongs lunge suddenly and I dive beneath them. They snap loudly in the air very near where my throat was before the dive. From the other side of the room I study the strange fireside scene. My father and Band-Aid are talking, Soraya's eating a carrot, my mom is holding the tongs by her side. I'm shocked by this casual behavior. "Band-Aid, Soraya! Let's go for a walk," I order.

Outside the surf is pounding and the sun is still shining.

"I see what you mean about these rocks," Band-Aid says excitedly. "Show me one of those long climbs you were telling me about."

We walk to the edge of a high cape that sticks way out in the ocean. From here we can look back on the whole seacliff to see where we want to climb. Over toward the house my dad's walking Dori with my mom skipping next to him. He still looks big from here. He's a rock, inching solidly across the cliff edge, and my mom is the bouncing fireball. I look at Soraya and I know we're a great team too. She whispers that she wants a kiss, so I lean down and kiss her.

I start to identify some scary climbs from my younger days, pointing out particular challenges, when I notice that Soraya is my entire audience. I look around. "Where is he?"

"He went down there," she answers, lifting her head toward the heavy ocean.

"Down there?" We're a foot away from the edge of this cape. "Did he scream or anything?"

She shakes her head.

I didn't want to go any closer for fear that a sudden wind would curl over the top of this cape and pull me over the edge and a hundred feet below to my death. Now I have no choice. I tell Soraya to back up and I drop to my hands and knees. With great caution I crawl forward to peer over the cliff edge. The sight that greets me causes my arms and legs to shake.

Band-Aid Man's head is three feet below mine. He has a pretty solid hold on the rock with his right hand, his left hand is pitifully grasping some brittle roots of a small dead bush with no leaves, and both of his feet are kicking freely in the air. He's looking up at me, smiling.

"How'd you get down this when you did it?"

"I never did this, Band-Aid. No one ever did this. It's unthinkable"

"Why'd you bring me here?"

"Because you can see the real climbing spots from here. You can't go down this."

"We're going down, Ames. Help me find some footholds."

I look around as best I can. "Band-Aid, even on a face that's all bad, you picked the worst possible place to climb down. There's no foothold in sight."

"Well, I can't pull myself up anymore, my arms are too tired. You're gonna have to climb down next to me and put my feet in places."

He's really done it now. "Soraya, baby, will you walk around to that part sticking out over there. I think you'll have a clear view of us and you can meet us wherever we climb up."

"Be careful," she sings.

I find the only place that isn't a sure dead end and I lower myself over the cliff. I climb next to The Band-Aid Man and look him in the eyes. "First of all, let go of those roots and put your hand right here as fast as you can." I grab his hand and pull it quickly toward me. On the way, our fingers brush the dead bush which falls off the cliff in one piece, roots and all, and tumbles over our backs into the sea. I press his hand into a crack near my head.

"Fuck, dude, can you see anywhere to put my feet?"

I climb down to see his situation. He can't come down that way. I push his feet up onto a little ledge and tell him to slide over. "Then you'll be where I was and you can climb back up."

He slides over and he's right above me. "Can't go up, dude."

"What?"

"Too dangerous. We're going to have to go down."

"You're lying."

"Just go down. We'll discuss this at the bottom."

"You know, Band-Aid Man... of all the stupid stuff we've done on this discharge, this is actually the stupidest. No question."

I climb down and Band-Aid's right above me. If I fall, he watches me tumble to my death. If he falls, he takes me down with him. This is turning into a better route, but the bottom's what I'm not sure about. I keep going down until there are no more footholds. My feet are dangling in the air the same way his were.

"Go, dude. I'm right behind you."

"Go where? This doesn't go all the way down, we can't just drop."

"It's like a six foot drop. That ain't shit."

"We can't do that."

"Bullshit. You mean we've jumped out of military aircraft eleven times between us and we can't survive a six-foot jump?"

I don't see what one has to do with the other, really. Besides, it's not the drop that worries me. It's what we're dropping into. This is forty-degree water down here, cold enough to make you forget how to swim. And even if it were ninety degrees, these waves are still smashing against the rocks with fury. We'll be pounded into the cliff and turned into sand right in front of my girlfriend's eyes. Soraya's on top of the next cape, I lift my right hand and wave across the water to her.

"Look, Ames, the water pulls back far enough sometimes and we can drop onto the ground and run across to that rock that goes to the cliff."

"Sometimes? How can we figure on something like that?"

"Dude, the ocean has a pattern just like everything else in nature.

Every seventh wave pulls out all the way so we can run to that rock. We'll wait for one, then we'll count seven waves and you'll drop when it goes out."

We wait a long time before the first wave pulls back far enough so that I could have run across to the rock if I'd known. My teeth are chattering. "That was a lot more than seven waves just for the first one."

"It was a multiple of seven," he says confidently.

"What multiple?" My question goes unanswered as the surf pounds the cliff under my feet. The vibration nearly shakes me off. I know I'll jump sometime, but I can't help thinking we'll be chased right back up here and we'll hang by our frozen fingers overnight until the Coast Guard comes.

Whatever pattern Band-Aid Man was talking about is too complex for me. And seven has nothing to do with it. If there is any pattern at all, it's a very high prime number and never the same one. I'm getting sprayed every time a wave crashes below me and I'm cold even with nervousness heating me up.

I look across to the rock that's supposed to be our destination, it looks a lot more slippery than when I first saw it. It's green with that sea algae that's ten times slicker than a banana peel. I'm shaking from cold and fright.

"Get ready to go! This is seven!" shouts The Band-Aid Man and I ignore him. One thing I have noticed about the waves, though – the ones that come in hard pull back hard. So I've got to bet on a big one, just hope it's so big that on the way out it knocks back everything coming at it and leaves me a dry path to freedom. If that rock out there really is freedom. I look at that slippery green rock again, what a pathetic object to reach for. I've had some pretty sad goals in my life before, but that green rock is up there with the saddest. Another wave crashes underneath me. I'm getting ready to jump, I'm going to do it, just have to time it exactly. Jump too late and I'll be beaten into the rocks, too early and the riptide will suck me out to sea where my body will go so numb from cold I won't even feel the sharks tearing me apart. Here's a giant wave right now. Boom! It hits the cliff so hard my right hand slips off. It got my feet, even. I watch it pull back, pull back, come on, baby. It's almost gone and I drop. Feet and knees together, legs bent, I hit the hard sand and fall forward. I push myself up with my hands and another big wave is coming in. I race as fast as I can to the big rock and my momentum carries me up. The surf crashes over my path and on three sides of this little jutting rock I'm on. I look over at my partner who's hanging from my old spot.

"Okay, this is two!" he shouts. "Count with me!"

I refuse to count, and I try to convince him to drop that method. I shout until my voice is hoarse, but he's still counting. I'm even more scared for him than I was for me, at least I had a fighting chance. *Stop, Band-Aid Man. You'll take your system to the grave.*

"Six!" he yells excitedly. "Get ready, here I come!" As that wave pulls out, I look at the one coming in. By the grace of luck, it's huge.

"Seven!" he yells as the wave crashes below him. The water sucks back and he drops. He doesn't fall, just hits the ground and goes. He scrambles up and I grab his hand. Owing it all to coincidence, he's with me. He made it.

"Science of the sea," he says, giving me a quick embrace. He turns around to size up the climb ahead, his back to me. "Time for a toast." He reaches into his jeans pockets and twists out two cans of Miller Genuine Draft. I hadn't noticed them before, but there they were this whole time, attracting as much attention in his giant rear-end pockets as spools of thread would in mine.

"My gosh."

"Prior planning prevents piss-poor performance," he says, turning and tossing me a can at the same time.

"What'll we make this to?" I ask, lifting the tab.

"To being close to our goal." The sun is over the ocean, mist is all around us, and the rush is still on. We lift our cans to Soraya high on the cape and then we drink.

"I'll lead from here on, dude," he's walking toward land. There's hard climbing ahead.

"What are you looking at?"

He grabs my shoulder and points into a crack in the cliff. I can see a pinpoint of sky deep in the rock, the crack goes all the way to the top. "We're going through," he says.

Courageous call, I've been burned by these tunnels before. Sometimes you get to the end and find the hole's just big enough to put your head through. I can imagine that happening to me and Band-Aid now, the tide chasing us up, the ocean slopping around our feet while our heads poke side-by-side through the surface of the earth. No comeback.

"This rock is slippery as hell," Band-Aid says before running across it to the base of the crack. I run too, momentum is more valuable than caution on this green slime. I wave to So, and Band-Aid attempts to signal what we're doing with some strange hand and arm movements. He climbs into the crack and I climb behind him. He's leading now on the upward phase, so all that I was saying when I was leading on the descent, about his taking me with him if he falls, is still true. And this is some tricky climbing. We're ascending in a crack where a rock sheared apart ages ago and these sides are smooth. Our only option is to press ourselves against the opposite walls and to scale by pressure. He starts and it's working. He's climbing fast, racing, like a Corvette up a mountain. And the crushed aluminum can circles in his back pockets are the Corvette taillights. Zoom! The passage is big enough this time and we're on top. In the open.

Soraya greets us with hugs and congratulations. The sun's right on the water, going over the edge, we watch it sink.

Inside, my mother brings dinner to our table. My dad barbecued steaks on the grill and she made everything else. I devour a third helping of her mashed potatoes and I remember I had to ask my dad something.

Oh yeah, it was my bank card problem, he's with the same bank. I tell him and he says he'll take care of it.

I put a big spoonful of hot fudge sundae into my mouth and Band-Aid's talking about some of our Army experiences together. My mom's reacting with an occasional "My word!" but my dad's just sitting back in his chair, smiling. Nothing's surprising him here, he doesn't get surprised. He's lived a lot, a relaxed man with a laid-back toughness that people recognize. Not a bully who flies off the handle, but a cool head who knows he can handle anything and does.

Unlike his ancestors, my dad never made general, a result of his having accomplished all his missions quietly, with all concern for his troops and very little thought of his superiors. Colonel is the highest of the non-political ranks, and I think it suited dad best. As a consequence, unlike the rest of the military heroes in my family, there's been very little written of him and his military accomplishments. And since dad doesn't tell war stories, all I've ever gotten is crumbs his friends have let slip about the Master Parachutist (Gold Star), 82nd Airborne Ranger infantryman who raised me. How the spinal injury that still nags him is the result of his having jammed his head at the top of a ladder while trying to save Vietnamese civilians. How there was no change of command at his remote military advisor assignment, because the advisor he replaced had already been killed. How dad was blown off course in one of his combat jumps with the Vietnamese Airborne and got hung up in a tree, where he swung quietly in the moonlight while an enemy patrol walked directly beneath. How he saved a drowning soldier, but turned down the Soldier's Medal he was put in for, because, he said, "It was nothing."

I guess that's why people say I have no respect for authority – no one's ever matched up to the first authority figure I ever knew. If you're wondering why I didn't apply to West Point and why I almost didn't join the Army at all, the answer is I knew I could never live up to dad.

In the living room, I watch my father place a log in the fire with one hand. The angle of his forearm reminds me of a picture my mom has hanging of a general shaking my young father's hand in the early days of Vietnam, the leading edge of all that hell. My dad's jungle camouflage sleeves are rolled up in the picture, his powerful forearm flexed in the grip of the general's palm. There are several other troops in the shot, and once I asked my father if he still remembered those other men. He told me that of course he remembered them, and that they were dead now.

Sometimes it strikes me that the most incredible truth of my own existence is all six generations' worth of career soldiers in both of my ancestral lines actually survived long enough to keep those bloodlines going through my birth. The odds against it strike me as astronomical, particularly in the frame of all the wars they fought. Not that enemy fire is the only way for military personnel to go out in the line of duty: my own godfather, artilleryman Robert Basha, came through Vietnam's firefights and counter-battery, and then died during the Cold War, before I knew what a godparent was, when his Huey helicopter lost its tail rotor over a German village and crashed on the edge of a sugar beet field.

My father nestles the log into the fire and calmly withdraws his forearm from the flames. He turns to my partner and speaks: "How about the story behind your moniker, there, Band-Aid Man. Is that one Top Secret?"

"Yes, sir, it is Top Secret," Band-Aid looks sideways and squeezes his jaw. Eventually he says, "And, Colonel, I know you have clearance."

The Alert Roster and How The Band-Aid Man Got His Name

I have no idea how long it took us, we put together a legal-length roster of amazing superheroes the world had not yet seen. But everything else was random. We rolled the cube and scratched crimefighters off the list, sometimes alliances at a time with big ink crosses, until that die pinned us down to a trio. Three superheroes for three mild-mannered lieutenants. The last cast would be for assignment. Critical. The die stopped at the edge of a long wooden coffee table in my Italian penthouse apartment. The first week I'd arrived in Italy, a local had randomly offered up this place to me as a rental, and I found myself moving into the best piece of real estate in the entire town of Portogruaro. My apartment was the third floor and roof deck of a commercial building (the ground floor was a popular pizza restaurant) overlooking the cobblestoned town square. With the windows open, you could hear the fountain. Everybody liked coming over.

"It's decided," Sweetser said. "Ames is Disguise Kit Man, I'm Backwards Man, and Russell is The Band-Aid Man."

The newborn Band-Aid Man cracked a fresh bottle of Jägermeister and took a deep gulp. He said nothing. The idea of rolling a die to determine what characters we would thrust on the local populace struck him as ridiculous. He missed A&M and the Corps of Cadets. While I donned various disguise elements and Sweets to reversing his clothing, The Band-Aid Man remained flopped back on the sofa in his regular house attire of Army galoshes and a pair of tight white underwear.

There was a knock at the door. One of my lovely Italian sisters came in, dressed up and appealing. She sat playfully on the exposed lap of The

Band-Aid Man. I slid on a pair of brown Army glasses and blinked. Sweets spoke to our guest in Italian. Their conversation became heated. She leaped up abruptly and left us, we heard her feet tapping down the stairs. At first I assumed Sweets had said something to set her off, but then I glanced at The Band-Aid man and witnessed another possible motive for our guest's quick departure – an erection straining against the fabric of his underwear.

"Get up, you pervert!" I ordered. "We need to roll."

The Band-Aid Man disappeared into my bedroom. Half of the Jägermeister was already gone. I wiggled my plastic mustache to get a more comfortable fit while Sweets buttoned his shirt behind his back.

Band-Aid Man emerged wearing my clothes. My slacks were floods and the sky-blue shirtsleeves stopped in the middle of his forearms. He had on one of my grandfather's oldest green-yellow ties with the skinny part pulled lower than the wide. Most striking, though, were the adhesive bandages. He wore strips on his wrists, fingers, across the bridge of his nose. He had patched his neck and one eyebrow, his chin was covered with a heavy square. A sleek one taped over the earlobe. He polished off the Jägermeister and bounded down the stairs without warning.

When Sweetser and I found him he was rocking before a plate glass window of the fanciest restaurant in town, confounding diners. Night had fallen, he was standing under a floodlight. We called to him and he wandered away from us into the street. Motorists swerved to avoid him or slammed on the brakes. Passengers cursed. He bounced off one car and careened into a sidewalk crowd.

"Christ!" Sweetser winced.

The pedestrians gave him space, but there was a certain logic that allowed them to comprehend this monstrosity. Any other man so covered in bandages would make people wonder about the nature of the accident. But The Band-Aid man was displaying such an obvious lack of motor skills that no one could wonder. This was an individual, clearly,

231

who scraped himself often in his everyday life.

I saw The Band-Aid Man approach an intercom of an apartment where a soldier in my unit lived. He depressed a button. Sweets and I rushed across the street in time to hear our friend break his silence.

"This is Captain Demerick!" Band-Aid shouted into the intercom. Demerick was my unit commander. "What the hell is going on in there!"

"We're asleep," the soldier replied. "Sir, it's late. Are you all right?"

"Hell no, I'm not all right! You'd better get alert, son. I need your help."

"What's wrong, sir?"

"This is serious!" Band-Aid screamed in desperate Captain Demerick cadence. "I want you in full battle rattle!"

"Sir, I don't have my Kevlar. I told the First Sergeant —"

"They're pouring over the wall! I'm getting my ass kicked!"

"Who's coming over the wall?"

"The Eye-talians! Fuckers turned on us. This is war! Get in full battle rattle and over to my house pronto. I'm getting murdered while you're in there swabbing each other's cocks!"

The soldier was shaken. "Sir, I don't have my helmet!"

"Good," Band-Aid Man replied. "If there's one thing we learned from Desert Storm it's that helmet straps tighten up in the heat of battle. That's how they found the Zydow Patrol — frozen in place, choked to death by their own goddamn chinstraps. Worst sight your sore eyes ever saw! I want you in standard soft cap, earflaps down."

Sweetser let out a low whistle of alarm. "We can't talk about the Zydow Patrol."

It was true that the Zydow Patrol was classified, but since its hideous sudden demise had in fact been attributed to biological weapons and not helmet straps, I didn't think The Band-Aid Man was technically divulging state secrets. Seemed more like a fine misinformation campaign. Besides, I was overtaken by a more immediate concern. Military combat units have something called an alert roster. When a commander gets orders to send his troops into battle, he grabs the roster and contacts the man below him on the flow chart. That man calls the men below him, and the sequence plays out until the last soldier has been alerted.

I was just praying that the soldier Band-Aid Man was scaring out of his mind in his apartment wasn't mistaking this for an alert. If I remembered correctly, the soldier was pretty far down the roster, so the majority of my unit would be skipped, but if even a few soldiers got called, this could be a pretty significant incident.

"I'm coming, sir!" the soldier shouted in terror.

"Hurry!" Band-Aid fired back. "My wife is their wartime concubine." The Band-Aid Man held his finger on the intercom button and began to sob. Real tears streamed down his face. "They put her on a goddamn lazy Susan! She's spinning around and swabbing any cock she can get her hands on!"

Sweetser got a running start and knocked Band-Aid from the intercom the way one might knock an electrocution victim from surging voltage. The drunken giant started back into the street, weaving through nighttime traffic. We tackled him there, then dragged him to my car. He collapsed in the shotgun position and Sweets crawled over him into the back as I drove at top speed to the beach.

He wouldn't budge for hours, Sweets and I had to leave him parked while we presented Disguise Kit Man and Backwards Man to the Italian disco scene. We returned to The Band-Aid Man twice, each time to find a fresh puddle of dark vomit outside the passenger door and no change in his position. "Band-Aid Man!" Sweets shouted, shaking our friend by the shoulders. "Band-Aid Man! We're going to another club. You're coming with us." But none of it registered.

When the discotheques finally closed us out deep in the black morning, we took my Lancia for a windows-down drive back to town. We passed a pair of hitchhikers a few blocks down the road and Sweets announced: "Evens we keep rolling. Odds we U-turn and pick those two up... And it's a five."

I cranked the wheel around all the way and bore down on the couple, blinding them in my headlights. They stepped aside. Sweets unlatched Band-Aid's seat and kicked it forward, dropping the giant's bandaged forehead into the dash. An early-twenties boy and girl slid into the back of the car. They seemed comfortable until I gunned it and they started to take in their surroundings.

"Where are you from?" Sweets asked.

"We are from Sweden."

"I don't speak Swedish. Would you rather speak English or Italian?"

"Italian." The boy was on the hump and he caught my reflection in the rearview mirror just as I was tightening my pirate's eyepatch. Through my good eye I recognized his mounting discomfort.

"Fantastico!" Sweetser declared.

"You can let us out here," the boy announced suddenly.

Sweets held the die up in one hand and put an arm over the boy's shoulder, "Not so fast, friend. The die instructed that we pick you up and take you all the way home. We're going to your doorstep."

I turned slowly and smiled to the hitchhikers, my lips spreading to reveal rotten horse teeth. I held the position for a long time, speeding down the road all the while. The Swedish couple hugged each other tightly.

"The die also told us to kill someone tonight," Sweets stated.

"But not you," I clarified.

"...necessarily," Sweets clarified further.

I banked a hard right through a farmer's field and The Band-Aid Man's unconscious form lurched through the seats so his head fell back onto the hitchhikers' knees. The girl shrieked. I stepped on the pedal through the field, dust was kicking up all around us. When I came out onto the main road I slowed at a red light for a second out of reflex. The Swedish boy instantly tore at the seat latch with one hand, shouldered Band-Aid Man's seat forward, and swept the door handle with the other. Both he and his girlfriend scrambled out onto the pavement. "Help!

Help!" they shouted. "Killers! Help us!"

I think it was Sweets who first noticed they were running toward an Italian Federal Police vehicle. "This just went multinational," he said. "Drive your ass!"

I floored it straight ahead. Another *carabinieri* car screeched to a halt in the intersection in front of us, blue lights flashing. "It's a coincidence," I said.

"You wish!" Sweets exclaimed. "Get off the road!"

I turned us down onto a dirt trail. That weird European siren noise began to fill the air.

Sweets shoved The Band-Aid Man against the car door. "Push him out of the fucking car, Ames! It's him they want!"

"You disloyal fiend," I muttered. "You're in as deep as the rest of us, Sweets. Deeper." I bounced over a main avenue awash with blue lights and dropped instantly over the other side. We raced parallel on a byway hidden by tall stalks.

"Band-Aid Man! Band-Aid Man!" Sweetser shouted at the top of his lungs. "Look at this fuckstick. He's responsible, Ames! We're just actors. He became his character. He is The Band-Aid Man!"

I maneuvered under a bridge and out onto a low-lying trail. Part of that "actors" jabber was nonsense, but I had to agree that The Band-Aid Man had become his character. Jammed in high gear I reached over the shifter and grabbed my unconscious partner's hand. I squeezed him warmly and took in the magic of the man who was now and would forever be The Band-Aid Man.

"Kill your lights!" Sweets cried urgently. "Stay on these back roads! And who in Christ are these assholes?"

I looked out my window and it slowly sank in that I had taken us into the sleepy town where my commander lived. There Captain Demerick was standing at the edge of his lawn, surrounded by a dozen soldiers. I tried to sink low in my Lancia, I prayed for the effectiveness of my disguise eyepatch and plastic mustache, but my unit peered in at me as I passed. They were in full battle gear, except for helmets. Instead it was soft caps all the way around, earflaps down…

The Civilian and the Hill Covered with Dead Boys

My father responds to the story with a comprehending nod. I have never heard Band-Aid tell it to anyone else.

The hot tub calls me, so I go change into shorts in the bathroom. When I emerge my mom comes at me with the tongs again, "You're fatter than I thought. You really need to be measured with the calipers."

"Mom, I weighed one-ninety-five two weeks ago, that has to be close to acceptable for a six-foot-one man."

"That all depends on your muscle-to-fat ratio. You need to change your diet."

I jump out of the way of the snapping tongs and run outside. Band-Aid offers me a beer from a six-pack while I lower myself into the hot water.

"Your mom looks primo hot," says Band-Aid. "I'm serious, she looks good."

"She could model," says Soraya.

"Yeah," I say, "she'd be a great model-spokeswoman for calipers. Do I really look that fat?"

Soraya shakes her head, "You look perfect."

Band-Aid laughs. He probably knows So would say the same thing if I weighed 300 pounds. "Dude, another thing. Your dad is cool as hell. I expected after all those rough combat years in Vietnam and thirty years in the Army he'd be loud and uptight and shit."

"I've heard that before. I used to think about that too, and one day my mom told me a story that made me understand everything."

"What story?" he and So are looking up, interested.

"Well, my mom and dad were having dinner at a restaurant with a reporter and his wife, and this reporter guy didn't know my dad well, but he'd heard about his combat experience. The waiter came to the table and knocked a full bottle of wine into my dad's lap. The waiter was apologetic, making a big deal, but my dad just smiled. He wiped himself off and said it was no problem. The waiter left and the reporter told my dad, 'You were completely good-natured about all that, as if it didn't bother you at all. I thought after all you've been through you'd be intense and explosive.'

"And my dad said to the reporter, 'Once you've walked down a hill covered with the bodies of dead boys, it's hard to get upset over a spilled bottle of wine.'"

Band-Aid looks out over the ocean. "God damn," he says. I can tell that short story had the same effect on him that it did on me. Finally he turns back to me and says, "That's how different our fathers are."

"How's that?"

"My dad would've decked the waiter and the reporter." Band-Aid stares into the clear night. He speaks again, "Well, we'll never be our fathers."

"That's for sure," I second.

"No, I mean we're not even trying to be anymore. That's done. Our fathers went off to war and fought for America and served their whole lives. They're military heroes, we're not, and that's it. We're out of their shadow. We took this trip to make you a civilian, right?"

"Yeah."

"Fair to say we did that. Look at you in the hot tub with your woman you love and that smile in your eyes that says you're ready to blaze your own goddamn trail starting now. You're a civilian, bro."

"What about the dog painting?"

"What dog painting?" asks Soraya.

"Band-Aid said I had to turn in the dog painting to A&M to complete my discharge."

"Goddamn you – we don't refer to it as a dog painting! It's called *Reveille*, it's a priceless historical painting by a renowned artist. And we're still returning it one of these days, but now we'll be turning it in as civilians. It'll be one of your great lifetime achievements to define your civilian legacy."

"But I still don't know what I'm going to do with my life."

"FIDO," he's grinning now, rolling. "Ames, it's *good* that you have no clue what you want to do. That's what civilian *is*. Now it's your turn to find your own identity and your own plan. It was the regimented Army machine that made you have to know your next move. That's prison, dude. And *you're discharged*," his hand breaks through the water's surface and drips in the open air.

I grab his hand in my own and squeeze Soraya closer with my other arm, I'm so happy to be with them both this instant. I think about the transformative cross-country, cross-cultural journey that brought us here. The D.C. airport was another world ago. I look in his eyes, "I owe you for this, Band-Aid."

Band-Aid swings his legs out of the hot tub, "We'll be even when we die."

We're under a completely starry sky, the waves are crashing into the rocks, the moon is big, the beer's good, and Soraya looks miraculous in her bikini. Band-Aid heads inside. "Hey, Ames," he calls from the door. "If our fathers could ever get drunk enough, they'd tell us – in their own goddamn way – that we did all right."

I try to reply, but I'm distracted. So's already pulled my shorts off with her feet. The moon grows even brighter before I carry Soraya inside and set her down on clean sheets in her bedroom. She falls asleep before my eyes.

Sisi, I could hardly sleep at all as my recall date neared. In just a couple days I was going to have to board a plane for Fort Sill, Oklahoma. I felt beyond rescue. I could barely bring myself to discuss any of it with my beloved. More even than The Band-Aid Man, my soulmate Soraya had opened up my civilian life. Band-Aid had been there for me in those initial critical days, and many more days since, but I'd been living with Soraya for almost a decade. Soraya was a girl who grabbed me by the hand and pulled me around the planet, literally. From my starting point as a kid who grew up eating nothing more exotic than what my mom bought at the commissary, I could now walk into a Thai restaurant and order a five-plate dinner, *in Thai*. Soraya was a woman who sat with me at a balcony table at a glamorous restaurant on the Amalfi Coast, and, by her mere proximity, made me and everybody else know that I really belonged there. Soraya was my key to the world.

I couldn't stand to put Soraya through any of this. Now of all times. With the Army on the verge of seizing control of my life and mind again, I dived into a bottomless depression. I heard the telephone ringing somewhere, insistently penetrating. It rang several times before I mustered the strength to pick up.

The caller was animated, throwing out scattershot strategy I couldn't quite understand. "Need one outside man," Rusty Spray intoned. There was a commotion on his end – I pictured him at his command desk, barking military orders to underlings all around. "No way you can be officially connect to me. Bruddah Ames, you listening?"

"Uh… yes. Did you get me in your unit?"

"Sorry, brah. You too late."

I sighed tragically.

"So enjoy yourself, cruise fo' couple months. Call you den."

"Enjoy myself? I'll be in Fort Sill guarding tennis courts."

"Dat's ova, brah. Now you freelance on my team, fo—"

"Over?" I asked. "How is it over?"

"I told 'em I get amend orders to bring you on my team. To stop me da Army have to prove ownership of you. Army neva can do it."

I contemplated this revelation with wonder. Rusty had finally forced the U.S. Army's hand by telling them he'd changed my orders. If they wanted to stop it, they would have to prove they had a claim to me – and they'd been unable to prove anything of the kind. "So, I don't have an obligation? The Army admits it?"

"Tink about it, Ames. Da Army have you on da books as lieutenant fo' fifteen years. How you can be one lieutenant fo' fifteen years? Eeda you make captain or kicked out. Army no can have it bof ways so you get no benefit – you neva get promote or retire – but dey can use you fo' each war."

I'd never thought about that. The Army might have had a leg to stand on if they'd elevated me to captain at some point, but to keep me as a lieutenant for fifteen years – far beyond the time the U.S. Army prescribes a lieutenant must be promoted or fired – they'd made their position indefensible by their own standard. I asked, "Did you know that from the beginning?"

Rusty's pidgin broke for a line: "You and me deployed together would have been cool."

"Yeah."

The call was silent for a long interval of both our minds running wild.

Finally, Rusty broke it: "Now I use you fo' special-contract, da kine military neva touch. You in Iraq as one civilian tourist, like da guy who got his head cut off."

"Good." I saw he was resuming talk of some kind of behind-the-scenes role he had planned for me. I didn't quite understand it, but I knew I could learn that when the time came. All that mattered now was that my nightmare was over. I was discharged. I was a civilian.

"I give you one gun at da flight line—"

"Rusty. Thank you, brother." My friend had done it.

Over the sound of the Northern California surf, I hear The Band-Aid Man say goodnight to my father in another part of the house before they head to their beds. I give sleeping Soraya a kiss and then get up to catch Band-Aid before he lies down. We regroup at the cliff edge to stare out over the midnight ocean.

Nights like this have a star glow that stays with you forever. If you're going to restart your life from scratch, it's hard to imagine a better launch point than the Golden State, looking across the Pacific.

"Mission complete," The Band-Aid Man declares, "You goddamn puke civilian."

Band-Aid and I are both a little choked up. We keep thanking each other, but there are so many people to thank.

Epilogue: Sisi and the Most Glorious Day

Sisi, on the subject of gratitude, the very day of my report date in the 21st century, I stood outside my mailbox for several minutes, rereading the official documents and even the official Army envelopes in which they'd come. I'd trusted Rusty with my life from the start. I'd trusted him when he recruited me into his combat brigade bound for the war zone, and I'd trusted him when he told me it was all over – the Army didn't own me after all. But to hold in my hands the Army's confession, in the form of fresh printed orders revoking my mistaken recall, was a concrete victory that jumped the gates of faith.

In a larger envelope, separate from those revocation orders, was a certificate of Honorable Discharge that glowed off the page. I gripped it with both hands and felt the warmth travel through my arms to heat my entire being. This was my second lifetime discharge, and at that instant it seemed as glorious as the first.

To top it all off, I received a genuinely nice e-mail from onetime nemesis Major John Bivens, who was no doubt as relieved as I that my recall had been an error and that the war had not gone so "sideways" as to put a man like me back in uniform.

From: "Bivens, John MAJ, HRC-St. Louis"
To: Ames Holbrook
Subject: Revocation of Mobilization Order M-04-400681/A02
1LT Holbrook
Please be advised your mobilization order M-04-400681/A02 has been revoked. Also, you will be receiving an order of

243

discharge, in which your military obligation to the U.S.
Army Reserve completed.
On behalf of the U.S. Army Human Resources Command-STL, I
want to thank you for your service to the United States
and U.S. Army.
Regards,
MAJ JOHN L BIVENS, MP
Human Resources Command

I didn't look for an explanation, I knew the Army would never give me one. I didn't look back, either. As a precaution, to make sure he didn't have to go through the same thing, I did ask my dad not to answer his phone for a while.

That really happened, Sisi. And here's another thing that's true: it came down to the wire. That glorious day the Pentagon offered me their surrender and officially revoked my recall orders, I had two plans at the ready. Plan B: I was going to fly to Fort Sill, Oklahoma, for Army retraining and immediate follow-on assignment. Plan A: I was going to the hospital. Thankfully, that official revocation arrived in the nick of time and, instead of boarding a plane on government orders, I was there to drive Soraya to the hospital.

Plan A was the preferred plan, but it turned out to be freighted with scares of its own. Soraya's condition went from complicated to perilous, and suddenly doctors were around me explaining critical terms like *eclampsia.* They declared an emergency procedure was needed right away. Administrators rushed in with printed waivers I had to sign promising I wouldn't hold the hospital responsible if Soraya didn't survive.

I watched from the edge of the operating table as the blades went into my Soraya's skin. I saw the layers inside pulled out. I saw my wife, whom I'd married in 2001 on the best day of my life. I saw all the good times I'd shared with her, as her eyes rolled back suddenly and she lay still.

I wanted to wake Soraya up so she would breathe, but smocked workers pushed me out of the room so I couldn't see anymore – "If you get out of the way, the doctors can do their job." I stood in shock, alone, on the other side of a locked door. I don't know how long I was there.

Eventually, a doctor stepped in my room. He read my face. "No, it's okay," he announced. "She's fine."

I asked, "Who?"

"Both," he answered with a smile. "Congratulations."

And that's how it turned out that my having vanquished the United States Army wasn't even the greatest thing that happened to me that day. The greatest was becoming a father. In my sun-bright glare of victory, I held my daughter and smiled. She was a couple weeks early, but healthy. And you know that daughter was *you*, Sisi. I just kept looking into your eyes and I felt blessed by luck, and by God, and by the beautiful universe we inhabit. I smiled uncontrollably with your mother – Soraya – my true love on the discharge road trip and my true love still today.

And then, reward on sublime reward, Sisi, I got to be with you for that next year and a half that I couldn't have even laid eyes on you had I not won, had it not been proven that the Army didn't own me after all. And, you won't remember it, but that year and a half was perfect. By the end, I'd lost track of all the times I'd beaten the odds, but I never stopped being grateful for you and all the days I got to spend with you.

Sisi, I wrote this book for you, and you can keep whatever you wish for yourself. I dream it will drive you to make your own choices, and live your life on your own terms, and always keep fighting for what you think ought to be – no matter how much the machine seems geared against you. And that is, by the way, what American servicemembers have always protected for us, and what I hope they always will.

Oh, right, Sisi, there's something else.

I was on a trip, my first night away from you and your mother since you'd been born. It was a short time but another universe later, after I'd put my last military documents to rest in their cardboard home, that I remembered the other path. Had the stars not aligned, had the mistakes not been corrected and my inverted world not inverted again, how different life would have been. I shook the military images from my mind. I determined to close the box on the U.S. Army and never look back.

I'd forgotten one detail.

I'm summoned outdoors by a heavy scrape in the driveway and a persistent horn bleat. Hot off the road and overwhelming the driveway is a Cadillac, pinging and creaking in a four-thousand-pound forward lean.

By the time I get out to greet him, my friend has two shots of Crown already poured.

I clink his glass. "Here's to my baby's godfather: The Band-Aid Man."

Band-Aid's eyes well with tears and he beams. "Was that Soraya's idea?"

"Yeah."

"How long did you argue with her?"

"A long time."

"Soraya's right, fucker. I'll be the best goddamn godfather a kid ever had."

The whiskey goes down beautifully.

The Band-Aid Man collects the glassware with urgency and jumps in the car. He leans across the Cadillac bench and throws my door open. "Dude, get in. If we don't make Sill by tomorrow midnight we're AWOL."

"What?"

"I've got orders," he grins, waving a stack of papers in his hand. "We're back in on the buddy system."

"Band-Aid. My orders were revoked!" I declare urgently. "We've got to cancel yours."

A grimace stretches his face. "I signed up. My orders can't be canceled."

"Yeah they can. We've been out too long." I try to explain it to him just the way Rusty did to me, "The Army can't make us lieutenants for life. They don't own us."

Band-Aid's eyes roam, as if he's trying to make that logic work but cannot. "Dude, you don't understand." He stresses, "I'm a *volunteer.*"

The distinction wrenches me. I sit shotgun in the Cadillac and pull the door in. The Band-Aid Man throws us in reverse so we hit the street in a bloom of sparks. He knocks the shifter into overdrive and stamps the gas. "Is Soraya cool with you taking a side trip?"

"Are you kidding? She thought the Army was taking me away. This is like a free eighteen months."

"Call her in the morning and have her fly out with Sisi. They can meet us at some Oklahoma resort where generals' mistresses stay."

I nod assuredly. "So, you know where that junkie is?"

"I know where a lot of them are."

I suggest, "We should get an old Deadhead. When he starts telling the Army he's not you, they'll think he's still crazy from the acid."

"He'll wind up in the V.A. mental wing," Band-Aid agrees. "We can milk this for years." He hits the freeway and flattens the accelerator all the way to the floor. It's suddenly more important than ever that we get there on time.

I realize Band-Aid's cell has been chiming from a woman, or women, wanting to FaceTime him. All in *the now*, he knocks his chiming phone aside and I see it slide away between the seats. I won't be surprised if he doesn't touch it again this trip.

How wild that phones and navigation systems and female grooming can change so radically over the years, while the really priceless things stay the same. The deep breaths of freedom we're sucking in right now can't feel any different from what flooded the lungs of our Founding

Fathers.

"Did you sign up for direct deposit?"

"Of course." Band-Aid flashes his bank card, and then slaps the wheel in a burst of inspiration, "Dude, we should get Jammer. He can use the treatment."

"Perfect." The dreams are really spinning now.

"And we should finally turn in *Reveille.*"

"You still have Reveille? Band-Aid, you never brought back that painting?"

"I've had a busy life, fuck."

"We're picking it up?"

"Maybe not this trip."

"Oh, geez. Hopefully the authorities have forgotten all about Reveille."

"Oh, no, they're still looking for it, trust me," Band-Aid shakes his head solemnly.

A red truck on the oncoming side of the freeway abruptly spins out and hurtles our way on the grassy median. For a moment I imagine it's going to bounce all the way over and land right on our speeding Cadillac, killing me instantly.

But it won't happen, not now or ever. Nothing's going to take me out until I've seen the whole nation from under the bill of this Saints cap. There will be more trips. I look at my partner and I know he can't die either. The nuclear bombs can fall and we'll watch the flash in our rearview. 'Cause we'll survive, baby, and we'll return that painting, by God, if we have to do it in the last Cadillac made, cruising the bulldozed roads of America with Montecristos glowing and a booby-trapped gas tank. We'll knock the mutant zombies' heads off like golf balls and we'll charge them directly, feeling their poison breath while we fight valiantly with fireworks, broken Miller bottles, and purple Crown Royal sacks filled with batteries.

I salute reverently out the open passenger window — my gesture aimed at Rusty and all of the other soldiers, whose sacrifices are *not* wasted – while my brother drives on. We devour the country around us, Band-Aid Man through the windshield, and I through that right-side window, still holding the salute like a majestic parade in review.

Sisi, I ask only that you keep our veterans in your mind and heart. When you encounter them in the future, let them know you appreciate them. And, if you have a chance, please pass on this message.

One of the ironies of the American military experience is that, while they are serving, American service personnel are an unshakable Number One – members of the mightiest military force in the world – but, when they get out, American veterans are always certified underdogs – society's misfits, struggling against the odds to make their way into the civilian world that everyone else takes for granted. It can be a rough landing. Sometimes it can be rough for a long time.

But, Sisi, I want you to tell them that life has a way of getting better. Often, in fact, life comes around and finally figures out a way to pay them back in full. Assure the veterans you meet that beautiful surprises are inbound to their locations. In case they want some relevant real-life proof, you can tell them how things played out down the line for your Uncle Band-Aid Man and your daddy.

Yes, The Band-Aid Man worked like a dog for Miller beer in his early post-military run. And from there, he sank. I vividly remember his drained telephone voice informing me Miller had let him go after he ran over a fire hydrant in a marked Miller van, well outside of work hours, naturally, and he was being pressed to pay all the damages even though he had nothing in the bank and his income stream was finished. *FIDO.* Band-Aid's plight motivated him to return to his construction-engineer roots. He got into the federal construction universe, took classes when he could, and drew on his military background to work his way up to a career with one of the biggest U.S. companies doing government building projects around the world. As I write this, The Band-Aid Man is in Laos, serving as the quality control manager of a $126,000,000 U.S. Embassy project in Vientiane. I double-checked, that is the correct number of zeroes and commas. As you know from the postcards he sends you regularly, your Uncle Band-Aid is living in grand style, working his dream job, and not slowing down.

The month after the original discharge road trip ended, I was pulled away from San Francisco, the city that had raised me and a city I still had love for, by the irresistible draw of boiling gritty raw New Orleans. On the way, I stopped in San Antonio, and there Band-Aid put me on a Greyhound bus at 11:00 p.m. on Christmas Eve and sent me off to my new home. I arrived in New Orleans at the same time everyone else was leaving. The first local paper I picked up featured a cover story on the city's murder rate, which would go on to set a record that has never been matched by any major American city in history (and which was acutely higher in my new Central City neighborhood, according to the paper's murder map), along with an editorial on New Orleans' crushing lack of jobs. When I went out looking for work, most potential employers willfully ignored my military experience along with every gig I'd held before I got in, and treated me as if I were a fresh-faced child attempting to enter the American workforce for the first time. I was finally offered a job as a janitor, and I took it. It felt like a significant life demotion, particularly considering I'd been a janitor once in my teens, for better pay. Fortunately, not long after I began my second janitorial career, a U.S. Marine veteran at the French Quarter Marriott recognized my potential and offered me the best position he had – parking hotel guests' vehicles on the graveyard shift. As grateful as I was to have that job, I tried, further down the road, to improve my professional circumstances by applying at a New Orleans car wash, but I never got a call back, even though I continued to see the Help Wanted banner hanging on the cinderblock exterior every time my bus rolled past.

It was right about then that an old Army buddy set me up with a job as a Deportation Officer. It turned out to be the perfect career at the perfect time. For the next several years, I ran with the New Orleans aggravated felon unit, where I apprehended and managed the cases of dangerous criminals from over 100 countries and personally escorted the most violent hardheads to their motherlands. I performed my Deportation Officer duties with such aplomb and personal dash that I managed to jump up the ranks of Homeland Security and, along the way, sell movie rights to my life as a federal agent.

I quit the Deportation Officer job, wrote a book about my desperate hours wearing a gun and badge on the streets of New Orleans (the book I'd told Colonel Rosato I was working on), I appeared on over fifty TV and radio shows, and then – in one of my all-time great civilian coups – I convinced the Department of Homeland Security to hire me back with a two pay-grade promotion. As a *writer*. The whole experience is one I couldn't have imagined when I was sprinting the concrete ramps at the parking garage, deep-breathing carbon monoxide for 40 hours a week while my coworkers, including the ones living in the brick projects, made jokes about my neighborhood.

And there was another beautiful surprise. When my literary agent called to inform me of big movie deal offers, it turned out the winning bid was from a guy I'd served with at Fort Sill. I hadn't heard from Stephen Lile since artillery school, but he came out of the woodwork with a vengeance, having fulfilled his journey from his public-housing / absentee-father roots, through a ten-year stint in the military, ultimately to king-of-industry tycoon status.

All that goes to show that those who have served never can tell what will become of their old trench buddies, and, likewise, as discharged veterans, there's no limit to where civilian life can take them.

Sisi, when you see my fellow veterans, let them know.

Tell them: Just *Go*. It's sweet out here, I promise. The civilian world needs you to dive in headlong and add to the wonder. *Go* lay your own tracks and make your mark. I'm pulling for you – we all are. *Go* enjoy the U.S. Grade-A Freedom you once defended.

Sisi, my baby, tell them thank you so much, and when the world slams them on their backs, remember, *FIDO.*

And never stop until you're happy with the world.

With all my love,
Your Lucky Daddy

P.S. Officer Raker and the Dog that Came Back to Bite Us

Oh, yeah.

Sisi, remember I told you that this story closed the same way it opened, with a telephone call of catastrophe at an ungodly hour? And the opener was that call from Horse-pelt telling me I was a deserter? Well, here comes the closer. The only difference is that instead of your father getting a call from the Military Machine, this time it was your godfather getting a call from the Police State – that sky-splitting telephonic lightning strike followed immediately by the thunder of The Band-Aid Man calling me to relay the shock.

"Laura Coffeecake turned me in to the police."

"What?" The name of Band-Aid's A&M ex brings in a flood of memories, none of them fresh. I hadn't thought she was part of his life anymore. "For what? Defamation of her modern-day character? Failure to let her repo the rest of your wardrobe?"

"No, Ames, this is serious," his tone leaves no edge for laughs. "*Reveille.* The cops tracked me down and they want it back."

My first thought is that he has to be putting me on. This wouldn't be the first time he's pulled me into a ruse, like the one where he picked me up after he'd volunteered to go back in the Army. There was more to that one, but all you need to know is that, while he truly had volunteered, Band-Aid greatly overstated the degree to which the Army had accepted his offer. It was more that the Army had sort of accepted the *possibility* of his re-upping, and Band-Aid had manufactured all the urgency from there. I wasn't going to be duped that easily again, "Come on, Band-Aid, the cops tracked you down at your embassy job *in Laos* over a painting

253

that's been missing since the nineties? Reveille's not that important."

"Well, evidently it's important as shit in Texas," he corrects. "Type 'Missing A&M Painting' into Google right now."

I follow his instructions and feel apprehension grip me when the search returns multiple results. I click the first one, a genuine newspaper link from the Bryan-College Station Eagle. The byline's from Thanksgiving week and I haven't started shopping for Christmas yet – this news is fresh. I know by the first paragraph that Band-Aid Man is telling the truth, and my anxiety heightens as I read on. By the time I'm midway through, the article makes me feel like a full-on menace for my role in depriving the public of this priceless art, and I don't want to read any more. "Holy smokes."

"Yeah, believe me now, fucker?" Band-Aid's call through the Laos phone system has picked up an echo, making it seem as if he's calling me "fucker" over and over.

"Sweet Jesus, how did they connect it to you?"

"I told you: Laura Coffeecake turned me in. The whole Reveille controversy got out of control, they had three different police departments questioning witnesses for the past month trying to crack the case, and one of the cops – Officer Raker – got to Laura Coffeecake and she told him she remembered the painting hung up in my room when she was banging the shit out of me for two months."

"The cop told you that?"

"Yeah. I mean he described her without naming her, but when I said her name he made an affirmative noise and—"

"Wait," I initially interrupt him so I can ask him to mimic Officer Raker's "affirmative noise," but more worrisome thoughts swarm that one out of the way, "Did you admit you have the painting?"

"Of course, I'm not going to lie to the cops," he declares naively. "I told him it's in my storage locker in San Antonio, all padded up real nice in cardboard and sealed plastic. Officer Raker said I've got a week to get it to him, before he brings in the FBI because I'm technically an international art thief who fled the jurisdiction of the crime."

"What? You've got to be kidding me."

"Ames, for the sake of time, because I'm paying out the ass for these Lao international cell rates, can we just assume everything I say on this call is the truth? Trust me, I ain't got the time to joke around right now. I have a Top Secret clearance for my job, and some cop hard-charger asshole is threatening to fuck me out of it. I gotta go to my jobsite now, in fact, so I just need to ask you one question first, okay?"

"Go."

"If I arrange for the storage facility to let you and my brother Bob in to get Reveille, can you go out to San Antonio for one day this week and do that?"

"Of course."

"All right, don't worry about the cash – I'll buy your ticket, we'll be even when we die."

I laugh. I bankrolled most of our discharge road trip, and we've swung back and forth ever since, based on our individual degrees of wealth/poverty at any given time. The world's best accountant couldn't call it one way or the other. I feel my chuckle fade into a sigh, "This isn't how I dreamed it would happen, Band-Aid. I thought we were going to return Reveille to A&M personally."

"Yeah... fuck," he lets himself slow down for just a moment. "We should have." His tone conveys more than his statement. This one's going in the Regret column and it hurts.

My spirit flails against the inescapable death of our vision, "Why don't you stall the cop till you can get leave to come back to the States?"

"No, I'll lose that game. Besides, it's not like we have anyone to blame but ourselves. We've had that painting since the nineties, and check out the calendar – in three weeks it'll be twenty-fifteen."

"Wow."

He snaps back to business, "Just look for the itinerary in your e-mail today or tomorrow."

I slip my phone in my pocket in a fog of dejection, but I have to admit it isn't all bad. I will get a chance to spend some time with Band-Aid's brother, Bob Brown, and I will liberate Reveille, even if not in the manner that, as younger men, we dreamed. I keep a watch for that e-mailed New Orleans-to-San Antonio itinerary that night. I check again the next morning. The itinerary doesn't come.

Days later, when I finally do get an e-mail from Band-Aid, I open it to discover a fact-filled letter explaining that his company is taking him off the Laos job, which has finished its first phase, and is sending him to be the quality control manager at an even bigger embassy job in Chad. Band-Aid will get a 25% raise as part of his intercontinental leap, and company bigwigs will be able to sleep more easily since employees are required to use local drivers in Chad and may not drive themselves, whereas The Band-Aid Man has personally wrecked three company cars in his year and a half in Laos. The move seems like a big win for The Band-Aid Man, his company, and the people of Laos. Band-Aid's e-mail makes me smile, but I'm somewhat at a loss since it includes no airline itinerary and it fails to acknowledge in any way the stolen art crisis. I would've accepted even an offhanded reference to the painting in a postscript or a low-grade animated GIF of Reveille the dog, but Band-Aid gives me nothing. In the absence of any news, my instinctive optimism takes over, and in the ensuing days I manage to convince myself that the whole Reveille storm has blown past.

The next late-night telephone peal shatters my optimism. Turns out the Reveille storm is now a hurricane. Band-Aid's voice is more distraught than it was the last time around, and the speed of his words conveys a new brand of urgency, "Everything's changed, Ames. Officer Raker turned evil on me real quick."

"How? When?"

"I just got off the phone with that fucker and called you."

"What did he do to you? You sound as if you've been pistol-whipped."

"I know, I feel like it. Wait a minute, I need some Crown."

"You can get Crown Royal in Chad?"

"Yeah, I had to take out a liquor distributor," I hear him shift the phone to drop some ice in a glass. "She has a mustache and her apartment smells awful, but luckily she got wasted and passed out, so the next morning I told her we fucked."

I grimace, "That sounds unethical." It strikes me as something Band-Aid should have a personal code against, even a stock lecture: *"Never ever tell a woman you fucked her when you didn't. A man's dick is only as strong as his word…"* I'll have to circle back on that another time, since, as is often the case with The Band-Aid Man, there are more pressing matters. "Get back to the story," I fix myself a Crown-rocks in solidarity.

"So, this time Officer Raker is pissed. He says I told him I'd coordinate everything within a week, and I didn't do it, and all these other wild accusations."

"Are his accusations true?"

"Well, yeah, they're true, but they're still wild. Raker's a wildman. He's not taking anything into consideration. I told him I just moved from Laos to Chad on a new embassy job, and I've had a lot of things to take care of since I've been in N'Djamena. When I mention that, he goes off on my ass about fleeing justice, says I left Laos for Chad to avoid extradition and all this shit."

I wash back a gulp of Crown, "Band-Aid, why didn't you just have me and Bob give him the painting the way you planned?"

"I *can't*. That's the other part I ain't caught you up to. So, the owners of my storage unit used to be family friends, the guy was a Vietnam vet stationed in Vung Tao where my father was. It's a beach province and he actually surfed there, so I always used to call him and say, 'Charlie don't surf.' Anytime I wanted, I'd just call him up and tell him my brother Bob is coming by, or whoever, and he'd let 'em in. Well, come to find out, he died two months ago."

My ice cracks in the glass. "No."

"Yeah, his kids sold it to a new storage company, and this new company's some premier global outfit that treats their storage lockers like a Swiss bank. No one gets in except the owner in person."

I groan softly.

"So the whole plan with you and Bob getting Reveille out is shot to hell. I figure the last resort is get 'em to let Officer Raker in personally, but as soon as I mention that plan, the VP at the storage place cuts me off and says no cops without a warrant. Then she announces they're 'turning it over to legal' and hangs up. And I'll be goddamned if they've answered any of my phone calls since. This is like when the Army stopped taking your calls during the recall."

I do a shot of Crown out of the cap, not bothering with ice anymore. "At least I had only one adversary. It was just the Army against me, but you have the Swiss storage locker conglomerate and Officer Raker coming in like pincers."

"Yeah. And, believe me, that dickhead ain't slowing down on account of my circumstances. Raker chewed my ass. Said he's been talking to people who know me and my family, and if I don't give him the painting by New Year's Eve, he *is* gonna get a warrant."

"Oh, God."

"Yeah, says he's gonna write it up for possession of stolen property, and if he finds the painting in there – which you and I both know he will – then I'll be charged and prosecuted in the State of Texas."

I'm looking for a way out somewhere, "That doesn't mean he can come get you. Raker already said there's no extradition."

"Dude, my company does billions of dollars of business with the U.S. government – they're not gonna risk their reputation having their Quality Control guy be a convicted art thief. Raker knows he doesn't need to come get me. I lose my clearance, I'm done here. I either head back to the States or become a Chadian, pouring concrete on my site for twenty dollars a day."

"Then Raker's got us," I despair. "If you ignore Raker, he'll get the warrant and charge you, and your company will fire you. But if you up and leave your worksite your first week on the job to fly back stateside to hand Raker the painting, I'm sure your company will fire you for that, too. You're done either way."

"Weeell," Band-Aid draws out. I think I hear him pour another Crown.

"Well, what?"

"There is one glimpse of hope in the picture."

"There is?" I haven't felt any hope since I picked up the phone. "What is it?"

"New embassy, new man in charge," Band-Aid drawls.

"Go on."

"My new boss is an Aggie."

I step off my airplane in San Antonio and get a text from Band-Aid saying he just landed too. This means that in a stroke of divine orchestration, Band-Aid has managed to route me from New Orleans, one state over, and himself in from N'Djamena, two continents over, and have us hit the floor in his hometown at the same time. I walk from my gate A9 and spot him walking my way at around A4. I freeze for a second in the concourse and behold the wonder.

Without meaning to, I flash back to the original discharge, when he met me in the D.C. airport. Those elapsed years show up a couple places in the smiling giant before me now. First off, he's got about 45 pounds on his end-of-the-millennium counterpart. Aah, make it 65. It's as if, at some point, Band-Aid decided he was done with his Greek god persona, and he flipped the switch into full-on party animal. In Hollywood casting terms Band-Aid went from a blue-eyed Benjamin Bratt to a more blown-out Vince Vaughn. He also has some gray in the stubble he's sprouted during his 30-hour migration out of N'Djamena International. None of that gray in his hair, though, which is constant over the years – still an unassisted Mexican black, and somehow perfectly styled off the plane. Unchanged also are his pale blue eyes, them and his smile lighting up the concourse even now.

I step in and give him a big hug. There's a bar next to us, so I grab us a couple of shots of Crown. When the bartender asks me if we want the double for only a dollar more, I tell her of course. I catch us in the mirror and I can't help but notice I've got a lot more mileage in my face than my partner does. My frame may not have the extra pounds, but even from here I can see deep creases like grill marks in my forehead and permanent saline-implant bags under my eyes. Seems I've finally reached the age I've long pretended to be. Wrong side of 40 to dive into the stolen art business, but who are we to question our destiny?

We down the shots and head to the rental car counter in a golden glow. My partner successively charms the girls at the rental car desk and the boy out on the lot, winning the latter over with an off-the-cuff "Big Bang Theory" analogy that I don't get, but which really fires up the boy.

"I'm gonna give you an upgrade," the boy enthuses. "What do you like?"

"We got precious cargo, we need some space. How about that Ford Explorer," Band-Aid points to a glistening SUV still dripping out of the car wash.

"No Cadillac?" I challenge.

Band-Aid shakes his head sternly, "That's just what the fuckers will be expecting."

I can already feel magic working. The Band-Aid Man on fire in his home state, drawing power from the Lone Star earth and air.

He tears us out of the lot and I immediately start drilling him with questions. My e-mailed itinerary notwithstanding, communication from Band-Aid leading up to this has been in spare bursts. He hasn't had time to fill me in.

"So your Aggie boss approved this?"

"Oh, yeah, I just told him I had the Reveille painting, and he gave me his unqualified blessing."

"Awesome! What about Officer Raker?"

"He's our problem," Band-Aid's testing out the SUV's basic functions: horn, sunroof, acceleration, seat recline, and the rest, while he rolls his hometown streets. He jacks in his phone to feed the stereo his playlist and seems satisfied when we're assaulted on all sides by Lil Jon at ear-crowding decibels. I turn it down just enough to get my partner's attention so he understands I'm waiting for a more complete answer, which he finally issues, "I told Raker he left me no choice but to fly in and give him the painting personally, and I'd drive Reveille the two-hundred miles to A&M to make the delivery."

"And?"

"He was already too pissed at me. He said if we hit the road with that painting, then he'd arrest us on the spot for transporting stolen art."

I release a startled cough.

"Yeah, with Officer Raker it's his way or no way."

"What's his way?"

"The terms he dictated – and I mean dictated like a dictator – are that we meet in front of the storage locker on the thirty-first and take him in to get Reveille."

"Why does he care how he gets the painting, as long as he gets it?" as soon as I voice that question, I'm already figuring it out. "Oh, so he wants all the credit. Raker's already bragged to the whole station that he cracked the cold case and tracked down the stolen art from the nineties, and now he wants to make the story richer by saying he had to travel to San Antonio to confiscate it from the thieves in their hideout." I sigh, "So that's the plan."

"That's Officer Raker's plan. That ain't our plan. You gotta fly back to New Orleans tomorrow night to be with Soraya and Sisi, right?"

"Right."

"That means we got twenty-seven hours on the ground. That's our window to get Reveille out of storage, return her to her true home on A&M soil, finish that four-hundred-mile round trip back, and get you to the airport in time for your flight."

"Oh, that's all, then?" Band-Aid's phone is buzzing nonstop from his hometown buddies, some are even texting me to find out what's going on. I'd answer them, but I still have no idea. "So, Band-Aid, you want to grab the painting, even though the police said we'd be arrested."

"Police ain't got no idea The Band-Aid Man's in town. I told Raker I was coming in tomorrow, so we'll be a day ahead of him the whole time."

I draw a deep breath and release before I try to issue a controlled response, "Band-Aid, police don't rely on suspects' promises for their surveillance. These guys have lookouts in all the systems. You used your credit card to buy your plane ticket, they know you're here. Same with this rental car, they have our make, model, plates. They'll get hits from your storage locker facility—"

Band-Aid spikes the radio volume to cut me off, before he lowers it again so he can seize the floor, "I'm so sorry I don't know the newest law enforcement techniques."

"Not new. Like since the invention of computers."

"Do you want to do this, Ames?" Band-Aid's challenge hangs in the climate-controlled air of our rolling SUV.

Here's the thing. Normally, I make it my policy to stay in the good graces of law enforcement officers. At this point in my life, I've *been* a law enforcement officer. It's not my character to flout the law. However, the choice to be made here is not a choice between one good/legal outcome and one bad/illegal outcome: to return Reveille or not to. The good/legal outcome of Reveille's return is a given. Band-Aid has already made the right moral choice by coming here.

Our only dilemma is whether we return the painting under the terms Officer Raker dictated, or we return it with no rules other than the whim of The Band-Aid Man. And the tradeoff between those two alternatives is freedom versus risk. If we go the Band-Aid Man way, our souls will feel better for being let loose, but we will also bring upon ourselves the certain hellfire of a cop defied, with the full arsenal of prosecutorial and enforcement resources that he may choose to rain upon us. Honestly, I'm scared.

Then again, The Band-Aid Man flew from the other side of the world, and brought me in to be with him, all at his own great expense and professional risk. I take a look at my boy maneuvering our upgraded rental through the San Antonio traffic, and I make an on-the-spot decision that, as a good guy just trying to do the right thing, Band-Aid deserves to exercise some free will in this ugly situation.

"Yes, I want to do this," I manage finally. "But let's not pretend we're a day ahead. Let's operate on the correct premise that they're hot on our trail. We need to get to that storage facility and get Reveille now before the cops head us off."

"Fine," Band-Aid peels off the main freeway, onto a parallel frontage.

"That's if the Swiss Storage Army even lets us in to get it," I say pretty much to myself, since Band-Aid turns the radio back up at the same time.

It's not long before he pulls us up to the compound. We drop both backseat rows flat. I toss my sunglasses on the dash, so as to arouse less suspicion, and follow Band-Aid through the door. There's one storage agent at the desk, a Latina blonde, and she's in a strained engagement with a pair of customers. There are pleas and tears from the customers, followed by angry outbursts directed at the Latina blonde. For her part, the agent doesn't wither in the least, just stays stony cool.

Band-Aid plays it cool too. He stands patiently and quietly as if he wouldn't mind being ignored all day, and when the agent finally does lay eyes on him, she is pleasant. Band-Aid gives her his ID and she shows no flicker of emotion, but when she punches him into the computer, her eyes get big. She reins it in and walks calmly to the key locker, but around the edge of the door I see her pull her phone out and start texting.

"What about us!" the original customers start clamoring again. The older woman customer cries.

That seems to throw the storage agent off balance, she drops Band-Aid's keys on the counter. She reports, "These are the keys we have for you," which strikes me as an odd statement from a storage business that safeguards your keys in a secure area. I don't know what she saw in the computer, what she texted, or to whom, but Band-Aid and I are already moving down the hall. It's clockwork now, he turns us down one corridor, stops at a metal roll-down door, and pulls out the keychain.

He slips the first key into the lock. It doesn't work.

The second key he's still wiggling. All I can think is this had better not be a set of dummy keys to stall us while the cops sweep in.

Click. The lock turns. Band-Aid throws the door up and the light flickers on. He says, "There it is. Right there."

The painting is huge. The first thing that comes to my mind is that it's going to be close, even for our big SUV. We grab the package, pull down the container door, lock it tight, and move out. When we hit the door, the Latina blonde breaks away from the agitating customers and insists Band-Aid sign some papers. She takes her time getting the papers, everything feels like a stall to me, and I hit the front door with the painting myself. I pop the hatch and get the frame in securely, the huge painting easily covers the whole back area, at least 5 feet long by 4 feet across. I can't see the subject, though. The whole portrait is wrapped securely in cardboard and plastic, just the way Band-Aid said it would be.

I rush inside to grab my partner, his pen flying across the pages, his eyes reading none of it. He drops the pages on the countertop and thanks the Latina blonde storage agent. She appears to want to say more, but the original customers are really up in arms now. Band-Aid and I hit the door, get in the car, and pull out. From his phone playlist, a club hit called "Animals" blares all around us through our getaway truck's speakers, providing sublime escape music. The Latina blonde rushes, cellphone in hand, and throws open the glass entrance door.

"Hey, she has something else to say to you, you'd better to go back."

"Yeah, what a great idea," Band-Aid says, and we both laugh. He squeals the SUV out of the lot and onto the main road. We're in the wind.

As Band-Aid navigates the streets, I spin to assess our cargo in the back. Even bundled up, Reveille is an impressive bitch, I can feel the history radiating. *We have her*, I keep saying to myself. *We have her.*

We're still far from safe. The storage facility was one danger overcome, but there's no doubt now the police know we have the art, which means it's open season on The Band-Aid Man and me all the way to A&M campus, where, if we're lucky, we can drop Reveille off in unobserved silence and disappear into the night.

I remember the original discharge road trip, when every police stop was a near heart attack for me because I imagined the stolen art was in our trunk. My anxiety then turned out to be unfounded, because the painting wasn't really with us. Right now, though – this is no misunderstanding, nor is it a classic Band-Aid Man ruse. This is all the way real. The priceless stolen military painting that triggered a manhunt is inches from my elbow. Long-lost Reveille is taking up the whole back of the SUV, it's impossible to wish away.

"Oh, man," I moan ruefully, "we should've found a way to turn Reveille in a long time ago."

"You're missing the silver lining," Band-Aid counters.

"What's that?"

"We're civilians now – Leavenworth's off the table."

True, we're just facing regular prison. That is the glass-half-full way to see it.

Band-Aid's doing a lot of surface-street driving, which is confusing me, because I was sure we'd be on the freeway by now, hammer down for College Station, the only course of action that might keep us a half a step ahead of the cops. "We are going straight to A&M, right?"

"Oh, no," Band-Aid says in a bless-your-heart tone. "That was never gonna happen." He's cruising slowly through the paved tar sea of a

Texas-sized parking lot, which is mostly empty to add to the run-down feel of our environment. Band-Aid pulls into the parking space in front of the lot's least enticing tenant, a used mattress store, and kills the engine. I take a second look up through the windshield at the giant red letters spelling "Mattress FIRM Clearance Center" above our heads.

Gripping my temples in confusion and despair, I ask, "Why aren't we going straight to A&M?"

"Dude, I ain't slept in 30 hours, I ain't makin that drive today."

"I'll drive."

"No, my brother Bob wants to join us."

"That's great!" The prospect of a clear-thinking ally excites me. "Give me the wheel, let's go pick Bob up."

Band-Aid exits the car and I jump out after. I head around the back, expecting to cross him as we switch places, but he's actually walking away from the Explorer, now heading for a small door in a one-story establishment that looks only marginally less sketchy than the used mattress store. I race after him and, as soon as I grab the door handle, a darkening realization overcomes me so that when I do swing the door open and see the naked Latina strippers, they correspond exactly to what I've already just forecast in my mind.

I break straight to the restroom, simply to separate myself from my partner's influence for a minute and try to think my way out, but, just my luck, there's an active bathroom attendant inside who has no one else to pay attention to. He's all over me, asking questions, tearing things off, and hitting the faucets with zeal, all while offering up numerous bathroom goods and services. No thinking to be done in here, and this attendant's costing me money too. I've already tipped the guy my last two singles for various good deeds, and if he does anything else I'm going to have to ask him to break a twenty, which will no doubt kick his hospitality into an even higher gear. I thank him again and escape back into the bay of flesh.

A seated Band-Aid gestures to our tabletop, where the strip club black lights impart an ominous shade to the amber beers and onyx shots he has laid out for us, "Jägermeister in honor of the original discharge road trip." He's raising his, so I join him.

It feels good going down, but I need to contain this situation. Band-Aid has us at the furthest table from the stage, which would be comforting if it weren't irrelevant. I wouldn't see the strippers if they were right in front of us, my whole mind is consumed by the image of our bundled priceless painting in plain sight in the back of our SUV. Rear license plate sticking out for the cruising police. Desolate parking area at the forlorn mattress store for the criminals. Maximum vulnerability to all the things that can go wrong.

The semi-naked waitress comes back by with a second round of shots, Band-Aid peels off a hundred from a huge wad of hundreds wrapped around his IDs. The two San Antonio natives discuss their neighborhoods and high schools before she asks, "Can I bring you men some ladies?"

"No," Band-Aid mercifully dismisses the notion. "My buddy and I have a lot of catching up to do." He starts showing me pictures of his latest girlfriends on his big-screen phone, sweep after sweep of naked women in selfie mode, the scoop of one clean-shaven armpit on the camera-holding side, and, orbiting those armpits, smiles and breasts and everything else. Then there are the shots with ladies posing in different tropical homes for a photographer, presumably Band-Aid Man himself, and I start to glance around to see if we might be offending anybody with this carousel of nudie pics, but then I remember I'm in the one place where no one could be offended, a strip club – for no good reason, since I'm blind to the strippers the same way I'm blind to the girlfriend photos, because the mattress parking lot image keeps piercing my brain.

As soon as the waitress walks away from another beer delivery, I hammer him, "This is insane, Band-Aid. We're already on the run from the law for transporting stolen art. Even if we beeline it for A&M, we're liable to be picked off at any point along the way. But, as bad as that is, that's still our smartest play, way less dangerous than leaving the painting visible through every window with our car parked out there."

"It's not visible, dude. It's all wrapped up."

"That's worse – thieves will assume it's valuable. Can you imagine if it gets stolen? And we're at the strip club? There's no way to explain that."

Band-Aid fishes for his rental keys, "Fine, we'll bring Reveille inside."

"We will not. You're just going to pay dancers to give Reveille a lap dance. Photos are going to go up on Instagram, these shenanigans are going to blow up on both of us…" as my voice drones on, I start to hear what Band-Aid Man hears: just noise. He's already made up his mind. I've been under the mistaken impression that Band-Aid flew me in to keep him out of trouble, and there may be a shred of truth to that, but the bigger truth is he wanted me on this ride to enjoy the trouble with him.

The return of Reveille will wait for tomorrow. The Band-Aid Man has his own plans for today, plans that include hometown friends and bars, maybe an icehouse, and cigars and Whataburger and laughs and toasts and whatever surprises may come. His approach to life, the way he seeks out the path of greatest exposure to risk, is maddening to me. I can't think the way he does. Right now I can't think at all, because I'm on that ride and my mind's already reeling. I gulp two aspirin with a kamikaze and vow to get it all right in the morning.

P.P.S. Bob Brown and the High-Stakes Run to A&M

In the bedroom doorframe stands Band-Aid Man's tall form, rapping the hollow-core suburban door, "Let's go. Time to shower and hit the road."

I hold my watch in front of my face: 6:20 a.m. We've logged maybe three and a half hours of sleep. I taste the cigar in my mouth and go brush my teeth even before I shower. When I get out to the kitchen, Band-Aid Man tells me to put on a better shirt. I return in something that Band-Aid assigns only a marginally higher grade. We serve ourselves up a breakfast concoction of eggs, ham, biscuits, and heavy cream that has been prepared for us by the host whose house we just woke up in – Pat Lynch was with us for most of last night's frolic, he and Band-Aid have been tight friends since the second grade. Through the garage entrance comes Band-Aid's brother Bob. I give him a hug and he holds out a sack of tacos that he's picked up on the South Side and which all of us immediately tear into. This is a professional crew. The gears have switched to business, and I'm reminded of a fun Band-Aid Man fact: in all his hard-partying nights in all the years I've known him, he has never called in sick. This may not be a workday, but there's work to be done.

We hit the road by 7:00, Pat sending us off. No room for Pat, barely space for the three we have in here. We've secured the Reveille painting at a 45-degree slant now to make use of one seat in the second row. I'm sitting in that spot, according Bob the shotgun respect position. Bob has a familial resemblance to Band-Aid, despite possessing neither the height nor the blue eyes. You can see they're related, even though Bob's more obviously Mexican than his kid brother and his voice carries a rhythm that throws San Antonio's South Side in your ears with every line.

269

"Had a dream about us, *Roscoe*," Bob announces. Unlike the folks who ran with Band-Aid in his Army days, Bob doesn't refer to his brother as The Band-Aid Man. Bob does often address him as Roscoe, his personal bastardization of Band-Aid's Christian name, Russell. "House in the old neighborhood was on fire and we were rescuing everyone. Hell of a fire, house went up quick, but we kept bringing the kids out. It was a younger version of you."

"How could you tell?" Band-Aid countered.

"Cuz you were too *skiiiinny*, motherfucker!" We all laugh together, and then Bob adds thoughtfully, "You had a couple kids on each shoulder down the stairs, I don't think your knees could take that now."

Because Bob isn't emotional, his littlest scowl stands in for thundering disapproval, and the smallest smile is a belly laugh. Bob is unflappable, almost inert, which I take to be the natural result of his being big brother to The Band-Aid Man. I feel as if Band-Aid nearly kills me every time we're together, and I didn't start running with him until he was already in his mid-twenties — when science would say his brain was already properly formed. How crazy must Band-Aid have been as a kid and a teenager? And I know that Bob, more often than not, was the guy bailing Band-Aid out (even literally — when Band-Aid was arrested for motorcycle theft, for example, it was Bob who drove from San Antonio down to the coast to get Band-Aid out of the Corpus lockup). What kind of levelheadedness would a man have to develop over decades of exposure to Band-Aid behavior? Not that Bob Brown has always been a textbook mentor — he did shoot The Band-Aid Man once, with a 22-caliber rifle. Not a graze, a direct shot.

"You know, Bob, the first time your brother and I hit the American road together, it was in the Cadillac rented in your name, since Band-Aid's credit-card and driving-record challenges prevented him from renting his own vehicle. Look how far your kid brother's come!"

"Roscoe done good."

The three of us fly through little towns in the big state of Texas, cruising north, and I'm shedding a little discomfort with every mile we get closer to the target. Band-Aid suggests we tour the painting to an Aggie uncle of mine he likes, for history's sake. I embrace the suggestion because it will be cool to see my aunt and uncle, plus the detour through Austin will take us off the main trail for a while. In my mind that makes it less likely we'll be picked off.

"Officer Raker again," Band-Aid reacts to the buzz of his cell. Raker's hitting Band-Aid with childish messages. Law enforcement officers can be spoiled brats in their demands to get what they want, when they want it. I tip the phone my way and look at the latest, which reads: *"Any news?"*

"Aren't you supposed to be on a plane right now? What news would you have?"

"Obviously, he figured out we changed the plan," Bob says. I feel even more grateful for our detour. Band-Aid drops his cell in annoyance, as he does each time, and each time I remember that on the other side of that message is a livid cop tearing his hair out, barely keeping it together as Band-Aid runs further off the script.

Turns out my uncle's in the hospital, but we do get to spend a few minutes with my aunt, who brings us in for refreshments while we tell her about our mission. My aunt comes out and admires the cloaked picture before we pull away.

Band-Aid pulls us onto the highway, and a right-lane speeder nearly plows into us before the driver snaps his truck into the left lane. "Fucker almost made Sisi a rich girl," Band-Aid comments.

Sisi, that would be a reference to the life insurance policies your Uncle Band-Aid Man and I both have that list you as the beneficiary.

"Don't get any ideas, Band-Aid. Please drive defensively from now on."

He sets the cruise control for something within reasonable range of the speed limit and settles in on the mostly empty State Highway 71 West. "Hey, Ames, what exactly was it that kept you and Soho from having another kid?"

"You know we planned to have a few kids... We had Sisi soon after we started trying... but after that Soraya couldn't have any more. Even though she was still young, she had a condition." Out my window there's a giant field that the sharp-bladed combines have sheared close to the ground. Big rolls of hay lie quietly on their sides, like tipped over saltshakers on a green table. "It's really wild to imagine, but it turned out that Sisi was Soraya's last good egg."

"Damn," Band-Aid squeezes the wheel and looks my way. "It's a miracle."

"Yeah. All I can feel is grateful."

A&M signs begin to appear. I can feel the confidence infusing my teammates on this mission as we near campus, and a little of it is seeping into me, but I'm not quite in their frame yet. I remember something I've meant to bring up since the storage place, "Hey, Band-Aid Man, you know what I noticed about your locker?"

"What?"

"That's everything you own in the world, right? Aside from maybe a suit and a duffle you brought to Chad?"

"Right."

"With the exception of one big flat-screen I saw, there's nothing you bought in there."

"True, it's historical furniture. That bedframe was the bed Bob's and my grandmother was born in in."

"Wow."

"Aside from that TV, everything in there's family heirlooms."

"You're like me – we have pretty close to zero possessions. Ever wonder where our money went?"

"Memories, baby." Band-Aid cracks an over-his-shoulder smile my way, "You rather have a massive hangar full of new shit, or stories like we have?"

Bob cracks, "Ames is waiting to see how this story ends."

We laugh together. When our mirth quiets down, Band-Aid says, "Hey, Bob, when we get back to San Antonio, I'm gonna get my shit moved out of the Swiss fortress and back into a mom and pop place that'll give you access. You can grab that flat-screen anytime, it's yours."

"Then you'll own zero new stuff," I say. "And the TV becomes Bob's family heirloom."

"That's how we do it. Thanks, Roscoe," Bob's opening browser windows on his phone for some of the various news stories on the lost painting, including its history and "mysterious disappearance." He starts scrolling to the bottom of the articles to share the posters' comments, "Hey, *Extremely Fast Driver* posted at 10:15 pm on Wed, Nov 26, 2014: 'No one will ever find this painting because the sad fact is that staff of A&M are not mindful of art... Total waste. This painting is gone forever. Someone threw it away.' "

"They got the 'someone threw it away' part right," Band-Aid vouches. "But lucky for posterity, The Band-Aid Man showed up and pulled it out of the garbage."

"Oh, shit, did you guys know the Reveille painting has its own Facebook *paaage?*" Bob's South Side rhythm turns the question into music.

I lean forward in my seatbelt and peer over the back of Bob's seat at the Reveille page. Hundreds of likes and shares. And a seemingly endless column of user comments for us to quote in our best-guess impersonations of the posters' voices as a way of breaking the tension as we zoom closer and closer to Reveille's home.

"Christine Gehler Mott: *Interesting and I hope this piece of history is found soon!*"

"Mike Casper: *Stolen or misplaced?*"

"Sally Cosgrove: *Bring her Home! No Questions asked!! Just Thank You from All of US!*"

"Brian Wilkin: *Am I the only one that wants it returned with lots of questions asked?*"

The fact that this painting means so much to so many is working on me, and I can't help but get excited about Reveille's repatriation. But seeing all this tribute in print also reminds me of the principal crime we're a part of. We are art thieves. We justify what we're up to – what criminal doesn't? – but none of that takes away from the underlying prosecutable facts: we are in possession of stolen art, and we are transporting that stolen art on America's Interstate system. As an aggravating factor, I would add that we are committing this crime in direct defiance of the recorded orders of a sworn officer of the law. There will be no quarter granted if we get caught at any point along the way, nor will we plead for any. We are what they say we are.

More indicators of A&M campus are showing up: the agricultural fields, an A&M-blazoned water tower on the horizon.

"We'll be in the Dixie Chicken having a beer in no time," Band-Aid predicts. I'm excited about the Dixie Chicken too. I've been hearing Band-Aid refer to that Northgate bar in his stories since the first day I met him. Far beyond its being the watering hole that, in my brother's five years as an Aggie, facilitated more of his hookups than any single establishment before or since, Dixie Chicken is a vault of Band-Aid Man history. It is where he met friends he has to this day. It is where he celebrated grand achievements and drowned the sorrow of catastrophic failures. It is where the owner pointed a loaded pistol at him. It is where Band-Aid broke a giant wall mirror with his fist, escaped with a blood trail behind him, and then returned the next day to confess to the manager, Larry Odell. It is where the owner forced Band-Aid Man to pay for the broken mirror with a combination of cash lent to him by Bob, plus two weeks of work for no pay. It is where Band-Aid worked so hard during that unpaid two weeks that the owner brought him on full-time and where, consequently, Band-Aid spent years of his A&M after-class life changing kegs, mopping floors, dusting animal antlers, and scrubbing the boys' and girls' bathrooms on his hands and knees. It is also, according to Band-Aid Man, home to the best burgers in Central

Texas.

"I can't wait!" An idea springs into my mind, "Band-Aid, we should hang Reveille up in the Dixie Chicken. Let's stop by a hardware store and buy a bracket!"

"No, we ain't hanging Reveille in the Chicken. I'm giving it directly to the cop."

"What?"

"I'm handing it to Officer Raker personally."

The confidence I was just allowing to grow in me is gone all at once. My jaw hangs. Color drains out of my visual field. "Why?"

"Why not?"

"Raker threatened to arrest you if you deviated from his plan. Why would you disobey his orders and then bring him the painting?"

"I told him I'd give him Reveille."

"That doesn't make sense." I'm having an allergic reaction every time Band-Aid opens his mouth. "You've defied Raker in every other possible way. You were supposed to give him the painting *tomorrow*. At the *storage locker*. In *San Antonio*. You were supposed to let *him drive down* for it—"

"No, Ames, all that other shit is what *he* told *me* to do, so that's different. But *I* told *him* I'd give him Reveille. I'm keeping my word."

I lean forward to assess Bob's reaction to this news, and I see no reaction at all. Bob is going to let his kid brother charge into the combine.

Oh, God, so close to victory and suddenly we're plummeting to rock bottom. Before this minute, I had never imagined it was possible to be at a worse place than the used mattress store / strip club junction. Ever since we snatched the painting under the noses of the Swiss Storage Army, I thought the only way to play this would be to drop the painting off anonymously somewhere really cool at A&M and vanish. But here's this other way, scripted by a maniac. "So when you were disobeying the cops every other step, was your point just to make them angry before we present ourselves for arrest?"

"One of the articles said, 'No questions asked,'" Band-Aid offers with a smile.

"That article was not written by the cops!" I yell in exasperation. "Writers can't offer up amnesty to criminals – I know you're just saying that to be ridiculous."

"No one else has to be there with me," Band-Aid replies, fully aware that no one in this car came all this way to sit on the sidelines for any part of this mission.

My former giddiness is gone. Getting closer to campus no longer makes me feel happier, now it's the opposite. This feels like a suicide mission.

The Last P.S. The Fallen Warriors and the Dixie Chicken Shrine

The SUV rolls up to the Dixie Chicken and we all three unload. Band-Aid knows I'm headed for the bathroom, "It's a wall of honor in there. You'll see."

The bathroom's in the middle of the wooden bar, as soon as I cross the threshold I understand what Band-Aid means. Bannered across every wooden surface, amid the other bathroom graffiti, over the urinals, above the sink, on the ceiling, are the names of A&M Corps of Cadets graduates who have been killed in action. Some of the KIAs are stenciled reverently, others are scrawled grievously in dark Sharpie. Some call out from prior wars. Some are so fresh the ink looks as if it would wet your finger if you touched it. Birthdays. Death dates. Never forget.

I come out humbled, wiping my washed hands on my pants. Beers seem in order, I buy three large Shiner drafts at the bar. Band-Aid tours me through the place. I hear more stories, see the rattlesnake tank, stand under the ceiling plank by the entrance where his initials are and have been since he inked them there as a senior, and of course he shows me the wall mirror that replaced the original he broke and had to work off. He and Bob and I grab a table next to it, and we haven't been sitting down for two sips when a guy runs up and calls Band-Aid by his given name, "Russell! Russell Brown!" Band-Aid looks up, at first not sure who it is. "It's me, Larry Odell."

"Larry," Band-Aid jumps up and hugs his old manager, the guy he'd turned himself into the day after he punched the glass. "I was talking about you – just showed these guys my mirror."

Larry laughs. He's here as a pure customer now, no longer

professionally connected to the Dixie Chicken, just picking up his Aggie son from campus. Fluke of timing. He and his kid both sit down at our table with their burgers. After some reminiscences and catching up, Larry asks, "What brings you to campus?"

"We're returning Reveille. The missing—"

"*Yeah*, the long-lost painting, we all know Reveille – how'd you end up involved with that?"

"I've had it the whole time."

Larry takes a hurried bite of his burger.

"Well," Band-Aid corrects himself, "minus the time the Army misplaced it with the rest of my household goods."

Larry's looking out of the edges of his eyes at Band-Aid, "You just decided today was a good day to bring back a priceless piece of A&M history?"

"Yeah, pretty much. The cops kind of forced the issue, but that was my intention from the start."

Larry casts a protective glance at his son.

"It's mostly society's fault," I explain. "This can't be blamed on The Band-Aid Man – it's not like the mirror."

Larry reflexively glances at the famous mirror, perhaps catching a glimpse of his own face, and looks quickly away.

"No, not like the mirror," Band-Aid repeats eerily.

Larry swallows down the rest of his burger and signals for his son to do the same. His eyes make a fretful track around our area, "Where's Reveille?"

"In my rental out front," Band-Aid indicates, and Larry's eyes shoot nervously that way. "Still have to work out the handover with the cops. Might have to bring my lawyer in too. We don't know how this is going to go."

Larry's on his feet, already policing up his and his son's trash, "Real good to see you." The goodbye isn't quite as tender as the greeting was, but there's still warmth, and I'm pretty sure that if Larry hadn't been with his son, he'd still be here at our table instead of out the door. Not really the right situation to pull a kid into, I understand.

Band-Aid's cutting straight to the chase, his phone's connecting already, "Officer Raker, hello."

He has his cell a couple inches off his ear so Bob and I can hear.

"You landed in San Antonio?" Officer Raker already interrogating. His voice suggests a muscle-head in his thirties who's been an enforcer long enough to have developed a general contempt for everyone outside his circle.

"Landed yesterday," Band-Aid telling Raker what Raker already knows.

"Where are you now? Where's the painting?"

"College Station, I'm here to give you Reveille."

"That wasn't the plan," Raker snaps. He should be happy to get the painting, but he's too outraged at Band-Aid's improvising. He takes it as a challenge to his authority.

"I understand that, Officer. But it's been me and my buddy's dream to bring Reveille home — ever since we got out of the Army. It's an unfinished chapter of our lives."

"And I said I'd pick it up in San Antonio tomorrow. You remember what I told you."

"Honestly, Officer, it wouldn't have fit in your cruiser. I'd just like to hand her to you at the police station."

"It's my day off."

"Mine too."

"I got the kids today," Raker hisses, and I can't help filling in more details in the Raker picture: divorced cop whose own wife couldn't stand his company any longer. "Now I gotta come all the way in to the station."

"I came from Chad, Africa," Band-Aid states flatly. "Let's do this."

"Be there at two o'clock," Raker orders, seizing control of the time, at least.

Band-Aid drops the phone off his ear and visually confirms he's been hung up on. "That'll give me time to contact my lawyer." Band-Aid scrolls through contacts, drills in a text, and then asks me and Bob, "You guys remember Terrance, my first roommate at A&M?"

We nod. The name's familiar, anyway.

Band-Aid sends a text while he's talking, "Yeah, Terrance is a big-shot attorney now. Works out of Boston and D.C. a lot, but he lives here and I think he's home for the holidays." I'm picking up just the slightest hint of desperation from Band-Aid while he discusses Terrance. My partner is flexing his jaw, definitely nervous. He's not as uneasy as I am, but even a hint of anxiety from Band-Aid is rare, and that makes it all the more disturbing. Both Band-Aid and I have careers that likely won't stand up to any kind of criminal conviction, much less an associated prison term. He may be thinking of that. I'm more consumed with my daughter.

Sisi, how could I explain to you that Daddy's a convicted art thief?

Band-Aid and I both look to Bob, who is strikingly unfazed. It's obvious that this is just the sort of fiasco he expects every so often from his brother, and seeing that in Bob's eyes pulls my spirits back up – or at least momentarily stops their freefall. But Bob doesn't have a daughter. The comfort goes only so far.

Attorney Terrance's reply text buzzes in.

"He's gonna meet us at the police station at quarter 'til," Band-Aid reports.

"Beautiful," I take a gulp of my beer to go with the best news I've heard all day. Our drafts are done, and I make the command decision to cut us off there. The large Dixie Chicken beers I bought us are more like three beers each in a mini-pitcher, and I don't want us skidding up to the police station with an obvious buzz. No telling how the cops would take that.

Raker calls Band-Aid and pushes the time to 2:30. I think he just wants to be ahead of us, maybe rally his squad, so I convince my company to stick to the original time.

Band-Aid gets us to the police station at 2:00 and kills the engine. We all peer out, hoping to identify Raker when he arrives. Sedans roll around us and a couple uniformed cops come and go, but I don't make any of them as Officer Raker. "Oh, there he is!" I point through Band-Aid's window where a good-looking guy in a sweatshirt and sunglasses is walking across the lot. He's fit, but not quite the muscle-head I imagined. He strides in the main entrance.

It's Band-Aid who identifies the next driver who rolls up, "Terrance!" We leap out of the Explorer, the former Aggie roommates hug out on the asphalt. "Thanks a lot for coming."

"Sure, it's good to see you."

Terrance takes a look at the wrapped painting in the back of the SUV, but they don't talk about Reveille much. More catching up on each other's lives. I'm still scanning the horizon. I see the station doors pop open and out come two cops: Officer Raker, still in his sweatshirt, and a uniformed officer in tow. The uniform is close enough now that I can read his nametag: Rodriquez. The officers step to us, very serious in movement, with grave expressions to match.

Band-Aid introduces us all. The nervousness is gone from him. Terrance's presence is part of it, and the other part is that The Band-Aid Man is just clutch. He does his best work at the edge of the precipice. I don't move, but somehow I mentally step back from this circle and take in my partner, with his perfect hair and his giant-toothed smile, as he nods encouragingly while providing cartoon-like explanation to his audience. He's gotten under the armor of the officers, emotionally disarmed them. Band-Aid Man transfers their attention away from us and into the SUV, to the cargo – to Reveille, the prize. And there the officers go, into the back of the Explorer, under the flipped-up gate, gloved hands around Reveille's padded frame.

The cops pull out the wrapped painting carefully. This is priceless treasure. A smile stretches across Raker's face. He has won. That it didn't play out the way Officer Raker dictated is wiped away, forgotten this instant in a triumphant sunflash. Raker moved a man across the oceans to close this legendary cold case, probably the finest piece of detective work this department has seen in years. Officer Raker is a relentless, tenacious bastard, and exactly the kind of cop I'd want chasing down a criminal who wronged anyone I care about. That does not mean that I regret having made unflattering/untrue comments about Raker when, through extraordinary circumstances, I wound up on the bad side of his caseload. If you find yourself in a situation like that, the regular rules go out the window.

The cops are inside the station now, the painting in their possession. I mentally rejoin the circle as we trade stories in the parking lot. Before long, the officers come back.

Raker says, "We've pulled off enough of the paper to see that it is Reveille. It is the genuine historical painting everyone's been looking for since the nineties."

"Yeah, I didn't come out here to bring you a forgery," Band-Aid replies.

Officer Rodriquez steps forward now. "Well, this is a criminal incident, as I'm sure you all know," he begins. "We have to file a criminal report, and as part of that, I have to run a contact on you." He's looking at The Band-Aid Man.

"What does that mean?"

"I just need to run your driver's license in connection with this criminal incident."

Band-Aid pulls his wallet out of his pocket and flips it open with his usual overboard flair. I see him fingering his Laos driver's license, and I involuntarily close my eyes. Concentrating with all my might, I communicate telepathically with my brother: *Come on, Band-Aid Man, let's not mess this up. For once in your life just do the easy thing and don't make these officers think you're screwing with them.*

I open my eyes in time to see Band-Aid bypass his Laos permit and retrieve the Texas license for Officer Rodriquez. Rodriquez calls it into his radio.

"I've got a Top Secret clearance with the U.S. government," Band-Aid offers. "You're not going to find anything that hasn't already been settled."

A minute later, the desk crackles back through the radio, confirming what Band-Aid just said. My partner is clear. Rodriquez bids us a good-natured farewell and heads back toward the station's main entrance.

It is Raker who has the final word, "You know, in trying to get this painting back, I interviewed a lot of people." He faces Bob. "I even learned about you."

Bob returns Raker's look, no change in Bob's expression.

Band-Aid says, "I can't believe Laura Coffeecake turned me in."

Raker turns back to Band-Aid, "It wasn't just your girlfriend. I talked to a whole lot of people about you. I heard, *'I'm not surprised.'* I heard, *'He's crazy.'* I heard, *'Outlaw.'* After a while, I couldn't help it: even *I* started liking you."

Officer Raker – whom I take for a man who doesn't extend a hand if he doesn't mean it – reaches out to The Band-Aid Man. Band-Aid takes the officer's hand and shakes it. At the moment of the handshake, I can't help liking Raker, either. And, weeks later, in 2015, when Reveille would be unveiled at a full-tilt ceremony loaded with dignitaries of the highest Texas political and military tiers, and the entire A&M Corps of Cadets in dress uniform, including Band-Aid's old unit, the Animals of A-1, howling in tribute, and the news story of the priceless long-lost painting's return would hit the Associated Press wire and get coverage in hundreds of outlets, the man at the center of all those stories, in print, radio, and television – the man actually performing the unveiling – posing proud in the paparazzi lights, charming the press with his factual wisecrack that the painting was worth more than his salary, would be Officer Raker. And I wouldn't begrudge Raker a minute of it. I would feel then exactly as I feel now as I watch him shake Band-Aid's hand.

Did Raker get nasty and put the screws down? Yes. He put the fire to us, and now a painting that disappeared when Raker was ten years old is back where it ought to be. And, even though he could arrest us and bring us into the station right now, Officer Raker, at the moment, appears to be letting us walk away.

As if to confirm that all is clear, Raker disappears into the station for the final time, the main door swinging closed behind him and staying closed.

Mission Complete. Dream fulfilled. We pull away from the police station, leaving priceless Reveille behind, destined for a special wall all her own, in her proper historical home, and all that fanfare she will receive at her very public unveiling.

No jail time for anybody. The Machine keeps coming for us, we just keep landing on our feet, and I guess that's how it's always going to be.

Band-Aid, Bob, and I celebrate without delay at the Dixie Chicken. Bob has a trace of a smile on his face right now, which, on the Bob Brown scale, means he's full-on laughing at me for ever having doubted this would end well, just as it has now, over beers and burgers that more than live up to the dreams I've been carrying with me since my trench buddy first told me about this roadhouse in the last millennium. Band-Aid pulls the Reveille Facebook page up on his phone and, amid the crowded field of zealous posters' comments, he surgically airdrops in his own for official record.

His historical understatement reads, "The band aid man has returned the painting."

He glances at his watch, "Looks like we need to get Ames back to Soraya and Sisi."

I check the time too and realize I've been on the ground with The Band-Aid Man for exactly 24 hours. A person doesn't get many days like this in a lifetime.

"Hey, tell my goddaughter I'll swing into New Orleans after New Year's, on the way to Chad."

I smile in anticipation, "We'll all love that."

Those two head out to the ride, but I peel away and detour into the restroom shrine one last time.

When we pull out of the Dixie Chicken lot, our vehicle aiming back where we started, I think again about those KIAs on the wooden walls. I reach over and squeeze my brother's shoulder. We're no longer warriors, but our blood surges with what the warriors keep protecting in us all.

The Band-Aid Man jacks his phone into the rental's stereo and his playlist explodes through the speakers all around. I've never heard this song before, but it strikes me as just perfect for right now. The highway rushes at us and we feel like such free dogs. The world is ours for the taking. We're in one of those weightless bounces off rock bottom, and we're sure we'll just keep going up.

47191974R00162

Made in the USA
Lexington, KY
01 December 2015